BORN AGAIN TO FIGHT: THE UPRISING OF AN EXORCIST

Peter McMaster

Born Again to Fight: The Uprising of an Exorcist
© Copyright 2024 Peter McMaster

All rights reserved. This book or any portion thereof may not be reproduced or used in any manner whatsoever without the express written permission of the publisher except for the use of brief quotations in a book review.

For more information contact soulwinners@bigpond.com

ISBN: 9780975641408 (paperback)
ISBN: 9780975641415 (ebook)

www.soulwinners.com.au

Publication Date:

February 2024

Disclaimer:

This book is memoir. It reflects the author's present recollections of experiences over time. Some character's names have been changed.

To my darling wife Poss. Thank you for so much support. And for putting up with my faults and failures and always encouraging me to keep pushing on. Even when you were a target too at times.

Thanks to our friends in Uganda who taught us the reality of prayer and its power. Who opened our eyes even more to the war in the heavenlies. And how to fight to win. God bless you in Jesus name.

Thanks to all who believed and knew the war was real. To just have some open ears to share with helped me to persevere. And to those who were in the battle also and the words of wisdom and encouragement you gave when I needed it, however they came. God bless you all in Jesus name.

Thanks also to 'Jill'. You are a real warrior. Thanks for coming out of the darkness and sharing your insights and testimonies that has helped us take Tasmania back. We are so grateful for that. And showing me that fear is an enemy that must be conquered. You showed none at all. No matter what was thrown at you.

And others who have prayed for me wherever you may be. God bless you in Jesus name.

And thank you to Kylie for showing an interest in this book and taking the time to tidy things up. I am so glad God filled in this gap with you. And the souls that are awakened after reading this book will be your fruit also. God bless you in Jesus name.

A Prayer for the Reader

Father God. I ask you in the name of our Lord and Saviour Jesus Christ to bless the people who read this book.

Grant them more spiritual understanding and knowledge of the deeper things of the war for souls and excite them and encourage them to seek your face in a greater way.

Help them to find the good works that you have prepared for them beforehand and teach them how to fight the enemy and not just defeat but crush them. Help them to not be discouraged or to turn away from the fight but to overcome all obstacles, and take control over their lives, their families and homes as you guide them.

I ask you to totally destroy every spirit of darkness that has blocked and hindered their fruitfulness, stolen their joy and bound their hope.

I now bind all fear and doubt in Jesus name and loose strength and might and power to be more than a conquerer to those who look into these pages in Jesus name. Let them never be the same again.

It's time to take the land. Arise and go forth. The harvest is ripe! The God of above and beyond what we can ask or even think is waiting for you.

Chapter One: Destiny Awaits 06
Chapter Two: No Farting in Church 12
Chapter Three: Shot in the Guts 19
Chapter Four: The Search for the Truth 25
Chapter Five: The Road to Salvation 33
Chapter Six: The True and Living God 40
Chapter Seven: The Name Above all Names 47
Chapter Eight: If You Believe 57
Chapter Nine: A Cold Reception 62
Chapter Ten: The Wilderness 68
Chapter Eleven: And They Overcame Him 78
Chapter Twelve: Full Gospel Business 85
Chapter Thirteen: Voices and Dreams 89
Chapter Fourteen: Time to Pick a Fight 98
Chapter Fifteen: The Mountain Beckons 105
Chapter Sixteen: The Four Letter F Word 111
Chapter Seventeen: The Spiritual Kingdom 119
Chapter Eighteen: Africa, Here We Come 131
Chapter Nineteen: Kony Country 139
Chapter Twenty: The Crusaders 147
Chapter Twenty One: Kampala, the Return 160
Chapter Twenty Two: Africa, the Return 165
Chapter Twenty Three: The Underwater Men 174
Chapter Twenty Four: Another One Bites the Dust 196
Chapter Twenty Five: Reliving the Fun 215
Chapter Twenty Six: Tassie Life Goes On 222
Chapter Twenty Seven: Another Fight to Pick 229
Chapter Twenty Eight: 42 Degrees South 236
Chapter Twenty Nine: Things Warm Up 250
Chapter Thirty: Wicked Witch of the West 259
Chapter Thirty One: The War Begins 265
Chapter Thirty Two: Gone Nuclear 273
Chapter Thirty Three: A Different Battle 292
Epilogue 302

CHAPTER ONE
DESTINY AWAITS

"Awww God, do ya really want me to do that?" I already knew the answer, but was hoping without hope that He would lead me away from this direction or speak to me somehow, whether audibly or the still small voice of the Holy Ghost to say something like, "No, that wasn't me, it was the devil". Or maybe He would say, "Yes, but I just changed my mind, don't worry about it".

It was Dec 1st, 2008 and I had now been a believer for almost 9 years. I had experienced His leading and guidance and knew that this was a fight that he wanted me to enter. It certainly wasn't the first and certainly more than that, wasn't the last. But this was going to have bigger consequences than I had faced before. There was no doubt in my mind about this. It was no weird thing for me to know that God can speak when He chooses. He doesn't hide this fact.

> Joh 10:27 My sheep hear my voice, and I know them, and they follow me:

I had heard the still small voice of God speak in the past, and was beginning to recognise that voice. Sometimes though, it has to be said, it is harder to discern who the speaker is. And knowing that the enemy can speak in lots of ways and also the voice of our own flesh that can certainly influence our decisions, gave me more desire to know who was who and what was what. But over time the errors had been lessening and my discernment was being honed. I had made many mistakes, in my zeal to serve the One who had given me so much freedom and Life. And I was still struggling with the flesh that didn't want me to let go of my pride and who the world was saying I should be. But God knows who we are and extends much mercy and grace towards our weaknesses and failures. And as long as we are moving forwards, He seems to overlook so many of our errors and mistakes.

And a lot earlier in my walk He led me through this following, to give me more confidence in Him, who knows the end from the beginning.

CHAPTER ONE: DESTINY AWAITS

> Isa 46:9-10 Remember the former things of old: for *I am* God, and *there is* none else; *I am* God, and *there is* none like me, Declaring the end from the beginning, and from ancient times *the things* that are not *yet* done, saying, My counsel shall stand, and I will do all my pleasure:

After continually asking Him every day, and I mean every day, at least once, from day one of my Salvation, "What do you want me for, what good am I to you?" And being filled with self-condemnation, insecurities, rejection and all sorts of rubbish from a lifetime of over indulgence of fleshly activities, I really did want to know, did God have any plan for my Life?

He had to have, I was positive about this. He had warned me with the two dreams of getting shot. And the same week it happened, and now with hindsight, I knew He was watching. Was there a path He wanted me on and was there something He expected from me? I was willing to repay Him anyway I could, because He had turned me off the path of Death and towards Life. And there was no mistake about this.

So after around 2 years of this asking, He said, "After 3 ½ years you will know". Now there are prayers that we can accept by faith and they are answered, and there are prayers where persistence is needed. This is where I learned an invaluable lesson of pushing through in prayer.

> Luk 11:5-13 And he said unto them, Which of you shall have a friend, and shall go unto him at midnight, and say unto him, Friend, lend me three loaves;
>
> For a friend of mine in his journey is come to me, and I have nothing to set before him?
>
> And he from within shall answer and say, Trouble me not: the door is now shut, and my children are with me in bed; I cannot rise and give thee.
>
> I say unto you, Though he will not rise and give him, because he is his friend, yet because of his importunity he will rise and give him as many as he needeth.
>
> And I say unto you, Ask, and it shall be given you; seek, and ye shall find; knock, and it shall be opened unto you.
>
> For every one that asketh receiveth; and he that seeketh findeth; and to him that knocketh it shall be opened.

> If a son shall ask bread of any of you that is a father, will he give him a stone? or if *he ask* a fish, will he for a fish give him a serpent?
>
> Or if he shall ask an egg, will he offer him a scorpion?
>
> If ye then, being evil, know how to give good gifts unto your children: how much more shall *your* heavenly Father give the Holy Spirit to them that ask him?

I began a countdown, from the day I was saved, which was on 21st Feb 1999. I was equipped now with a date, and excited about God and how my destiny on this planet, and purpose in life, was going to be revealed. This was about one and a half years off into the future, so I had to wait a bit. But I knew it was God that spoke 100%, so I wasn't put off, and I was happy knowing it was coming.

In the past there had been a problem that all the date setters that I had believed had almost drove me insane by their false prophecies and end of the world predictions. And I had buried food and tools and even dope seeds in case things got real bad. At least I could stay stoned. But that was the Old man, before the Spirit of God entered. This date coming in the future had given me hope. Unlike all those others, that were Hell bent on destroying it.

The three and a half year date eventually came and was about ten days away. I was now constantly thinking about it. The closer it got the more excited I became. Then my Father phones up and says, "You better come over, Mums only got a month or two left to live". I had never got on with Mum, she had her problems and I had mine, but I didn't expect her to go so early. She was around 60 or so. So I didn't talk to Dad much either, and the phone call was out of the blue.

I couldn't go over to Western Victoria from Tasmania because of work and lack of finance and other things that I can't remember now, but I did wonder if this has definitely something and somehow, to do with my destiny and the Word I got almost 18 months before.

But now my head was filled with other thoughts too. Regrets and guilt and shame about the part I had played in building the wall between my mother and myself. And as much as we were so far apart and even at enmity with each other, I didn't want her to die. My father loved her and my brother and two sisters, so I began to pray. I got some time off work then started a three day fast. The four letter F word for Christians. It wasn't too hard because I was repentant to God and wanted him to restore the things the thief had stolen. Jesus promised us Life and more abundant and that was what I needed for my mother, and myself also, weighed down by guilt and remorse.

> Joh 10:10 The thief cometh not, but for to steal, and to kill, and to destroy: I am come that they might have life, and that they might have *it* more abundantly.

And I believed that He could heal, I just needed to get his attention.

> Mar 8:2 I have compassion on the multitude, because they have now been with me three days, and have nothing to eat:

I can't remember if this was my first three day fast or not. But it was one among many that I would do in the future, after seeing and again experiencing the truth of His Word and the power and miracles that are in the Kingdom of God, that are available for every believer. We only have to ask. But not ask Amiss, like many do. Chasing worldly lusts and desires, they will receive nothing.

> Jas 4:3 Ye ask, and receive not, because ye ask amiss, that ye may consume *it* upon your lusts.

The day before the expectant big day had arrived, and I had arrived at my father's house situated on the sheep and grain farm he owned and where my brother's house was that I was staying in. I wasn't expecting the welcome mat out for my return.

We grew up well off. Eating well and sleeping full and warm. But there was dysfunction there, no financial hardship but more emotional and hidden, but we weren't as bad off as others. I walked up to the house and Dad answered the door and I said, "G'day Dad, I've come to see Mum." I knew the reception for me would be cold or so I thought, and true to my perception he said "She is asleep, come back tomorrow," which was fair enough, I certainly didn't want to wake her up then try to get in a "How do you do"?

Things were going to be hard enough. But I was broken and contrite and was ready to wear what I had to. But it had to wait for tomorrow. So in the morning I prayed and also a fair bit the night before and just before I wandered up to the family home I had spent some time on my knees. I was feeling weak and all sorts of things were going through my mind. But I have learned since that this is a good place to be at in the Kingdom of God.

> 2Co 12:9 And he said unto me, My grace is sufficient for thee: for my strength is made perfect in weakness. Most gladly therefore will I rather glory in my infirmities, that the power of Christ may rest upon me.

So this was the day. Three and a half years since becoming a believer in Jesus Christ to the very day, and the thoughts of what was coming next were in my mind, but not as much as just seeing Mum and trying to resolve something of the past and the resentment and bitterness that we had been walking in.

I walked inside and put my head around the doorway that led into her bedroom and looked, and immediately a loud inner voice said, "Cancer, Death". I knew it didn't come from me, so I knew that I knew it was God telling me that there was a spirit of Cancer and a spirit of Death, which was the problem. Not that I had much idea really how to deal with them, but it was a Word of Knowledge that increased my faith to understand that God was present and wanting to help.

So what I seen was my Mother, skinny as a rake and no hair and looking like a skeleton, or death warmed up as some would say. And that was a perfect way of describing what I was looking at. I burst into tears and got on my knees and asked for forgiveness. My father was there too and he started crying also. I had never seen him cry ever, maybe half at his father's funeral, but I wasn't really looking, I was fighting a losing fight trying to hold back my own tears there also. Not the manly thing to do.

But seeing Mum in this state all of a sudden brought forth the sorrow and grief and all hardness seemed to vanish. It was an instant massive shock, instead of watching her slowly fade away. I am not sure which one would be easier on anyone though. I had little to do with death before this. A few friends went suddenly in car crashes, but no-one that was near constantly. I told her I was a new creation and that I was Born Again, and now not the person I used to be. After asking her to forgive me I could see that she was softening.

She was an old Catholic with Nuns in her family and was a believer, but not living it. Maybe tried but failed like many do. Without the Holy Ghost it is impossible to live the Righteousness of Christ in one's own strength.

> Rom 15:13 Now the God of hope fill you with all joy and peace in believing, that ye may abound in hope, through the power of the Holy Ghost.

So I talked about what had happened in my Life for about 15 minutes, with her not wanting to give me much recognition, but as I mentioned being Born Again and how you can be saved with a prayer, (this is all I knew at the time, after saying the sinners prayer and shaking like a leaf, and the demons that had been yelling in my head were removed, I thought this was the way. And sometimes it is just this simple.)

I got my Mum to repeat the prayer after me and as soon as she had finished, almost to the minute of the three and a half years after my salvation; at around 11 am in the morning when I was led in a prayer up the front of the St Helens Christian Fellowship; where I was made speak it into a microphone as a public acknowledgment of my desire to give God control of my life; when Jesus Christ moved into my spirit and washed me clean from all sin, by his shed blood on the cross of Calvary, (I'll get into more on that later).

Now I had faith that she had been brought over to the side of the Light, just enough to cast out those spirits of Cancer and Death. I truly believed this.

CHAPTER TWO
NO FARTING IN CHURCH!

But first we'll go back to my childhood days of the farm. My Parents were both Catholics, but not really practicing. Not that I knew what that was anyway, from what I'd seen, everybody went to church, and I thought only the real heathens never did. But they weren't much different to anybody else really, as far as I could tell.

And in the small country town of Lake Bolac, where the population was about 180, or whatever it was, give or take 20 or 30 or so, (I did remember reading that number somewhere so it must be right?!?!) it wasn't hard at all to keep tabs on everyone, which was a pastime for some and there was nowhere to hide and everything was brought up eventually.

Most attended the sport in the small country town and the local High School serviced about 5 or 6 other small communities. Lots of farms and machinery with shooting and motorbikes and old cars to bash about in, all sports, and a lake for fishing and boating, Bolac was not a bad place to grow up in, and the lake of course was a fun thing in Summer. Nearby to it was the Catholic Church which had a prime spot overlooking the lake. My great Auntie had donated the land to them, which is now prime real estate in Lake Bolac. This was where the religious part of my life took place.

I remember being made to go to church as a young kid. My mother eventually tired of it and I can't remember my sisters going much but Dad took me and my younger brother. I was rebellious, but my brother Kevin was cleverer in his tricks and planning. So where I was straight out resistant to some authority, he would think things through, and no doubt this mentality of mine of let's just get to the fun bits, brought about the rule on Sunday morning. "No Farting in church".

It was either Auntie Norah or Auntie Daphne, who were both Nuns, brought my mother home a clear plastic bottle shaped like the Virgin

CHAPTER TWO: NO FARTING IN CHURCH

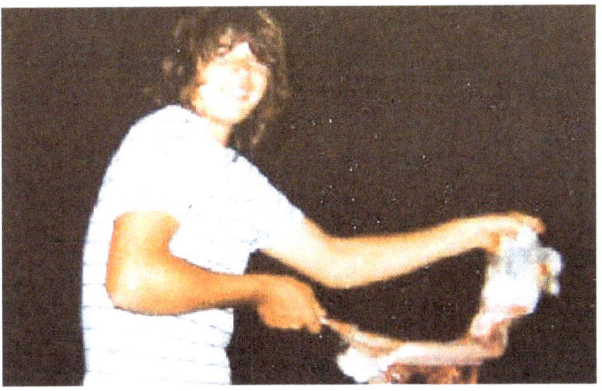

Mary full of some of what they called holy and blessed water from Lourdes in France, where she was to have appeared to some woman there. Mum would take a dab and touch our heads and say that we were blessed. Probably now I would say it was putting curses on us all but we never felt any different.

But Kevin had a plan to be more holy and righteous than the rest of us and I caught him out. He had the plastic bottle of the Virgin Mary and he was sitting on his bed and it I caught him drinking it. I knew his plan straight away and snatched it off him and finished it off. Then I thought immediately, looking at the empty bottle, what do we do now? Mum will know it's empty. But Kevin had planned well and just said; "fill it up with normal water. How will she know?" And he was right. She never did find out.

Everyone's looking for shortcuts in religion. But they are always the long way around, and usually dead ends. There were all sorts of Idols and images around the house that Mum had. St Christopher always came driving with us. He was always going to save the day if needed.

Even when Mum or Dad were drunk driving. Maybe that's why they needed his help. Because some nights as a small child, I was curled up in the back of the station wagon praying to the Catholic God and hoping that He would hear me, to stop Dad from crashing, because I knew which side of the road we were meant to be on, and a lot of times we weren't.

There were three sets of Rosary beads in the house too. How do I know there were three? We watched a Vampire movie one night and when it finished my brother and two sisters ran to the drawer they were kept in and put them on like their life depended on it. And I searched the house high and low for more and the cupboard was bare. I got pretty frantic as I seen the fear in my sisters and brother subside as they donned the protective amulets and how they were happy they were safe. I slept with one eye open all night worried about some Vampire coming in and biting my neck because I never had any protection.

Probably just before the time I was going to high school I was getting sick of the Sunday ritual. So I decided to hold back the release of any wind Sunday mornings until church and then let rip on the wooden pews, where it was absolutely incredible how much of an echo, when you got the right angle, that would come from them in the brick building with bare floorboards. This was the beginning of the resistance.

My Brother thought this was the funniest thing and I laughed out loud the next weekend when he had decided to join in the game. After a few weeks we had perfected the timing in the church rituals to where it was the quietest and instead of one long ripper, we trained to let them out in short sharp bursts so we sort of played a farting symphony, if you like.

Then for a short time, church became a giggling house. With a mate who was there with his parents and some others who we could see, thought it was a great joke too. The older religious ones never gave a smile. And my mate Jezza would never join the rebellion, which was disappointing to me, but he certainly rebelled not long afterwards in different ways.

So Dad was always threatening to belt us when we got home, and sometimes he did, and sometimes we took off as soon as the car stopped in the car port, to hide for an hour or so until the heat cooled off. But Dad became sick of this and thought up a different tactic to use to keep me at least, on what he must have supposed to be the narrow path.

CHAPTER TWO: NO FARTING IN CHURCH

With Priests and Nuns on both side of the family, it was a big thing to be involved in the Catholic Church. Although from what I seen with a couple of my mums sisters who were Nuns coming to stay and getting drunk with my parents, and the local church Priest doing the same at times, I was wondering what the fuss was about. I expected the shearers and farm hands and footballers and the alcoholics to do this, which was happening a lot in this small community, but not the righteous and the Holy.

Hmmmm…….. Questions were arising.

My Catholic Nun Auntie Norah could say a Hail Mary quicker than one could take a breath, or that's what she said she was saying. Most of the words were impossible to be recognized, but she didn't seem to worry. Whether because of some penance after confessional or some sort of race with the devil, I never worked out. But she could whip through the rosary beads like you wouldn't believe. Obviously never reading this,

> Mat 6:7 But when ye pray, use not vain repetitions, as the heathen *do*: for they think that they shall be heard for their much speaking.

Not that I knew any of this back then. I just thought that the Nuns must have had some sort of rosary race with each other to fill in the time of their boring existence. Anyway my Father asked me if I wanted me to be an Altar boy. I thought anything would have to be better than sitting in the pew like a stunned mullet, just wanting to be somewhere else. So I said, "Yep, I'm willing to give it a go". The boy, who taught me the process of the rituals or whatever you call them, was from a neighbouring town. He was a couple of years older. I had just started high school and was about 12 years old. I liked the priest who had some duck dogs and would go shooting and get on the grog and seemed a bit grumpy at times but I didn't care.

But there was another priest who used to fill in. Not very often. I had seen him once before I took the unpaid job on as Altar boy, and he had worn his St Kilda scarf to church, over his frock, or gown or the dress they wore. I had to put the dress on too when I was the Altar boy. It did give a sense of High and Mighty servant of God feeling that I know now was obviously a religious spirit of some sort.

Anyway the older Catholics were a bit shocked and angered by this, but St Kilda football club had just won their first game after a couple of years so I just thought, fair enough. Little did I know that this man

Gerald Risdale, had things going on in his life that would make even the most hardened shearers want to string him up.

Things were going on not too bad. I was used to the rituals and helping the older boy do the job, until one morning my Father walked in and woke me up and said, "Paul McKenzie was killed in a shooting accident last night". I said "How"? And he said "He was cleaning his shotgun and it went off". I thought this to be so strange. Even at that young age, we had good understanding of guns.

Lake Bolac was full of ducks and swans and all sorts of water birds. Plus the peppering of swamps in the district made it one of the most desirable places in Western Victoria to go duck shooting. And before the Myxomatosis and Calicie virus was released, the rabbits were everywhere.

And there were foxes to shoot with higher powered rifles and clay birds sometimes and a need to shoot sick sheep on the farm as well. Not to mention snakes and vermin and tin cans and sometimes anything that moved. So questions were in my head. You can't clean a loaded shotgun and as every young kid knew, you definitely check them before pointing the end that goes bang anywhere near your head.

It wasn't until a fair few years later that Gerald Risdale, who was not far away from the community where Paul lived with his Parents, at the time Paul was shot, was convicted of over 60 counts of pedophilia with Altar boys and some girls and causing suicides of them also. I worked out then what had happened. Or this is my theory anyway.

I did work with him once after Paul's death, and maybe he was keeping a low profile, but nothing happened to me, thank the Lord God Almighty!!!. The one time I did work with him, I saw where he hid the key to the locked cupboard that held the Holy Eucharist wafers and the Communion wine. So when he was in the other room getting changed, I opened the cupboard and took some big sculls of the wine and ate a heap of wafers. Not sure why. Maybe looking for a shortcut to some sort of Holiness that the attendees were seeking. Maybe it was some spirit that took me over to do this? I only ever did that this once. But it was the only time I walked out of church feeling a bit of a buzz, probably more from the hidden sin than the wine, or maybe a bit of both.

There were many rumours getting around about priests tampering with little boys and my mate James came up with the phrase, Altered Boys, every time he heard something mentioned about a Catholic

CHAPTER TWO: NO FARTING IN CHURCH

Priest, he would repeat this. And we would laugh so much. It was funny, but after a few things getting revealed, the joke became more of a rebuke to the pervert priests that were hitting the news a little more.

And I never forgot the time with the wine and wafers, thinking, if I wasn't doing that, I may have been changing out of the robes the Alter boys had to wear as well as Father Gerry, as he was called. I didn't like to walk through those thoughts to any possibilities, ever! I am thankful that I never became an Altered Boy.

So in the end I got sick of this, especially when I overheard a close friend of the family speaking to a group of Ladies saying, "Why does old man Hick bother coming, he should just stay home".

As if she was way above this poor alcoholic with seven kids who would come in after the start and leave just before the end and sit right up the back every time. I could see him from the front where the Altar was but most would miss him, unless they were sticky beaking.

I thought he's taking the effort to come with his whole family after drinking most of the night. He's probably closer to God than you are. So after that I had enough. The hypocrisy of the whole thing was offensive to me, even as a young teenager. I was not going to do the Altar stuff anymore. I needed to escape this fake garbage.

I decided to run away Sunday morning after arguing that I'm not going to church anymore at 14 years old or so. I took off over the back paddock and my old man was chasing me with the cricket bat. But I had jumped the back fence easy, being around six foot tall by then and very fit. And when he yelled at me I'm going to get the gun, I wrestled with the thoughts of will I get out of range before he went the 25 meters or so back inside to get it or not.

It was a .22 that hung in the back room, and as much and I wanted to escape, I decided to admit defeat and turned around. And for the next month or so I was always wondering if I would have made my escape. And I wondered even more if he would have pulled the trigger. He certainly seemed angry enough.

But not to be outdone, I just sat still in the pew that morning. Not standing, kneeling of repeating any prayers or confessions or whatever, just sitting with my arms crossed and sulking. So after a month or so, he didn't take me anymore, and it was soon after this he stopped going as well. I was happy about this but wondered also if all this was part of some torture experiment made for me and my brother.

Why did Dad stop going after we did? Anyway we were free to sleep in Sunday mornings now.

I did feel sorry for Jezza though, who was made to go for another couple of years. But his rebellion was already working within. He soon made up for lost time.

I have met around eight other altar boys who all became alcoholics or drug addicts or both all except for one. I know now that this cult that calls itself church was dangerous to all who get involved in some way or another. If they would actually read their Bibles they would know that kneeling before an image of the Virgin Mary, (who never remained a virgin) and worshiping images and idols, was a massive sin in the eyes of God, as well as all their traditions and hypocrisy that they are blinded to.

> Rev 17:4 And the woman was arrayed in purple and scarlet colour, and decked with gold and precious stones and pearls, having a golden cup in her hand full of abominations and filthiness of her fornication:

CHAPTER THREE
SHOT IN THE GUTS

"WHOA, What the F#$%……."

I woke up puffing like I'd just ran a marathon and sweating like I just did too. Holding my guts and in pain, but it only took a few seconds to realize it was only a dream.

But immediately sitting upright in bed, the girlfriend at the time, Roxanne said, "What's happening" and I said, "I just dreamed I was shot in the guts". She said something like, "Oh yeah, good onya" not showing the least bit of interest, which was understandable I suppose, it happened in my head, not hers.

Two days later however, I had exactly the same dream. Same puffing and sweating and real pain to make me hold my guts when jolted awake by this. This time when she woke up because of my violent awakening, I said, "I just had that dream again, I got shot in the guts".

She showed a little more interest in it this time which was a small consolation for me. And we did discuss it that night and the next day wondering what it could mean.

If I had been reading a Bible I may have spotted this.

> Gen 41:32 And for that the dream was doubled unto Pharaoh twice; *it is* because the thing *is* established by God, and God will shortly bring it to pass.

But I hadn't read the Bible or showed any interest in it. I was too busy running around chasing the sex, drugs and rock and roll lifestyle. Growing dope and playing football for money that I soon spent on alcohol, I was about 30 years old. Very fit but no direction whatsoever. No interest in spiritual things at all, but how that was all about to change, in a massive hurry.

Two days later I went down to my mad mates place on Christmas Eve looking for a party. On the way out the door I was thinking, "I hope I don't get shot tonight". It was not just a passing thought, it was a little stronger than that, but I ignored it anyway.

So I get there to Phil's house and bashed on the door like I was the cops and was greeted with a five shot auto shotgun barrel stuck through the crack in the door that he had opened. He had stuck it about a couple of inches from my nose and then said, "Oh, it's only you, what are you doing?!?!" with a fair rebuke. I already had a few beers so it didn't really faze me.

Phil was a lunatic, and this was normal behaviour for him. But later in life he must have upset some wrong people and went missing. Which was probably always going to happen eventually? If you upset a lot of people then sometimes it's the wrong ones. Phil then hung the gun up over the back door, and we started drinking and bonging on. Little did I know that he had forgotten to put the safety on and placed the trigger and guard over a nail to hold it up. Now Phil had a couple of kids so this could have been really disastrous.

We drank and smoked into the night when a couple of twins that were mucking around St Helens showed up. They were playing in a band and liked to party. One wanted to see Phil's guns that were hanging around. There were three of them up on the walls so he got them down and was showing them off. Then he got to the shotgun. And I was sitting about five meters away along the wall where the gun was hanging up, in a corner with my back up against another wall.

And then "KABOOM".

I was watching them check the guns out and when the shotgun went off I saw the wad go flying past and it just missed my head. I felt a bit of a hit and stood up. By that time there was blood running down my legs, and I knew what had happened. I did see the kettle on the bench blow up. A few weeks I did go back to Phil's house and there were pellets in the kitchen bench and a spread about the size of a large dinner plate right next to where my head had been of about 20 pellets. I mean only five or six inches beside. No wonder I seen the wad. If it was any closer it would have hit me between the eyes. I am very grateful to God now that is for sure.

I said, "Phil, you just shot me you C#$%". He just replied with the standard answer of "Get FU#$%D". I thought I better go to the hospital so I run out the back door and started to faint in the supermarket car park where the side gate to Phil's yard opened up to.

CHAPTER THREE: SHOT IN THE GUTS

The thought came to me, "Oh well, if I die I'll find out where we go". Then apparently the twins grabbed me as I was collapsing onto the car park bitumen. But the strangest thing, everything lit up with the brightest light I had ever seen and it was so weird how I could look at it and it wasn't blinding - I still don't know if it was God or not.

I woke up on the stretcher going into the hospital, which was only about 200 meters from Phil's. It may as well been a hundred miles away because there was nothing they could do there. I came around and there was no panic in me at all. I was at peace.

It was surprising to me, even when I could hear the nurses saying quietly to each other "He's bleeding from the mouth" which I thought, that mustn't be good if they don't want me to hear. I'd seen enough westerns on TV to know what it meant. Death was close by for me, or was in their minds anyway.

But then one Nurse looked in my mouth after I was stripped off and they were counting the holes and found that a pellet had gone through my lip and hit the plate of false teeth that I had and was causing the blood. It was still stuck between my lip and my falsies. They calmed down then. Didn't make any difference to me, by then the pain was growing.

I had copped two in my top lip, one just in the temple in front of my right ear, three in each thigh, and only one in my guts. Would have been a few more but they hit my hand and probably in the beer can I would have been holding on my lap.

I don't want to be crude but the best way I can describe what a red hot pellet of steel or lead feels like in your guts is if somebody grabbed you by the testicles and ripped them out. I could not think of anything else that would compare. Or that's what I imagined anyway. I did get a twisted bowel a year or so later after complications from the first surgery and that was not fun either, having to go under the knife again.

Because I had been drinking, there were no painkillers. The ambulance took four or five hours to get from St Helens to Launceston. It stopped on the road near Avoca for a lifetime and I was in agony, and they just parked there. They said they had to swap over. But surely 20 minutes or so more driving would not have upset much of anyone's plans. I was very confused about this. And the way they just cruised along. I swear I could have got more speed out of a pushbike. I do reckon they thought I was going to die so didn't push it. But I never did obviously, although it certainly felt like I was on the way. I'm sure the devil wanted me dead. And I still believe this.

The clock said around five AM when I got to Launceston hospital. And it was just after 12 midnight when in St Helens hospital. So it was a mystery why it took so long. St Helens to Launceston was a two hour trip, and in an ambulance, with a life threatening injury, I thought it should have been a lot quicker. I was positive of some conspiracy against me.

A fair few years later I was flown to hospital in a plane which only took 15 to 20 minutes to get there. My heart had been skipping beats really bad and I thought I'd better see what the trouble was. They went into a panic in the hospital and put me on the stretcher, into the ambulance and then were rushing me onto the plane like I was dying. In the middle of this I needed a leak. I told them and they said "No you can't have one". I thought if I don't have one I'm going to pee my pants, so I jumped up off the stretcher and ran behind a shed at the airport. I did just drive into town from Pyengana to the hospital which was 25 minutes. Surely a one minute toilet stop was not too extreme. But apparently it was. In the end the doctors sent me home without doing anything. Too much plaque in my arteries they said. Too many half cooked snags at footy club barbies was the reason I'd come up with. But it was a root of bitterness which I'll speak on later.

I compared the two events sometimes and think they got the whole thing back to front. Anyway my heart was sorted out after direction to forgive and a seven day fast from God, so all's fine now.

When they gave me the pain killer in the operating room after the shooting, it was so good. Although they must have given me a decent dose because I threw up really bad and it stunk so much, and the doctors were so pissed off. I felt a bit bad but couldn't clean it up. Then they prepared me for surgery. At least this part of the trip there was a bit more movement happening. I could tell these blokes weren't getting paid by the hour!

I woke up after the op and as soon as I opened my eyes I saw there were two detectives barking questions at me. Then I noticed there were tubes coming from everywhere and steel staples down the length of my stomach from my sternum to just above my groin. It was massive gash, and it was on my guts. It was all so surreal.

And lying in bed flat on my back, it was in view all the time, so that fact could not be ignored. The Ds wanted to know what happened and were saying all sorts of things. I definitely didn't need this so I told them to go away. I did say it was an accident though, because it was. Even Phil couldn't have pulled anything evil off that time of night on purpose. Not saying the devil couldn't though.

> 2Ti 2:26 And *that* they may recover themselves out of the snare of the devil, who are taken captive by him at his will.

Later when the local Sgt came around to the house after I got home from Launny Hospital, he said he knocked on the door on the night the shooting happened, and said to Roxanne that I had been in an accident. She said straight away "He's been shot hasn't he". This really made him think something was very suspicious, and when I tried to explain that I had dreamed it to happen twice, I'm not sure how much he believed it. But it made him think for sure, I could tell by the look of confusion on his face. He was maybe thinking, "Wow, this is spooky" or "does this idiot really think I'm going to swallow this one"?

The Doctors said I had one pellet go into my stomach, nicking my aorta which is the main artery, then proceeding through the bowel and finished near my backbone. He said he didn't understand why the aorta hadn't burst like a balloon and I just bled to death in a hurry. He thought it must have been because I was so fit. I was thinking that carting all the water in 20 litre drums, through the Tassie bush in the middle of summer to my dope plants must have been good for me, because the footy finished a few months earlier.

But that wasn't the last of the devils attempts. The nurse who hooked me to the morphine drip didn't connect it right and for three days and three nights I laid awake in agony with no painkiller. I must have pressed the magic morph button 100 times with no relief at all. They took it off me because they thought I was greedy and hung it away where I couldn't reach it.

None of them believed it wasn't working. Not only that but I was having spasms every couple of minutes and I really thought my guts was going to burst open and my guts would fly everywhere. Like one of those Alien movies I'd seen where the thing pops out of the guts, "SURPRISE!!!" It gave me more insight into their predicament. I could really relate to that at this time.

Then around five in the morning, three days and three nights later a nurse I had never seen came in and I told her that I thought I was going to die and she gave me a shot in the behind and I slept for two whole days and nights straight through. When that was over I was feeling OK. Although I was having full on nightmares, it was only because of the Pethidine. Which I was glad when I went onto the panedine forte, because then they nearly stopped.

Every time I read the story of Jonah in the whale for three days, I think, "I wonder how painful it would be to be stuck in a whale for three days", but being a little claustrophobic I thought I was better off probably, and I still do wonder though every time Jonah is mentioned.

This event though had totally changed my direction like nothing else could have. Like Jonah, he was never the same either.

Shot pellets still in the kitchen bench

CHAPTER FOUR
THE SEARCH FOR THE TRUTH

Lying in hospital I was constantly wondering who tried to tell me about the shooting. Was it a prophecy, was it a premonition, was I psychic or was it aliens or was it God? I didn't think it was God after the Catholic games but just believed that He was probably too busy to do this or not interested in me. There were little thoughts of anything else.

The dreams of the shooting had fascinated me. And that was now my purpose, to find out the truth on planet Earth. And having plenty of time on my hands because of only a sporadic at best desire to work, I put everything into the quest. After getting out of hospital I began. I was hungry for knowledge and after watching things on TV about Nostradamus as a kid I started there. It was easy to find the stuff, too easy really. And these days it's impossible to dodge. Like poisonous fairy floss, scattered across the land just waiting to be devoured.

Nostradamus had a few dates on the go that were getting closer and then there were New Age mags that I devoured and Ascended masters, saints of old, Nordics, Angels, the Virgin Mary and Christ consciousness (which I didn't know the difference between this and the real Jesus, those details were just a chore) and even Dolphins bringing messages to the human race.

A lot of these were saying how Christianity has got it wrong. And from what I'd seen they were right. Then the real games began. I saw in a magazine ad, "DO YOU WANT TO KNOW THE SECRETS TO THE UNIVERSE". I thought, "I sure do, what's needed"? It was an advert for the Rosicrucians, the Egyptian mysteries. After all the stuff I was looking at, it didn't seem much different, but had given the huge promise of the mastery of life. So I thought mine was a little off track, I'll give it a go. I sent away for the stuff they said I needed and answered the questions about why are you seeking this.

I told them about the dreams and the shooting and said, "I just want to know what was going on here on the planet". They wrote back and said I'd been accepted so that felt good. Then they charged me $300 to move on, which never felt so good. So the course was entered by snail mail. And in a week or so I got a little book and that was about it. I thought "hello they've ripped me off", and I had been ripped off by mail order stuff before. But I had nothing to lose now, the 300 bucks was gone, so I looked into it.

First thing I had to do was make a little altar. A mirror was needed and some candles to be perfectly positioned, and to turn the lights off and get into a meditative and passive state. It all seemed quite religious, but I'd had a bit of that in the past, so played the game. But I must have opened myself to receive, because receive I did. Probably because I wanted the truth and was willing to try anything, and another was the thought of the 300 bucks also that I didn't want to think I had wasted by getting conned into this. So I said the prayer.

"May the divine essence of the cosmos infuse my being and cleanse me from all impurities" or something like that. As I know now, that was the dumbest thing I had ever done, and I had made multitudes of mistakes in the past. My whole body started shaking and it was like I was shivering on the inside. I was thinking, "What's going on here, what's going on here?" It did freak me out a bit.

I was to stare at the mirror after the prayer and was to put in half an hour doing this. Then the instruction was to quench the candles with a candle snuffer. Which seemed a bit of overkill and far too religious for me so I spat on my fingers and put them out like that. With this attitude of irreverence, I was never going to make the grade into witchcraft, not that I knew that it was the path I'd just joined myself too. I'd been through all the religious junk under the sun so was just looking for the short cuts to the answers I desired.

A spirit or demon had entered, and because I had the dreams of getting shot I believe that it was a divination spirit that was sent with the material. And it was only a couple of days after the first ritual that I heard the spirit speak. I was walking to a mates place to help him do something, just to give a hand, like I'd learned growing up in the country. Help your mates and when you need a hand they'll be there. No reward or payment necessary. But a voice from within said, "See, you're better than he is because he needs your help". I thought, "What the hell was that thought. Where did it come from?"

That thought was so foreign to me and also very offensive. A bad start for the demon to tempt me with that but I did notice that my thoughts started to become more prideful, no wonder though, the demon that had entered was just like his master who said,

> Isa 14:13-14 For thou hast said in thine heart, I will ascend into heaven, I will exalt my throne above the stars of God: I will sit also upon the mount of the congregation, in the sides of the north:
>
> I will ascend above the heights of the clouds; I will be like the most High.

I would do the rituals with the candle and mirror fairly often with the same prayer and staring at the mirror, which was really getting weird. All sorts of faces were appearing and I was looking at myself then with a beard then long hair, short hair and others were showing up and all sorts of crazy stuff.

No wonder they made me take the oath of secrecy of having my neck cut from ear to ear and the top of my head cut off for the birds of the air to eat my brains and to be buried up to my head at low water down on the beach, and all the other crazy curses I uttered over myself. People would have thought I was insane talking about that stuff. Then almost as required, spit on the fingers, snuff out the candles, have a couple of bongs and head to the pub. The latter parts were my rituals, not from the book.

During this time I went to a dowsing course run by an old man. It was held in St Helens High school. I went with a friend who was interested in this also and we learned some stuff I wish I never. I had learned to divine for water on the farm at home by an old man who Dad got in to dowse out wells for windmills for stock water. He would use a willow branch. My brother and I would practice this and would follow the water pipes around the back yard and the streams around up the paddocks. The pull on the sticks was that strong that the bark would twist off the handles. No questions were ever asked, it just worked.

Then we progressed to steel rods, which were more finely tuned. I learned later on how to find the best flow in an underground stream on a large area, without having to criss-cross the ground. They would tell me if it was fresh or brackish, how deep underground and how many litres per minute. This was while I was playing with the witchcraft that I didn't know was witchcraft. I should have read this passage here but never did. It would have saved me a lot of trouble.

> Deu 18:10-12 There shall not be found among you *any one* that maketh his son or his daughter to pass through the fire, *or* that useth divination, *or* an observer of times, or an enchanter, or a witch,
>
> Or a charmer, or a consulter with familiar spirits, or a wizard, or a necromancer.
>
> For all that do these things *are* an abomination unto the LORD: and because of these abominations the LORD thy God doth drive them out from before thee.

The old fella at the school had a pendulum. I was working with them too and reading tarot cards. Anything to do with divination fascinated me. He taught us that not just could we use the rods to look for water; we could use them to look for anything. My friend Steve decided to test him out. He took the old fellas pendulum and stashed it in the building somewhere, then went and said, "Righto mate, you're doing a lot of talking, let's see if this stuff works, I just stashed your pendulum, show us how to find it".

It was a massive challenge laid down for the old boy that I was so keen to see. He picked up his rods, which actually had wooden handles that the steel would slip into (I thought these must be the luxury model of the busted coat hanger I used) and off he went.

He spun around and they pointed to the door. At the door they pointed right. Up the corridor we went following his every move thinking it absolutely incredible. And no doubt the old fella was glorying in this as he surely enjoyed showing off his powers. He told us all we could ask the wires questions. And they would answer. And he gave us a demonstration. Although firing away questions like this is a very stupid thing to be doing, which I very well know now.

But the seeds of deception and delusion within were watered again that day, and as for the result, how do you think anyone is going to end up anywhere, getting any wisdom and understanding by consulting a busted coat hanger? Because that is exactly what my wires/rods were. A coat hanger straightened out and bent back and forth until it broke in two.

Even though I could get 70 to 80 percent accuracy, (and there were others who were getting more), it was the 20 or 30 percent that you couldn't tell if were right or wrong. That began to drive me mad and there is no doubt that the spirits moving the wires knew this. Forming decisions from these errors was insanity.

CHAPTER FOUR: THE SEARCH FOR THE TRUTH

So the old bloke was on the move, past one door then we got to the cookery room. His rods pointed inside. We followed him and there were four or five sinks. His rod pointed to one of them. He walked over and under a minute from the start of his search said, "Well they tell me it's here but I can't see it". Then my mate was amazed and told him so and reached under that very sink and grabbed the old bloke's pendulum. We were so amazed and the possibilities were endless, I thought.

A couple of things I did, among others, in the small town of Ledgerwood, which got the people talking were these. I learnt to dowse out ley lines. The magnetic grid, that runs over the planet. There were larger grids, and smaller. I was learning to use these grids to affect areas in some positive way. Or the demons writing the books I was reading would call them positive. I had dowsed out intersecting lines and you would place a standing stone on them. Or from what I know now, an obelisk or a phallic symbol. But I didn't look at them as this. The stone would interrupt the straight lines and curve them into like a four leaf clover shape, where veggies would grow better than usual. Since then I have found that sheep and cow manure works even better, LOL.

Anyway, I needed a six foot 'Tower of Power'. That's what they were called. So I got an old concrete culvert. It was perfect size at about seven feet long. I buried it in the ground and filled it with concrete and it needed a pointy top on it like a witch's hat. But in my haste, I mixed the cement too soft and it had to have a rounded top. But I was happy with the result.

A friend pulled up out the front of the house and we were talking and he glanced down into the back yard. Then he glanced again and his eyes widened and said "How come you've built a giant dick in your back yard"? I thought, "How little does he know" and said, "That's not a dick, it's a Tower of Power, it helps the veggies grow better". He must've thought I'd lost it. We lived in such fertile volcanic soil that anything would grow well anyway, even if you knew little about gardening. Then he said, "Well it looks like a dick to me". I did have to agree with him. In hindsight, He was just seeing the obvious. It looked almost exactly like a six foot dick. And when I think back to my state of mind I laugh. If not I would cry. There are many walking in these delusions these days.

Another crazy thing I had in that backyard was the flotation tank. It was like a big coffin filled with very salty water. A heap of salt made you float. I would heat it up with a fire so it was warm in winter and

Old mate Jezza and my "Tower of Power"

climb into it very stoned, and spin out. It was a meditation device to enhance the experiences. Really weird stuff happened. All of it opening doors for the demonic to enter.

There was weird stuff happening in lots of things I was involved in that was not seen in the natural world. The supernatural was the hook that kept me involved. I know why witches become witches and new agers stay within these confines. They are searching for the truth. But there is no sense, in any of this. No solid foundation to build on like the Word of God, so no direction to truth or lies. Anything and everything went, for which I paid the price later on. All the doors were opened.

> Hos 8:7 For they have sown the wind, and they shall reap the whirlwind: it hath no stalk: the bud shall yield no meal: if so be it yield, the strangers shall swallow it up.

And most searchers I knew had rejected God, for the same reason I had. Religion! I had opened the lid to my flotation tank after the session of high strangeness and climbed out one day and the farmer at the back of our block was fencing there, and he yelled out, "What are you doing there mate"? I replied, "I'm trying to contact my dead Grandfather", which I was. But whether he believed me I don't know, although, maybe he did, because the tank wasn't far from the "Giant Dick!"

This went on for a while, going through the books and learning occult techniques and party tricks. The spirits were showing me things, but I thought it was coming from within me. I was god they taught; we are our own masters etc. I knew this was crap though, because I knew I was not the god or any god. So I wasn't playing their game quite right. Which no doubt frustrated the demons that were entering in more and more, because the doorways for their invitation, were many.

CHAPTER FOUR: THE SEARCH FOR THE TRUTH

> Pro 25:28 He that *hath* no rule over his own spirit *is like* a city *that* is broken down, *and* without walls.

The culmination of the whole thing was astral projection. Or that's where I was at when the course ran out. I could enter a meditative state lying on my bed, even stoned off my head, which I thought was a bonus, and leave my body. First time I got out I remember thinking, "What am I doing here, what am I doing here?", as I was sitting on the end of my bed.

Then I did it again and it was easy to leave. It really gave a sense of power that I had never experienced and created excitement. But being stoned and drunk a lot I thought "How am I going to know if I'm in my body or out and what if I get run over or jump off something and die".

They were scary thoughts and it put me off for a while. Then I started it up again and got another scare. I saw some eyes glaring at me in the meditation state that were very angry and that put some fear into me. Whatever or whoever it was, was not happy with me at all. That was obvious. And I do believe also that with anyone doing this occult activity, any righteousness they have will quickly disappear. They soon become a tool of the devil.

But in between all this I had lost the plot. Not reverencing the demons in the rituals and plus talking to others about my experiences made me a target for those spirits who had entered. Now with hindsight I know that witchcraft spirits and religious spirits not only enter the souls, but they can burrow deep down into the spirit as well. Because they have legal right and are welcomed in as an advantage in the earth, they can do this. And when they turn on you, it's not hard for them to grab the wheel. And this is what happened to me.

I got sick of the paths of so called truth that was leading me on wild goose chases and getting nowhere. I was looking into Buddhism, Hinduism, Lobsang Rampa, Rudolph Steiner, Aleister Crowley and all sorts of stuff that I can't remember now. I was spinning out and running in circles and getting nowhere. They all had paths to follow and all led to different destinations. It was madness.

> Isa 44:24-25 Thus saith the LORD, thy redeemer, and he that formed thee from the womb, I *am* the LORD that maketh all *things*; that stretcheth forth the heavens alone; that spreadeth abroad the earth by myself;
>
> That frustrateth the tokens of the liars, and maketh diviners mad; that turneth wise *men* backward, and maketh their knowledge foolish;

No doubt God put me through this path, and then He began to draw me. In the words of Jesus,

> Joh 6:44 No man can come to me, except the Father which hath sent me draw him: and I will raise him up at the last day.

I had been burying food getting ready for the end of the world, which most psychics and channelers were predicting, and Nostradamus, as in this famous flop, that went something like this, "In the year 1999 and seven months, the great king of terror will come from the sky, to resuscitate the great king of the Mongols. Mars will reign happily", whatever that meant?

But it was a favourite of mine as good reason to spin out about the end.

Even though I was saved just before this date, I still was freaking a bit, and had a stash just in case. But I had lived through many end time dates now and it was pissing me off bad.

Then I visited my old mate Jezza who was going out with a backslidden believer. She had some books by a man called Barry Smith, who liked to expose the Freemasons and the New World Order. Since the Rosicrucians were a lot like Masonry, I could see the things he was saying. I recognized the symbols and things involved and he was saying that it was satanic. He used lots of scripture out of the Bible and some prophecy scripture that had no dates but was very eye opening and God used it to draw me closer to Him.

Also I was saying the sinners' prayer when I would come across it. I never had anything against Jesus, even though I didn't know him much at all. But I never did use that name as a swear word. And when I started looking at Christian prophecy, there was a spark of faith that was placed in my heart.

> Eph 2:8 For by grace are ye saved through faith; and that not of yourselves: *it is* the gift of God:

And when I started to say the name of Jesus, was where my trouble began.

CHAPTER FIVE
THE ROAD TO SALVATION

The torments had started. All the spirits that I had invited in, unknowingly or in agreement had turned on me. They began to tear me apart from the inside out. Mental torments, fears and anxieties were in my head constantly. Their purpose was now Hell bent destruction for me.

No longer were they going to try to steer me into their agenda by telling me how great I was or how much advantage the party tricks could give me on the planet. It was now straight out death to this man who had opened the doors for their entry, and had not wanted to play the game they offered. More than that though, it was their absolute hatred toward the God who had kicked their master out of Heaven, and the Lord Jesus Christ, by whom, if I could make it toward Him and come into a saving knowledge of His sacrifice on the cross, they would have lost another soul and they may also lose their house, which now I was for many, as they had infested my soul, and spirit.

Their efforts were increasing all the time. I was constantly drinking and smoking dope, fighting and arguing with the girlfriend. Suicidal thoughts plagued me and once I had a gun loaded ready to pull the trigger and take someone else out also. But thankfully God was still watching, and a smaller and quiet voice spoke and said "Don't do it". So I listened and thank God I did.

I know about the thin line that many cross, that can destroy one's life in a split second. I had seen it in others and had come to this place a hundred times in my life. I had crossed many lines, many times, and some consequences were a lot worse than others. Some can take a lifetime to travel to these lines, but it is only a small fraction needed to cross to the other side and destroy all.

I was trying to cope, I got a job as farmhand out at Icena near Gladstone. I kept it for six weeks. I was put into the shearers' quarters which weren't too bad. But the first morning there was a crow sitting on the window sill, peck, peck, peck on the window, which was intensifying the insanity and madness that I was trying to hold back. I tried to scare him away by sneaking up on him and he would fly off but then return, peck, peck, peck. Arrgghh. It was making me trip out.

Then after a few days of trying to outsmart this dumb bird, I thought of the eyes we used to put on plastic ice cream containers, and wear them backwards, to trick the swooping magpies, so they thought they were being watched. Magpies and plovers always used sneak attacks from behind, never from the front, and once my little sister was hit by a Maggie and it cut her head open. This scared us all as little kids on the farm. So I drew a scary face on cardboard and put it on the window and it worked. I had outwitted the crow. Or demon as it was to me. But I only could handle six weeks of this work and the isolation and left to go to my father's farm in Victoria.

I was in bad shape. I couldn't work, read a book, or watch TV. All I wanted to do was drink, smoke and read end of the world stuff. I could actually read that, but it was only to my own destruction. Anything the demons didn't want me to do was so hard, and almost impossible. Also the nightmares were all night, every night. The devils plan was to get rid of me as soon as possible. Suicide was always on my mind. But the fear of Hell drummed into me by the Catholics, was a great deterrent.

This was my lot below, for far too long.

> Deu 28:66-67 And thy life shall hang in doubt before thee; and thou shalt fear day and night, and shalt have none assurance of thy life:
>
> In the morning thou shalt say, Would God it were even! and at even thou shalt say, Would God it were morning! for the fear of thine heart wherewith thou shalt fear, and for the sight of thine eyes which thou shalt see.

I did go to the Doctors and get some tablets which he said would take a week to work. Then a few days later I had an argument with my brother and ran to the pill bottle, just like one of my mates mother always did, when she was spinning out. And we used to laugh because to us, the pills were her god. They would turn her into a Zombie, but they were no cure for her. And this came to me, "Is this how I want to live?".

CHAPTER FIVE: THE ROAD TO SALVATION

I grabbed the pills and threw them out. I wasn't going to let them own me. I wish I could have said that about the drugs and alcohol, but I liked them, and was in agreement with their ownership of my life. I thought they helped to handle reality, but what a delusion those thoughts were.

There was no money, no work, and no hope. So I was as down as one could get, on the edge of the pit, then got down on my knees in the grandfathers old bedroom that I was sleeping in, what was now my brother's house, and I asked God for help.

Down and out

Not that I knew God but I knew that I needed help from a higher power than myself and it was the last resort. So I went to the God of the Bible in a last effort to find truth. The one that I had rejected because of all the hypocrisy I had seen in the past.

I had tried all the New Age garbage that was out there and experienced so many supernatural happenings, which were the hook to keep me involved and interested, but no real truth. The bait had looked good, smelt good, and tasted good so I swallowed, everything in sight. With no discernment or any testing, every door was open. All I wanted to know at the start of this quest was who told me and warned me about getting shot. And after a few years of constantly looking, I was no closer to this that I sought for.

But the Bible says that,

> Rom 8:28 And we know that all things work together for good to them that love God, to them who are the called according to *his* purpose.

I know now that Gods hand was with me in all these struggles, and teaching me firsthand the dangers of witchcraft, the futility of false religions to set the captives free, and the struggles of people who are tormented by the devil. So I prayed to God on my knees for a minute or so. That was all, and then a knock came on the door. It was my little sister who I hadn't seen for a while and though it interrupted the prayer, I never thought about that. Afterwards I wasn't sure whether it was seeing her or the prayer to God, but I was feeling a bit better.

I know now it was the humbling of myself to call out to my Creator and ask Him for assistance. Even though I would not get on my knees for a couple of years again, God was on my case. I can look back and see this clearly now. I got a job after this in the old home town grading onions and it wasn't too painful. But six weeks later I wanted to go back to Tassie.

I left Victoria and couldn't get any government benefits for six months because I quit my job on the onions, but got some work with a bricklayer who played football with St Helens and got some money to survive. I could still play footy, but the money I was given just went on alcohol. I also dug up a couple of my stashes of prepper food and ate that and lived for the six months.

I was still struggling inside but trying to cope and still able to drink and smoke dope no problem. I was living in a humpy out the road a bit from St Helens with no power or hot water but with a little effort you could have them. I had plenty of time on my hands.

During that time I listened to a tape set on a series of the Apostle John that was about ten tapes by a man called David Pawson. I had got them off Jezza's backslidden girlfriend after a visit to Bridport. Jezza was far from salvation at that time, but did come to know Jesus, after a few more years. Which his parents were very happy about; because they said to me after salvation of us both that they were praying that I would leave Lake Bolac. They blamed me for being a bad influence. I knew Jezza better than that. Some parents like to think the best of their children.

I stayed at Jezza's house one night in Bridport when he was by himself and it burnt down. He was running around in his undies in the street at five in the morning saying, "You burnt my house down Pete, you burnt my house down" but it wasn't me. He had dropped a smoke on the couch just before bed at about four in the morning. I woke up to see everything on fire and got him and another woman he was with, out before we were all dead. I did get burnt on the arm but it wasn't

CHAPTER FIVE: THE ROAD TO SALVATION

too bad. Green stuff dripped out of my nose for a few days. The devil had missed again. That was the second house fire I was in. Everything was crazy and depressing.

Then I met my future wife Poss. She was kind and gentle and was also an alcoholic, but nowhere near as much as me. She wasn't the loud and noisy type. But because I had played football at the small town of Branxholm that she lived in, I had a reputation of being out of control. And the last time I visited her house, which was almost straight over the road from her parents, her Mother had the cops come to hassle me. But the lies she told were soon discovered and they left.

Same night her father came up with a loaded shotgun. He stood out the back door yelling, "Where is he, I'm gonna shoot the bastard." Poss was panicking but I hid behind the kitchen door and thought when he walks in I'll grab it off him and scare him with it. But already being shot in the guts before, I changed my mind, which pleased Poss. I snuck out the front door and sat under a bush in the neighbours garden watching. He let one shot off in the air then went home. I sat out the back in the scrub for a couple of hours until I thought, "The old boy was drunk so he would have to be flaked it by now, I'll go back." And I was keen to get back, because I had my smokes but forgot my lighter, and was bustin for a smoke.

It took 10 years before I was allowed in his house which never worried me one little bit. I was actually relieved about this after that night. There was a lot of hatred and lies aimed towards me, all part of the torment, but some no doubt, linked to my own actions of the past.

Then Poss moved to St Helens and got a job, which brought some stability into my life, which was desperately needed. Things weren't perfect but we were getting along OK. I was still reading occult books and Christian Prophecy and had managed to read the Prophecy in the Bible. Revelation a few times, Daniel, some of Ezekiel, mainly Ch 37 and 38 and Matthew 24, Luke 21, and Mark 13. I was still trying to look for the dates to the end of the world.

Poss would listen to all my conspiracy theories, with some amusement and some excitement, and we were going well together. She did cry about her kids a lot because her ex-husband and her parents had made it just about impossible for her to see them. Their blackmail had an effect on her but the way I was, it probably wasn't a bad thing. I wasn't into responsibility and it didn't take much to stress me out. Kids would have made me flee, I'm sure.

Then we rented a house right out in the bush. We had a big dog that chased wallabies and possums. It was barking one night. I got up to kick it and tell it to shut up and he knew I wasn't happy so never came to me. I went back to bed and was awake. As I lay there trying to sleep I just played the game that I was taught by the occultists. Ask questions and let the inner voice give the answers.

So I asked a real simple one. "What's the exact time"? And "4:17" came to me loud and clear. I thought, "That's weird, it's only half past three". I did look at the clock when climbing back into bed. So I asked again "what's the exact time" and this time, loud and clear, "Matthew" came into my head.

I thought, "That's strange, Matthew 4: 17 is in the Bible, I'll check that out in the morning". I got out of bed in the morning and first thing I went for was the Bible, or maybe a joint, then the Bible. But when I searched through on my first mission from God, this is what was found.

> Mat 4:17 From that time Jesus began to preach, and to say, Repent: for the kingdom of heaven is at hand.

So I said to Poss, "I think Gods trying to tell us something, maybe we better go to church?"

So church it was.

A friend of ours called Danny, was born again a few months earlier, and was coming out sometimes and trying to convert us. I never hated the Jesus of the Bible, unlike some who really trip out about it. (They are so full of darkness. Their hatred is demonic.) We used to tell Danny, we are glad it's working for you Danny, but we are OK. But we could see a difference in him, even after a short time. His life had definitely turned around for the better.

And today was Sunday on the very day that Danny was getting baptized. Not that we were going to go to this, but we decided to show up, after the Word from the Bible. I thought the end of the world must have been going to happen, with the Kingdom of Heaven being near. That was my reason to show up at church. So a massive joint was rolled and smoked and away we went.

Six months before this, after a game of footy, we were driving down the street and the St Helens Catholics were having a Saturday evening service. I said to Poss, (after a fair few beers at the clubrooms) "Pull up". We walked in and they were praying the Our Father prayer near

CHAPTER FIVE: THE ROAD TO SALVATION

the end. I knew the order of things well, and I bet nothing has changed still. I showed a bit of respect and let them finish before saying loudly, " You want to pray a bit louder than that, because the Indos are going to come over here and eat you all". I did believe the Indos were going to invade, but probably not reach Tassie. Anyway with that bit of information given out, it was off to the Pub.

Sunday morning after the message from God (I was 100% positive of this, that it was God) I found myself standing on the side of the road with Poss near the St Helens laundromat, exactly opposite of the church. I had got to there and I sort of froze. I looked down the road towards the right about 100 yards, to the pub that I had frequented so many times. So many days and nights of madness had happened there and it was where most of my Tassie mates hung out. A cousin of mine had a book called roughest pubs in Australia, and the Top Pub in St Helens was number three on the list. It was a crazy place at the height of the Scallop fishing. Everyone had cash and all were in party mode. I had arrived in St Helens just at the tail end of this.

And here I was at the standing on the edge of the road, or you could say right at the crossroads of my life, looking at the church, which for all those years I never knew that this place even existed. So looking at the pub, church, pub, church I heard a voice say, "All your mates are going to see you and you will be the laughed at and seen to be weak".

I thought for a few seconds and thought, "I don't care, I think God wants me to go". And as an intrepid explorer, albeit a very stoned one, the first step was taken, which was a struggle, onto the road then over it and into the door of the church, without any evil intentions at all, or stupid drunken ideas. It had been many decades since I had willingly entered a church, or maybe never really in my own free will, that wasn't for funerals or weddings.

This was my second trip to a church in St Helens, counting the six months before, but this mob was a Pentecostal group. And I really can't blame them for looking at me like I was the devil, after the last church visit I had. No doubt they would have heard about it. But our friend Danny was pleased to see us and when some knew that he knew us, things eased off a bit, for a couple of them anyway.

CHAPTER SIX
THE TRUE AND LIVING GOD

Sitting in the church they all seemed happy. There was a lively band up the front which wasn't too bad and a lot of people were clapping their hands and waving them about. I remember a woman raised her hands in the Lake Bolac Catholic church once, and it was almost the talk of the town.

This is how far away from religion I had placed myself. I had never heard of Pentecostals, who jumped up and down and sang and clapped. I had heard of the happy clappers, but never seen it, and sitting up the back watching it all happen was interesting, but not for some.

The voices in my head were saying, "Get out of here, get out of here", but not wanting to miss the show or whatever was coming I was determined to resist as much as I could.

> Jas 4:7 Submit yourselves therefore to God. Resist the devil, and he will flee from you.

So a battle had started within me. Will I listen to those who were telling me to flee, or stay and figure out what the other voice wanted me to do. So I decided to ignore the other suggestions in my head and I hung in there for about an hour more. While we were in there, I could feel tears running down my cheeks and thought, "what's happening here, I'm not sad, or upset, this is very weird" and I looked at Poss and she had tears coming out too. And I said, "What's the matter" and she said, "I don't know". So I still stuck at it despite the resistance.

Then the preacher stood up and was talking, and an older fella stood up to give him a hug for some reason. I'm not sure how much of what was happening actually entered my head, because there was a lot of activity going on up there. Anyway when he gave him the hug, which was against all that I was at that time, and how I grew up, and what I thought about things, a voice said, maybe my own this time, "Aww come on, why doesn't he just put his tongue in his ear and be done with it".

And that was it. The demons had won and I went outside and played some basketball with the kids next to the church. Although somebody thought they had to keep an eye on me even doing this. I thought they're paranoid these people. And I was wondering too why the parents didn't make the kids stay in church, instead of letting them outside. Because it was nowhere near as painful as the Catholic mass that I was made sit through.

After they had all came out of the doors, we went around the bay to watch Danny get baptized. A lot of them stood around him and said nice things about him and I could recognize that they were speaking into his life by prophecy. All sounded good and amazing and from what I gathered, once this has happened to you then life is complete and all your dreams come to pass and the fairy tale ending is sure. I still knew nothing of false prophecies and men and women looking to put in spiritual hooks, whether for self-promotion, or mind control, or just trying to pretend they were something when they were nothing. But all this would come.

For now we were happy for Danny, that he was happy. And whatever it was in that place that had bought us to tears, we had to return the following Sunday.

The next Sunday we returned, and I managed to sit there the whole time, except for a couple of cigarettes in between which may also have been a break from those who were trying to control my mind and tell me to leave. After the service a couple of blokes came up and were friendly, telling me about their past and how they were back then and how changed they were now.

Gerry had played football for Carlton and played cricket for Tasmania and he got my respect, not for any great spiritual knowledge, but for the worldly feats alone, which God is not interested in one bit I have since discovered.

> Psa 147:10-11 He delighteth not in the strength of the horse: he taketh not pleasure in the legs of a man.
>
> The LORD taketh pleasure in them that fear him, in those that hope in his mercy.

So when Gerry told me to read a Bible, I went home and started to read. He said just read the red letters if you have trouble. But I had no trouble so I started at the New Testament and began to read it three times though, like I was instructed, before starting to read the start of the Book or the Old Testament.

I went to church every Sunday now for almost three months. I was close to finishing the New Testament the three times. We were putting more effort into dress and things and I thought this was it. There was a feeling of family here and we began to like it. The depression and tormenting thoughts were still present, and the nightmares had not stopped at all, but something was definitely happening, of what I had no idea.

During this time I had to go to court for my fifth drink driving charge that I had. And I was not looking forward to it. I was totally expecting a short stay at her Majesties expense, in the Pink Palace it was called, in Hobart. I fronted court and had legal aid, some girl who spoke to me for a couple of minutes then laid out all of these lies to the Judge that I hadn't told her at all.

I had asked God earlier if He would help me and I even had a letter from the Pastor of the church where I had been going for a couple of months. It was a good letter to use. I told God that I didn't care how long my license was suspended, but I didn't want to be locked up and didn't want a big fine.

So the legal aid did her thing, which when I heard her going on I couldn't believe it, and I'm sure the Judge saw the look I was giving her, of disbelief and disgust in her lies. Anyway I copped 18 months, cancellation of license, three months suspended jail, if I behaved for 12 months, and a $20 fine. I was amazed. A lawyer for someone else said to me, "Not sure what happened here mate but he was in filthy mood earlier, you got off real light".

*Almost three months after starting church,
one week before salvation.*

CHAPTER SIX: THE TRUE AND LIVING GOD

It was the judge who hated drink drivers because his Daughter was killed by one. So we were praising the Lord after that, and gave Him many thanks, even though we didn't even really know Him yet. But the thing that helped the most was only two of the other drink driving offences were bought up. The other two from the mainland were not mentioned. Which they hadn't forgotten the last times I had been up.

Not long after this, we were back in church on Sunday, when the preacher was up the front, asking people if they wanted to be born again. I didn't know what that was but something urged me to go up the front. This was a big thing for them. They made a show of it all, and maybe they had to.

They got the microphone and said, "Do you want to become a Christian"? I thought "What are you talking about, I've been coming to church now for three months and I'm dressing up and everything". This question confused me. I really thought I already was one.

Then the preacher said, "Do you want to give your life to the Lord" and I replied, still not sure of what response to give, "He'll do a better job with it than I've been doing". The preacher and his wife laughed and so did the people there, but I didn't care. It was like I was in some different dimension, and it was all happening at once, whatever it was. Like some altered reality in the Twilight Zone or X-Files.

He said "Just repeat after me" And started saying the sinners' prayer of a confession of faith, and repentance and asking Jesus to be Lord and Saviour of my life. And while I was trying to follow the preacher and repeat what he was saying, I started shaking from the inside again, exactly as I had when I did the first ritual for the Rosicrucians.

And I thought, "Awww, here we go again". While wondering what was happening, the spirits that were within me screamed, as loud as somebody screaming in one's ear. "NO, YOU CAN'T DO THIS," they screamed, "YOU CAN'T DO THIS, YOU'VE", then a very small pause as if they were stuck for words, "STILL GOT DOPE GROWING IN THE BUSH." I thought, "WOW", because I'd never heard them scream before, and I also thought, "What's that got to do with anything?" and "What am I doing anyway?"

I'm sure the preacher and his wife could see the shaking, although it may not have been as obvious to many, it was really happening deep within my being. And what I know happened now, was Jesus had expelled the spirits in my spirit, and He moved in, in the form of His Holy Spirit. And I was now Born Again. Praise the Lord. And this was how it happened.

> Rom 10:9-10 That if thou shalt confess with thy mouth the Lord Jesus, and shalt believe in thine heart that God hath raised him from the dead, thou shalt be saved.
>
> For with the heart man believeth unto righteousness; and with the mouth confession is made unto salvation.

I had chosen to believe and put my faith and trust in a being that I was learning about in the Bible. Someone I could trust that wanted the best for my life, and when I had made the public confession of this the Witchcraft demons and others had to leave from deep within my spirit. And my confession was made unto salvation. My spirit was cleansed and I felt good. I went home and we went back to another service that night and Poss made a confession of faith also.

When we got home that night, I threw all my dope in the fire, along with the hundreds of dollars' worth of occult books. Almost all of them went except the biggest most expensive one. It was an attachment that I had still to come out of agreement with, like other sin, and this happened later on. I went to bed, not expecting the thing that happened next. In my sleep I had a dream, massive numbers all on fire. The numbers were 26:18.

I woke up the next morning and was very surprised. I only had the one dream and it was the burning numbers. There were no nightmares and I felt total peace. My mind was still for the first time in years, and the torments of having to face the day were totally gone. I felt like I was floating on a cloud and wrapped in cotton wool or something like that.

I knew God had really spoken then and I realised that some major event had taken place, with the screaming, the shaking and now the dream and so much peace. I told Poss about the dream and we started looking for the answer in the Bible. She must have thought I said 6:18 and read something about Noah and said "He doesn't want you to build a boat does He" and I replied "I don't reckon".

It was funny and we laughed. But nothing made sense until we got to Leviticus 26:18.

> Lev 26:18 And if ye will not yet for all this hearken unto me, then I will punish you seven times more for your sins.

This was a warning I definitely needed. It came as a bit of a shock. So I said to God, "Whoa, OK, I'll be a good boy from now on, I don't want to be punished once, let alone seven times". And that hung over me for a few months until I got to this place in the Bible following my reading plan of three time new then once Old.

> Deu 26:18 And the LORD hath avouched thee this day to be his peculiar people, as he hath promised thee, and that *thou* shouldest keep all his commandments;

This taught me a lesson in searching things through. Not stopping short on what God may want to say. So the fear of sevenfold judgement, which was real, would have been softened by the grace given through the next scripture. But there were so many lessons I needed to learn, and I was hungry.

This God, who was now my God, had stopped all fear, depression, anxiety, nightmares, hopelessness, suicidal thoughts and the addictions of alcohol and marijuana, overnight. And I mean overnight. From one day to the next, I was free of all this.

I do believe that in my search when coming to Him, that the repentance I was feeling and remorse for past actions, had made me so ready for salvation. I had read in some of the Christian books that this is what He expected. But nothing changed until this one day. Feb 21st 1999, was absolutely incredible". This feeling lasted about three months.

I was saying to God, "You could tie me to a stake in the middle of a desert and throw rocks at me for the rest of my life and I would still be in a better place than where I was".

And I meant it. And this God who I decided to follow had just taken all my pain and hurt and suffering away in less than twenty four hours. I was so grateful. My mind was filled with God and Jesus, Life and Death, Heaven and Hell, Satan and Angels, and lots of stuff that had never been there before. And it was good. The Light of the World had entered. It was totally true what was said here,

> Mat 11:28-30 Come unto me, all *ye* that labour and are heavy laden, and I will give you rest.
>
> Take my yoke upon you, and learn of me; for I am meek and lowly in heart: and ye shall find rest unto your souls.
>
> For my yoke *is* easy, and my burden is light.

So the first part of this scripture had been completed, the rest had to be worked on, a lot. And I figured out that all my mess had come from the devil. Especially from what I read here,

> 1Pe 5:8 Be sober, be vigilant; because your adversary the devil, as a roaring lion, walketh about, seeking whom he may devour:

And I said this aloud to the devil, and put up the decree, only days after Salvation. "devil, I see that you had made a mess of my life and wanted me dead, and from now on, I am going to make your life as hard as I possibly can". I didn't know if I loved God more than I hated the devil, but what I had said I meant.

But there wasn't much help about. It seemed the church people didn't like talking about the devil. One person that was apparently higher up than others said, "Oh no, we don't talk about the devil, it gives him power." I thought this to be the strangest thing ever, and am so glad I resisted taking this deception on board.

Also a lot of them wanted me to stop reading the Christian prophecy books, which I really enjoyed, but I never. I was also devouring the Bible, daily, for hours at a time. I just couldn't wait to get into it. Although it was so hard to retain what I had been reading.

I had figured out what had happened after a short time. The devil had me open doors for him to gain access. Jesus Christ had come into my spirit and filled that place with light and removed the darkness.

But my soul and body were not renewed; I had to now work to bring it into alignment with his Holy Spirit, which was now the centre of my being, and my life. And I had free will to do whatever I pleased, but when I did the wrong thing it was as if a ton of bricks was placed on my back. The conviction of sin was so massive that it was easy to turn from them, and while some took longer than others to get rid of, I wanted to be obedient, so did all I could to follow the Lord Jesus Christ.

> Joh 16:7-8 Nevertheless I tell you the truth; It is expedient for you that I go away: for if I go not away, the Comforter will not come unto you; but if I depart, I will send him unto you.
>
> And when he is come, he will reprove the world of sin, and of righteousness, and of judgement:

CHAPTER SEVEN
THE NAME ABOVE ALL NAMES

The dope had gone and I hadn't had a joint or bong or beer for a month or so. Feeling good and grateful to the God, who was Jesus Christ, for this freedom that was still mine, although there were still things I had to let go of.

One was the hundred dollar book, full of pictures and diagrams. It did have a section on Jesus, but they said he was just a wise teacher, who was some special being, who taught some stuff. Not the Almighty Son of God, who died for us so we could be forgiven of our sins, set free and receive eternal life. I was beginning to understand this.

The supernatural release from the torments and weight of a lifetime and freedom I felt could not have come from some wise fella or even some Angel, which was nailed to a cross. He had to be the Son of God.

It said in the Bible, that He was God in the flesh. From what had happened to me, I could understand this or a little at least. And the words about eternal damnation I could hear also. Knowing that if our soul and spirit can exist outside our body as in Astral Projection/Soul Travel, then when the Bible mentions an eternal Heaven or Hell, I knew it was real. So every time I walked past the book on the shelf, I would get a twinge of conviction.

The Bible says,

> Deu 7:25-26 The graven images of their gods shall ye burn with fire: thou shalt not desire the silver or gold *that is* on them, nor take *it* unto thee, lest thou be snared therein: for it *is* an abomination to the LORD thy God.
>
> Neither shalt thou bring an abomination into thine house, lest thou be a cursed thing like it: *but* thou shalt utterly detest it, and thou shalt utterly abhor it; for it *is* a cursed thing.

God was onto me to destroy the last occult book that I had. I would walk past and look at it and think, "Nah, can't do it, can't do it" then in a few days it got to "Aww, maybe I better". Then a couple more and I couldn't stand it and thought, "Right, it's got to go.

And I burnt it. And felt a definite release from a soul tie that was between me and that book. Maybe this is what this scripture means, when we desire to be obedient to the Holy Spirit leading.

> 1Jn 3:9 Whosoever is born of God doth not commit sin; for his seed remaineth in him: and he cannot sin, because he is born of God.

The other alternative for me was this which I see many believers do, and it is all downhill after. They ignore the leading of the Holy Ghost, because they love their sin more than Jesus, and sear their conscience like a big burn scar.

> 1Ti 4:1-2 Now the Spirit speaketh expressly, that in the latter times some shall depart from the faith, giving heed to seducing spirits, and doctrines of devils;
>
> Speaking lies in hypocrisy; having their conscience seared with a hot iron;

Poss and I went to an evening service at the church, and a visiting speaker was telling the church "If you want to get close to God, you have to give him everything". I agreed because I had just given the book over and felt better for it, and in my mind that every time we let go of the wrong thing, it was for our benefit. The God Jesus we were following loved us and wanted the best for us.

But the thing was this person was staring at me the whole time. I was in the middle seats half way up the back and I felt like diving under the chairs. It was so uncomfortable. The thoughts I had went like this. "This old sheila knows I've got dope growing in the bush, I bet, she can see it on me or something". So not being able to escape her glare, I became so convicted I said, "Righto God, I will pull it all out when I get home".

And there was a lot. I'd been growing dope for years and this was my best season. Some of my shared crops I decided to hand over to the partners, which when I told them in the next few days, they were extremely happy about, but very confused as well. The dope close by, I went and pulled out as soon as I got home from this church meeting.

As I only had around 15 minutes of daylight left, I had told God on the way back to our house, which was in the thick Tasmanian bush, "Alright, I'll rip the dope out for you God". Being around late March or early April, about 2 weeks before the plants were ready to harvest, made it even harder to do, but for what I had received from God and what I thought He could do for me, I was willing to risk the sacrifice.

I got out of the car and ran up the bush and pulled one plot out and threw them in the river. I thought the wallabies won't get stoned if I do that. And getting back to the house, right on dark, I knew there was not time to get to the next plot. So I said to God, "I can't make it now, I'll do it tomorrow", which I did purpose to do.

The next day though I had to go into Launceston, over a two hour drive, and get a shotgun pellet dug out from above my ear, which was annoying me when I tried to sleep. It was creating pain and headaches when I lay on that side of my head.

So in we go, cut, chop, dig, and there it was, then home again after two more hours, and a bit. It was early evening, and I was tired and went and lay down on my bed. I was about to go to sleep when a voice spoke to me and said "Finish your washing". I knew it was God wanting me to rip the rest of the dope out, and I did say that I would do it today. But I said "Aww God, I'm tired, I'll do it tomorrow".

But what happened next, shot me off the bed and into in to a sprint straight up the bush. God obviously wasn't happy with my excuse, and with a very loud rebuke He said "NOW". It did frighten me a bit and at that time, as well as other times in my walk, I had upset him. I knew this God wasn't just the fairy flossy, Santa Claus that many are running after.

This is easy to see when one reads the Old Testament, and easy to see in the New, when the Old has been looked at. I did learn a fear of the Lord that day, which I did need and would need it very much.

I arrived at the plants and ripped them out and was dancing around waving them in the air, and throwing them into the bush saying, "How's this God, How's this," like some spoilt little kid who was made do something they didn't want to do. But this fitted perfectly the parable here.

> Mat 21:28-32 But what think ye? A *certain* man had two sons; and he came to the first, and said, Son, go work to day in my vineyard.
>
> He answered and said, I will not: but afterward he repented, and went.
>
> And he came to the second, and said likewise. And he answered and said, I *go,* sir: and went not.
>
> Whether of them twain did the will of *his* father? They say unto him, The first. Jesus saith unto them, Verily I say unto you, That the publicans and the harlots go into the kingdom of God before you.
>
> For John came unto you in the way of righteousness, and ye believed him not: but the publicans and the harlots believed him: and ye, when ye had seen *it,* repented not afterward, that ye might believe him.

Although it wasn't because I didn't want to do it, it was because I was tired and I thought it an inconvenient time. But I had told God that I would do it the next day and He let me know that the next day was "NOW" and I learned to not say things to Him or make oaths I wouldn't keep, and not to procrastinate.

> Mat 5:33-37 Again, ye have heard that it hath been said by them of old time, Thou shalt not forswear thyself, but shalt perform unto the Lord thine oaths:
>
> But I say unto you, Swear not at all; neither by heaven; for it is God's throne:
>
> Nor by the earth; for it is his footstool: neither by Jerusalem; for it is the city of the great King.
>
> Neither shalt thou swear by thy head, because thou canst not make one hair white or black.
>
> But let your communication be, Yea, yea; Nay, nay: for whatsoever is more than these cometh of evil.

This time however I was not even thinking on how stoned the wallabies, possums and wombats were going to get by eating the dope plants. That never even entered my mind. Word got around about this and my mates were so disappointed that they weren't chosen to be the recipients of the discarded dope, like the partners in crime were of the crops that were still growing.

CHAPTER SEVEN: THE NAME ABOVE ALL NAMES

Camera shy

I'm sure they would have thought me saner with the "Tower of Power" and the 'Flotation Coffin, than to throw all my dope away. To them now, I had really "Tripped out!"

After around two months into our salvation, we had wanted to get baptized. But the church said we should be married first. We were going so well. The torments had never come back and life was now happy. Compared to where I was, it was like a fairy tale. I was so appreciative of God. And if God wanted us to get married, I didn't mind.

I was happy with Poss. And she must have been happy with me because when we talked about this and I just said "Let's do it then", she agreed.

We were married, with the church doing all for us and most showing up and a few friends, it was more than we expected, although our parents never came. Poss was given away by an old friend Leo we knew and it was a happy day.

We went and got baptized after in St Helens Bay and it was freezing cold but a beautiful still calm day, and the scene just like a work of art I thought. And things were good. Then we went on our honeymoon.

On the ship to the mainland, we thought because we hadn't had a drink of alcohol for around three months, we could control it. But we were wrong. It started to overtake us in the next few months and then I started playing football and drinking again the next year and the conviction was heavy but no way to stop.

I cartwheeled down some stairs and nearly broke my neck and was in pain for six months. I went to a preacher who was healing people and the pain left and so did another complaint I had. God was amazing!

Also the thoughts of depression and anxiety and other torments were coming back. Nowhere near as bad but they became constant. They sounded like they were from outside, like a wireless being left on in another room. The Bible says this about what was happening, but I had to work all this out by myself. Thank God for His word.

> Mat 12:43-45 When the unclean spirit is gone out of a man, he walketh through dry places, seeking rest, and findeth none.
>
> Then he saith, I will return into my house from whence I came out; and when he is come, he findeth *it* empty, swept, and garnished.
>
> Then goeth he, and taketh with himself seven other spirits more wicked than himself, and they enter in and dwell there: and the last *state* of that man is worse than the first. Even so shall it be also unto this wicked generation.

So the demons that had been banished by Jesus when He saved me, had decided to come back and take back their house. And there were a few extras, no doubt. I could cope with this. It wasn't too bad, nothing like before, but annoying.

The visiting minister lined us all up in the church and said "Tell me what the problem is and I'll pray for you. So when I said "My mind is wandering" he sprang into action, grabbed my head like a vice and said "You tormenting lying spirits, come out of him, in Jesus name". I fell over and when I got up I had realized they were gone.

I thought, "Wow, they were demons, and this bloke could get them on the run." And because of hearing things like, Christians all have this authority, and reading things like this, and believing, I was going to worry the devil. I knew it.

> Mar 16:16-18 He that believeth and is baptized shall be saved; but he that believeth not shall be damned.
>
> And these signs shall follow them that believe; In my name shall they cast out devils; they shall speak with new tongues;
>
> They shall take up serpents; and if they drink any deadly thing, it shall not hurt them; they shall lay hands on the sick, and they shall recover.

I started to take authority over any torment and emotional struggles that I had. It was slow at first with a little bit of effort and persistence needed but then the demons would leave my vicinity quicker and quicker. I was starting to gain confidence in the Name of Jesus, and how He could use His people to take back the land. Or my land and my temple, and trespassers certainly weren't welcome.

> Php 2:9-11 Wherefore God also hath highly exalted him, and given him a name which is above every name:
>
> That at the name of Jesus every knee should bow, of *things* in heaven, and *things* in earth, and *things* under the earth;
>
> And *that* every tongue should confess that Jesus Christ *is* Lord, to the glory of God the Father.

It was a sense of power that I had and the fear of the unknown and defeat was melting away. Another demon that came out of my soul was a religious spirit. I was still struggling with alcohol but God was gracious and taught me another great lesson. I was talking with a man, who was asked to join the Masons, but he rejected them and their offers and he said they all drove past his house in a big procession and waved their finger at him, like the "Go Away" wave, which upset him.

I didn't like the Rosicrucians so we had a bit of a hate session on them, knowing they were witchcraft organizations. Then the topic changed onto the Catholic Church. I said" Ahh the Catholics are worse than the Masons" and straight away I felt like a cloak or garment had been ripped off me, and a voice started speaking within and said, "You've blown it now, you just blasphemed the Holy Spirit and can't be saved, and are now going to burn in Hell".

I actually started crying and told the man what just happened. I was devastated. After all that God had did for me I had just knocked the church and was doomed. It took me a couple of days for the grief to subside and for me to figure out that it had been a religious spirit that had come out. My rejection of Catholicism was the renunciation needed for it to lose its legal right and it had to leave. Even without casting anything out.

And I knew it left because now I never thought of the Catholic Church as being from God. All the respect I had for the Pope had vanished and my eyes had been open to the deception that this harlot religion is playing. It was an eye opener for sure, how God had done this within me. With deliverance, it can change the destructive thought patterns, and we can begin to go in a right direction. It's not just freedom from emotional things.

I went and told Jezza to renounce the Catholic Church as well, and he did. Another fella who I had helped to get saved, who had been brought up in the Catholic cult, couldn't even say the words, so I don't know if he ever got over it. I was happy that another demon in me had been banished. I definitely knew my thought patterns had changed. And I was starting to have more faith in God and His Word.

The roller coaster was still going full speed. High highs and low lows, no doubt enhanced by the fact that I was drinking during the week with my football mates and wracked with guilt and shame for a couple of days afterwards, and it was getting worse.

Some American Prophets, or so I was told that's what they were, were coming to the church. If you did a fast, God may give you more Grace and give you a good word I was told also. So I did 24 hours out of the 72 that I had aimed for. I was feeling condemned even for that. And I was totally expecting a smack on the bum from God for the drinking I was doing at the football sheds and Pub.

If the palm readers and dowsers and new age prognosticators that I knew in the past could see into the future and tell you the hidden things of darkness, then I was so worried that Prophets from the real God could see more.

But God isn't like our earthly parents, he is so much greater. This scripture became so real to me after what happened.

> Rom 2:4 Or despisest thou the riches of his goodness and forbearance and longsuffering; not knowing that the goodness of God leadeth thee to repentance?

I experienced His goodness in this way, and a big change came in my life. The Prophets spoke and both said amazing words that excited me and really sunk in deep. The condemnation and insecurities were weakened in me so much by these words of Hope. Poss was told that God was going to bless her, and we left the church on a massive high that wasn't deflated overnight.

I went to the football the next Saturday and had a few beers. But the thoughts of wanting to please God and if what the Prophets had said were true, then I needed to stop this sin and get clean. So that was the last time I drank alcohol.

When they laid hands on me, the words they spoke were imparted to me and I was lifted out of the snare of bondage by the goodness of God! And the desire to serve him overrode the desire to drink.

CHAPTER SEVEN: THE NAME ABOVE ALL NAMES

Another thing that happened was I asked God if I was ever going to preach. Now I asked him thousands of questions. And He answered in lots of ways. A voice, a scripture, another believer to tell the answer, TV, radio, even number plates on cars would give me scripture reference or confirm. There were dreams and a few short visions and quick picture flashes.

There was no shortage to the ways He could and would and was speaking. My eyes and ears were open. I was starving for Him. So this time He spoke through the still small voice and said, "You will speak to thousands".

Now I was slow of speech and my vocabulary wasn't real flash. I sounded like an old farmer, because that's where I'd come from, and wasn't sure how this would come to pass. But God confirmed this only a couple of days later.

In church I was talking to a man and another came up and he was meant to have a prophetic gift or words of knowledge. And he looked at the other man I was speaking with and said "I just feel God wants me to tell you, that you will speak to thousands". This excited me but I didn't tell him that the word he gave was right, but to the wrong person. Anyway I thanked God for the encouragement I had received from this wayward spiritual fire. But it only needed to land in my ears.

Also in this time we had been renting and on unemployment benefits. We have some chickens that were laying eggs and an old friend Terry used to bring us scraps from the supermarket for them. We were trying to tithe 10% of what we had and it would leave us short for a few days. But that was a small sacrifice to make, because surely the money was going to help get people saved, and as long as we had smokes though we were happy.

But in these scraps God was blessing us. If we needed veggies, there they were, if we needed bread, it was there, fruit, no problem. Sometimes we even got meat that was out of date only a day or two. It was amazing and we thanked God for His provision. Now I know some would say we were cursed having to eat like this, but little do they know. We thanked God for this every time.

We were sick of renting a house, and the dead money it was costing us, so we prayed for a house of our own. When we were finished I walked out to the kitchen and said to God aloud, "God, I don't care if I have to live in a tent for the rest of my life, I'm just glad I've got you" and went on my way.

I did truly mean it though. And God answered. The Word of God says this,

> Jas 4:3 Ye ask, and receive not, because ye ask amiss, that ye may consume *it* upon your lusts.

I had not asked amiss obviously and within about two weeks we made an offer on a house on an acre of land in a place that I had wanted to live for about the last ten years. And we got it for $15,000. It was an absolute miracle to us.

People couldn't believe it and sometimes their jealousy was easy to see. Some obviously thought they deserved it more than us. I thought the same. And it wasn't until we paid it off a couple of years later that I could accept it was actually ours. Even the bank manager was amazed when he put the loan request in and it was back within 10 minutes. He said he had never seen that before. And our repayments were just $80 a month.

Pete & Poss at the front of thier Pyenganna home

And that wasn't the end of the Grace that God put on our lives. Poss got a good job in the hospital working weekends, time and a half and double time.

Her 3 day week was good money, and if I needed anything, people would ring and knock on the door every time, with work for me. I never had to look for a job, they just came. And I knew it was from the prayer I prayed in the kitchen of that rented house, after telling him that He was more important and wanted more by me than any worldly possessions.

I still feel like this and we are blessed more than anyone I know. That is the Truth.

CHAPTER EIGHT
IF YOU BELIEVE

So here I was, the day of my destiny, or whatever purpose God had for me. Today was the day I found out what it was that He'd told me about.

But that thought was far from my mind while looking at what the spirits of Cancer and Death can do to a Human body. And also seeing the futile attempt of man to battle these demons, my business and concerns were basically non-existent in my thoughts and in these minutes that I was with my dying Mother.

The chemo drip was a nasty brown colour and it wasn't just hooked into her arm, it was getting pumped into a hole, right in front of her heart. A straight out connection, obviously to a larger vein or artery than the arm could supply, or even into the heart itself, I wasn't sure.

I wondered at the amount of money that Mum and Dad were forking out for this sort of treatment. This was obviously a last desperate attempt to cling to life that was fleeing away so quickly now.

The past of the tobacco and all the alcohol drank, being from a family of Hotel owners and big drinkers, although Catholics, had taken a toll, and whatever bitterness was in her spirit had possibly opened the door to these spirits.

My thoughts were on the chemo drip. I had looked into alternative cancer treatments and stayed with a man whose 82 year old mother was cured by a tincture taken internally and made from cloves, wormwood and the hull of the black walnut. It tasted like crap, but these bitter herbs had cured so many. The man's mother had made 20 litres of it and her son was giving it away for free.

I was at his house when a man knocked on the door and had come to thank him for the bottle of this parasite destroying mixture because it had healed his cancer.

I said "Wow George, that's pretty good." He said, "Yeah, he's not the only one" and pulled out 2 letters of gratitude from others who had written him thanking him for the same. So it wasn't just a one off or a fluke.

But right now, this info was useless. My Mother would be dead before any of that could even be sent in the mail, let alone have the desired time to work in her body. I'd spoken to her over the phone a while back and it didn't end well. It seemed that each other's close company always bought the worst out in us both.

I had visited some friends around Lake Bolac before seeing my mother for the first time in a few years. I heard this at least four times, the day before seeing my mother, "Sorry to hear about your mother Pete, sorry to hear about your mother". That was the standard response. And mine was, "Yeah, oh well, we'll see what happens". Even though my thoughts were, "fair dinkum, she's not dead yet, you've got her gone and buried already." But I hadn't seen her yet, which was probably a good thing.

By not having seen her state of health had kept the thief from stealing any faith or hope from me, not that I had any big expectations. I had yet to see anyone ever healed from a major sickness, even in the church. They were all just stories or testimonies that you watch on TV or in books. Minor miracles, yes, they had been numerous in our life. But to defeat a spirit of death itself, I wasn't full of faith, but I didn't doubt either. There were lots of thoughts, but none meant anything until tomorrow.

I had done this below without even thinking about the scripture, not because of the formula here, but because of the desire in my heart, for the relationship between my Mother and myself to be restored.

> Mat 17:21 Howbeit this kind goeth not out but by prayer and fasting.

Makes you wonder why some Bible versions have removed this scripture. Do a quick check. Is it in yours?

Immediately after my mother repeated the sinners' prayer, a righteous anger came over me. It was like my eyes were opened and my mother had disappeared, and I was all alone with the spirits of cancer and death. So I said this, which just seemed to flow out of me. There were no rehearsals that had taken place, and no pre planning at all. The words just came out, and I could feel the power and authority in them,

CHAPTER EIGHT: IF YOU BELIEVE

and also the compassion behind them, for my mother from me, but it also must have come from God too. Because I never knew this was in me.

I was amazed myself at the words. I know I had commanded the things that were tormenting me to leave in the past, and they would, whether it was depression, anxiety, confusion, condemnation, false guilt or shame, even a cold or two, but to attack something this big that had complete control over my mother was something totally new for me. I began "I take authority over you Cancer, and I bind you and rebuke you, and I command you to leave my mother right now, get out in the name of Jesus Christ!"

The righteous anger behind these words was so powerful. I was now operating in a faith that I had never experienced. There was no doubting or wondering "Did that work? Was that a good prayer? Did God hear that?" I was now in the realm of the place in the Bible that says,

> Mar 11:23-24 For verily I say unto you, That whosoever shall say unto this mountain, Be thou removed, and be thou cast into the sea; and shall not doubt in his heart, but shall believe that those things which he saith shall come to pass; he shall have whatsoever he saith.
>
> Therefore I say unto you, What things soever ye desire, when ye pray, believe that ye receive *them*, and ye shall have *them*.

I had never been here before and it felt like a good place to be at this time. "I take authority over you Death, and I bind you and rebuke you, and I command you to leave my mother right now, get out in the name of Jesus Christ!"

So that was it, the prayers were over, the righteous anger subsided and we just started talking again. No great manifestation, or coughing or vomiting out anything, just peace. But in around 10 minutes my Mother called out to my father and said "can you bring me some noodles, I'm hungry". She hadn't eaten in a fortnight.

I knew straight away that God had healed her and I told my father the same. He had trouble believing that she was hungry, and was speechless when I was saying that she was healed, being obviously full of doubt, but not me. I had been in the room for little more than half an hour when I got up and left the house and went back to my brother's house. In the middle of that same night, my mother had started vomiting up lots of this black gunk and they thought she was dying, but it was quite the opposite. The spirits that were told to leave had to go. And so did the sickness attached to them. And so she recovered.

I was thinking the next day about all the timing and the healing and started to cry, wondering why God would choose me to do this, and to hand to me the power to heal and cast out demons. It was all too much for me. So I was humbled, but in other thoughts I pictured myself as like the prosperity preachers on TV, travelling the world, being somebody. But little did I know that there was much testing and refining before these gifts would be a lot more consistent in my life. And some of those desires within definitely had to be dealt with. And they were quickly extinguished.

The next few times I prayed for people, thinking I had the magic wand, and the formula down pat, nothing happened. And I looked like an idiot. My father started going back to the Catholic Church after 20 years or so absence, maybe because of some vow he made with God about healing Mum?

My Brother went around the small town of Lake Bolac saying "Peter had come and prayed for Mum and God healed her". Then I heard him say that Mum went around town saying, "It wasn't bloody Peter, it was the chemo that has healed me". Which I had to respond in a letter to tell her to repent, saying "It is God who has given you a second chance, glorify him, and don't anger Him".

Anyway she ignored that. Which I knew would happen. When I got shot a mate asked her how I was going when I was in hospital and he said her response was, "They should have bloody killed him". So you can tell where our relationship was at.

Anyway Mum went to the doctor and he was amazed. The cancer was 95% gone. I knew if she just glorified God then He would deal with the rest of it. But in the Catholics mind, unless you are a verified saint, you can't do miracles. They are full of religion and ritual and tradition, which are very big blockages to the real truth.

I had a dream about eight months later and a voice spoke to me and said, "Your Mothers cancer has come back". I said in the dream, "That's OK; I'll just go and rebuke it". Which when I awoke I thought that a rebuke was all it would take. I traveled back to the mainland to pray again, but my rebuke and prayers didn't heal her this time, but she did say that she could feel them going in.

CHAPTER EIGHT: IF YOU BELIEVE

I still hadn't learnt persistence in the laying on of hands prayer. So I gave up and she died a few weeks later. But the relationship was a lot better. I spent a couple of days at home. She was in the lounge room on a stretcher and there was peace.

I did notice in the camper van that she had, a Jimmy Swaggart tape, that she must have heard I don't know how many times, on the drive she took from Western Victoria to North Queensland and back, after the healing that God gave her.

But there was no chemo now. I prayed with her and we talked. She had softened and so had I. And it was that God renewed our relationship, right at the end, and I am very happy about this. She died a few days after I left and I returned for the funeral. In which I cried, but all was OK now.

I do believe she was saved and the night she died I had heard that my sister had been feeding two orphaned healthy lambs for a couple of weeks and one mysteriously died the same night Mum did.

I still wonder if the devil had come for her and was denied, and so took one of the little lambs instead. There was so much symbolism around this. And though the lamb lost its life, I believed this was a sign, that everything was good.

CHAPTER NINE
A COLD RECEPTION

Arriving back in Tassie, I attended the home church on the Sunday. I was so looking forward to telling the congregation about the miracle that had happened with my mother.

They spoke about miracles and healings and prayed for people a lot, not that I ever seen too many healings, but they believed they could be done by believers. So I thought I would encourage them and excite them and give them my good news.

I told a few and although they tried to be happy, it seemed a struggle for them. As a matter of fact some looked in pain or something, like they didn't want to believe. I didn't think I was bragging or boasting that much. Maybe I was.

My mother had been healed of an incurable disease and I was rejoicing. I just thought it would be easier to round up some people who were happy for this also. But it seemed to me like if anyone was meant to heal anybody in that place; it had to be the elders and leaders. I think us babes in Christ weren't even meant to pray for anyone. But ex scumbags off the street, surely God wouldn't and couldn't work through them.

I thought I could detect an attitude of envy and jealousy, and things in the Sunday services began to deteriorate quickly for me. Things became a drag and I had trouble understanding why these people Poss and I had called family now, seemed to be coming against me. The scripture below gave me comfort though. I had not forgotten where I came from, so God confirmed His Word to me. Some hypocrisy was being uncovered.

CHAPTER NINE: A COLD RECEPTION

> 1Co 1:26-29 For ye see your calling, brethren, how that not many wise men after the flesh, not many mighty, not many noble, *are called*:
>
> But God hath chosen the foolish things of the world to confound the wise; and God hath chosen the weak things of the world to confound the things which are mighty;
>
> And base things of the world, and things which are despised, hath God chosen, *yea*, and things which are not, to bring to nought things that are:
>
> That no flesh should glory in his presence.

And in the next six months, things would really go south. The church had a platform speaking teaching where we all got to share a five minute talk. I spoke on hearing from God, where I knew He was speaking to me, but it seemed that others weren't happy with that, with an elder getting up, whose Husband had said out loud from the pulpit "I've never heard God speak", and she started to correct part of what I had said. She never corrected anyone else. I knew it was a miniature war on here, and somehow I had become the enemy, and I didn't know how to fight it. But God was with me.

There was a man there this night that was a young believer and asked a leader a question. The leader (We'll call him Brian) had already announced that the night was over and he was very short and impatient with him. I thought "Come on Brian, go easy on him and give him a go". Then to my surprise an audible voice spoke and said, "HE'LL BE GONE IN SIX MONTHS". I knew straight away it was God.

The voice was so calm and clear but from outside me. And I wondered if anyone else heard it. But looking around it was plain that they did not. Driving home I was asking God, "Who is going in six months? Which one? Are they leaving town", although I knew already that it was Brian and it may have been death.

I wrestled with this for a bit and said "If I see Brian getting crook, I'll go and tell him." After about four months' time, Brian started to break out in big black blotches. I knew it was close, but I didn't want it to be me that had to tell him.

So God gave me a way of escape, or so I thought. A leader of the church who I was working with in the bush came out to our house at Pyengana and said. "We know somebody knows something about

Brian, but they aren't saying". Maybe he had heard from a couple of younger believers in the church that I had mentioned this to but I'm not sure.

I said "It's me" and I told him what happened, and said that the six months is getting close. He said "You should go and tell the Pastor and elders'. So I did. The Pastor was new at the job, but not new in the church.

The other younger Pastor who was gone about 4 months before now, who I did like though, (because he had a background that was a bit wayward and I could relate to him), had come adrift. He bought a Harley with the tithe money, which some of the money men weren't happy with. He also beat up one of the congregation members sons, because of some adultery happening with the wife of a friend of his, and also got on the dope and the grog and was fighting in the pubs.

So the honeymoon seemed to be over in the church. It all went to crap. A lot of people had left and from what I also understand now, the witches were targeting it and cursing it severely. But when their theology was "We don't talk about the devil, it gives him power", and then just hope that the bad will just go away, there is no hope for any victory. This is a common problem in Christianity now. And many fall away because of it.

The Pastor and one Elder listened to me and I thought, "Great, they have to deal with it now, I'm off the hook". I did also tell them about what I believed that if Brian and his wife fulfilled the prophecy that was spoken over their life, then the sickness would leave. I did get that answer after travailing in prayer for Brian, because he was another who I liked and had helped encourage me in the past by his testimony. And if God had given me the word of knowledge to start with then I had no doubt He would give me the answer to this dilemma as well.

Meanwhile I had heard that the church was taking Brian here and there and having some healers come and pray but they were saying, "We don't know what is wrong. God isn't healing him".

I had already told them what I heard but it wasn't heeded and I was getting upset. I definitely didn't want Brian to die, and in my head, he was going to, on the same date I had heard. So I went to the Pastor about two weeks after I told him what God had told me and said, "Did you go and tell Brian about what I told you"? He said "No".

I couldn't believe it. My heart sank. I said "Why not"? There was a wrestle within me now because for whatever reason, I was ignored,

CHAPTER NINE: A COLD RECEPTION

and time was ticking. Whether they thought God wouldn't speak to me or they wanted to keep things positive, I don't know. But this frustrated me so much. Then the Pastor said, "You go and tell him".

So I said in my anger, "OK, I'll tell him, and if he doesn't listen, he will be dead on this date, give or take a week or so". I knew God had spoken and believed that God had given the way of escape for him through prayer.

I went straight to Brian's house and stood in the lounge room and told him what I had heard, and the way of escape and got it off my chest. I didn't do it in anger, I did like Brian and wasn't angry at him or his wife. We did have a little bit to do with them. And they seemed to take it well. It was surprising how calm they were.

About five days later Brian's wife rings up. And she said "Oh we prayed about what you said and we did have the money to do that what you said and were going to do it, but we decided to buy a car instead". I couldn't believe it.

I'm not sure what her thinking was with this response to what I had told them, but it wasn't received well from me. She would have been a lot better to say nothing, and I could not see any wisdom here. And so I said to her over the phone "OK, Brian will be dead on this day" (which was the day, six months from the time the audible voice spoke), and hung up the phone.

I had been a Believer now and involved with that church for almost four years exactly. And the first three and a half years we loved it. But things deteriorated badly and quickly.

But now I know for a fact (after praying deliverance for the High Priestess that was over the whole Tasmanian coven, who she said they visited it regularly) that the witches had been around St Helens cursing and bringing in sickness and death and division and strife and all sorts of things, exactly as they are in other churches around Tasmania still. They did their work and in the end succeeded.

And Brian died and I was angry with some of the people involved and couldn't believe how all this was dealt with. I wrestled with many negative thoughts against them. And those thoughts were winning. Poss went to Brian's funeral but I couldn't go. I was too angry, believing that it didn't have to be. Poss said it was more of a celebration than a sad departure, but I was not in a party mood.

A few days later the fella I worked with who was a leader in the church rang me and said he was coming to visit. I told him "Don't come out here, that's not a good idea, just stay away". He came anyway.

I do believe that he had believed me, but some of his attitude was not welcomed by me and he said something that he shouldn't of, and he was swiftly grabbed around the throat over the kitchen table and thrown out the door.

I did feel a bit, or a lot guilty over that and had to repent and apologise a while later. Even though I was arguing with God that he shouldn't have said what he said and deserved what he got. But I had to humble myself. It took a while to get around to it but he was good about it. I did work with him after all and we had played some footy together. And I think in some way he understood my frustrations.

Anyway, I was sick of church and wanted it to improve for me so I was on my knees in the lounge room praying, "God, please fix the church, make it how you want it to be". After about five minutes and audible voice spoke and said, "DON'T GO".

This was the same voice He had spoken with six months earlier, and told me about Brian. I got up and was looking around the room, as you do when a voice comes out of the blue, and I began to say, "Is that you God"? I had recognised the voice but had to say something. I couldn't just hear that without some sort of test.

I said "They are telling me I have to go to church or I'll go to Hell, that I have to tithe and obey the elders and everything they say, forsake not the gathering and that I have to come under the covering", and mentioned some of the other controls that had been put in place to keep the sheep from straying. And I have seen this technique in many places afterwards also that brings in the bondage to fear. And it works well for those in charge.

Then the same audible Voice said "ANCHOR YOURSELF IN THE WORD".

I leaped for joy. I'm serious. I was jumping around our lounge room like a teenager who just got tickets to the AFL Grand Final. I knew the devil would never tell me to read the Bible and I was so pleased I didn't have to return to church. It had become such a pain. I told the Christian man who I worked with and he said "God wouldn't say that" and I just said "Well He did" knowing what I had heard.

So I never went back to church and I heard that they were saying I had done witchcraft on Brian to bump him off and because I knew the date of his death, I must have been working for the devil.

CHAPTER NINE: A COLD RECEPTION

Which didn't help my temperament much, and no doubt God knew I couldn't return. I was far from perfected, and maybe this was the best thing for all of us.

There were a lot of things swept under the rug there in that last six months. But things can catch up to you when you least expect it.

> Heb 4:13 Neither is there any creature that is not manifest in his sight: but all things *are* naked and opened unto the eyes of him with whom we have to do.

CHAPTER TEN
THE WILDERNESS

And the wilderness had begun.

> Mat 4:1 Then was Jesus led up of the Spirit into the wilderness to be tempted of the devil.

There were many struggles and trials and temptations, fears and discouragements, and supernatural enemies. It was a place where I learned so much about God, mainly because I had no man's hand to hold.

And that was part of what I had to overcome. Years of rejection, self-condemnation, no responsibility and all sorts of insecurities had to be removed. If anyone had said follow me, I would have. But Jesus had said to follow Him. So I did. As best I could.

> Mat 4:19 And he saith unto them, Follow me, and I will make you fishers of men.

After a time I was happier here than what I had seen as the alternative. Being cloned to what the Pastor and leaders want and running in the same circles that a lot of the church is now, the game of follow the leader. Continually going around the foothills but never climbing the mountains.

> 2Ti 3:7 Ever learning, and never able to come to the knowledge of the truth.

But now if I needed answers, I had to go to Him. The one who gave me Life was the one I needed to trust to lead me through this season. However long it would last. But I enjoyed His Company. And I was enjoying the excitement of the Kingdom of God and what else He had for me.

> Jer 33:3 Call unto me, and I will answer thee, and shew thee great and mighty things, which thou knowest not.

CHAPTER TEN: THE WILDERNESS

I didn't know where the ride would end or how fast it could go, but I was in for the entirety, that I knew. I had found the truth and was determined to stick with it. Unlike many, who I had seen fall away. Some quick, some slow, but it was sad to watch. But nothing has changed in two thousand years. Back then they came and left also.

> Joh 6:66-69 From that time many of his disciples went back, and walked no more with him.
>
> Then said Jesus unto the twelve, Will ye also go away?
>
> Then Simon Peter answered him, Lord, to whom shall we go? Thou hast the words of eternal life.
>
> And we believe and are sure that thou art that Christ, the Son of the living God.

Also the parable of the seed and sower revealed the reasons for this as well. It was amazing to watch the truth of the Word of God take place, no matter how saddening it was.

> Luk 8:11-14 Now the parable is this: The seed is the word of God.
>
> Those by the way side are they that hear; then cometh the devil, and taketh away the word out of their hearts, lest they should believe and be saved.
>
> They on the rock are they, which, when they hear, receive the word with joy; and these have no root, which for a while believe, and in time of temptation fall away.
>
> And that which fell among thorns are they, which, when they have heard, go forth, and are choked with cares and riches and pleasures of this life, and bring no fruit to perfection.

There were so many things at war in my mind. About what had just happened in the church and amongst the people we had called family for a few years. Now I had become their enemy. Most had seemed to jump on the witchcraft story, so I felt condemned and doomed to Hell.

With the devil wanting me back in church, where I could be controlled, I wrestled much with those thoughts, but knowing that my God wanted me free; I decided to stay away from the place we had called home for four years. And living 25 minutes from St Helens, we were in a little sanctuary, except when we went to town. There we would sometimes see the people who were the believers. They didn't seem to greet us or say hello, and it became obvious to us that we were outcast and rejected. Though Jesus was rejected and this was part of the lessons I had to learn. Not that I knew that then. But slowly I would understand.

I wrestled with the condemnation of the enemy, saying it was my entire fault, you loser, God hates you now and you're doomed. There was another small group of believers in St Helens, and they had all been offended by the larger mob. So they were a renegade group. Both groups didn't like each other and that was obvious.

I had gone there a few times when I felt like it while being a member of the larger entity, and it wasn't hard to see this was frowned upon. Even visiting the Anglican Church right next door to the Pentecostal group I was in was looked down upon. And it was the same with the smaller group.

Around every second sermon in the smaller place, the preacher would be subtle and lay the boots into their ex church, and all would nod in agreement and say Amen. Everybody knew who he was talking about, even though he wouldn't mention names.

But this was the state of spiritual strength and righteousness in St Helens. Later on this church would close, after I had offended the Pastor so much, but not from my own planning, but in just another test of obedience for me.

I had a plan. There was a Pentecostal church up the road about 35 minutes away from Pyengana, and I thought, "Right, if I was to blame for all this mess in St Helens then I will see if it follows me to Winnaleah Church". I was determined to just sit still, say little and see what came next.

So off I went, sitting up the back. Only a couple of blokes came and said hello over a few weeks. One was Johnno, an old muso that would become a good friend over time. He had a story to tell and what happened in his later life, but no room for that here.

I attended every Sunday for 12 months faithfully, keeping quiet and trying to blend in. But that was almost impossible. They had obviously heard about what happened in St Helens, and most were very wary.

One of the Elders owned a farm, and a man worked there who was chasing a woman in the St Helens church. And I didn't have to be Einstein to figure out what had happened. Some people have itching ears and open them to anything. No doubt they had received the twisted version of the story of Brian.

CHAPTER TEN: THE WILDERNESS

I knew this to be so after 12 months of visiting every Sunday. Poss could only come every second week, because she was working the other weekends. But for those 12 months, I would walk in every Sunday, and the Pastor and his wife would turn away. It was so obvious. They only spoke to me about three or four times. You may say I'm paranoid and delusional, but there were only about 15 people in the church. It was a concerted effort to ignore me. But I knew what churches were like by now and made the most of it.

I did get my old mate Jezza to come and he got saved and then a mate of his got saved also, so things were going well. I wasn't too worried about the other stuff, now I had some people who respected me for caring. I did get a vision of a blockage in the church and town and delivered it to the Pastor. But nothing was done about it, and the thing I was shown caused a lot of trouble for them in the near future.

I went up the front once or twice when they thought the prophecy bug was biting to get a word. The quiet music was playing and everyone would act extremely holy. One word for me was, "If you submit to the elders and come under leadership, then God can use you". "Fair Dinkum, what sort of control spirit was that who had just spoken" I thought.

I'd already seen the fleshy prophecies of the churches and the twisted prophecies of the divination spirits operating in the church. I wasn't going to be cloned into their system. I'm not sure how they expected my submission to happen. They never knew how I thought; they had hardly spoken to me. Never asked if or what my troubles were, but made out that God was telling me to do what they say. Or obviously, I would end up in the eternal fires of Hell, damned for all time. It was a bit of a joke to me.

I don't remember getting up again for a word. This witchcraft mind control of intimidation and manipulation was in all the churches. It kept bums on seats and dollars coming in.

I was having many dreams and just after leaving the St Helens church, a massive snake, as round as a 44 gallon drum and as long as a cricket pitch, bit me on the side, around the rib cage. It was so scary. But the scariest thing was that its head was one of the women from the church. And that spirit, that attacks men, had attacked me and landed one on me.

Back then, I hadn't learnt any real defence to these curses. It is no wonder that the divination spirit that Paul drove out is also called a spirit of Python.

I had many dreams of snakes trying to attack, but now in my dreams I had begun to trample them and beat them with sticks. And I understood that when the women there in Winnaleah, who seemed to be under the same spell as the St Helens ones, tried to crush me or speak evil of me, I had to learn to pray and put a stop to their mouths. Or so it seemed.

I did learn later that this was exactly what was happening. God gave me grace to survive for this season. God was with me, and I was able to get people to come to church, only by asking them. This seemed to upset some.

They did ask me back at St Helens once, what I was doing to get them to come and I just told the truth. "I just ask them" I said.

One day the Pastors wife decided to have a go at me. She got up behind the pulpit and said in her sermon, "It's not about bringing people to church" and was looking straight at me. I became wild with her and Poss couldn't believe it was said either. I thought, "OK, I won't bring anyone here at all anymore". I thought about Jezza and Gazza and how they were saved by me, inviting Jezza to church.

Again, the manipulations and intimidations were not going to work. I was beginning to be aware of the spirits that wanted me to crawl into passiveness and be tossed to and fro with every wind of doctrine, probably because I was still reading my Bible, Old Testament once and New Testament three times in a year, every year.

So now I had read the Bible more than most believers ever will. And this was vital for me. I needed the firm foundation under my feet and it was being built. But I was still only a five year old now, but fed on the right food, the Word of God. So as a five year old, I was ready now for school.

And that was it. I thought, I'm leaving here. The 12 months were up in a couple of weeks so I planned my escape, and the way I would go out. I knew what to do, to make them see their own judgement were wrong about me. I grabbed the prophecy tape I received a few years ago from the American prophets, because I had heard their names mentioned, and gave it to the pastor and his wife saying, "Those men spoke over me once, would you like to hear it? They said "Yes, OK" and the next week they were almost waiting for me at the door.

They sat me down next to them and said how good it would be if I became a member of the church. By then it was far too late, I left that

Sunday, after my 12 months and only went back once after some months had passed to deliver a Word I was given, and the church would close two weeks after that.

After that year long season, I went back to the smaller St Helens group a couple of times. Whether I was meant to go or not, I went. After about the second or third time, God gave me this dream. No vision, just a voice that said this. "If (Billy, we'll call him) doesn't forgive (pastor of larger church) his church will shut down".

I knew the bitterness of Billy. I had heard it from the pulpit, and it was spreading there. A root of bitterness had no doubt entered, and now I'm writing this I know what that is, because I struggled with one myself, and I'll get to that part eventually. I am praying that these words will not be arrows towards any of them. This is part of my story and it needs to be told. I had let this go long ago. God is the judge, not me. For I also have learned, with what measure I mete will be measured back.

> Mat 7:1-2 Judge not, that ye be not judged.
>
> For with what judgement ye judge, ye shall be judged: and with what measure ye mete, it shall be measured to you again.

Poss and I went into the church Sunday morning. I had the intention of telling the Pastor what the voice in the dream said. And that's all it was. I thought he would understand. I never said it was God, although to me it definitely wasn't the devil, saying that forgiveness had to occur if the church was to stay open. I knew the devil would never say that. So I delivered it.

You would have thought I'd smacked him around the ear. He started going crook and saying that's been done and it's not right. He'd made up with the other man and given him crayfish and stuff and justified himself. I just said, "I don't know, it's just a voice that spoke in a dream Billy, that's all".

I was wondering about how all these churches would speak about the supernatural power of God, but if it didn't line up with their theology or their ideas on what and how they thought things should work, then it was offensive to them.

Like I said before, I knew that God could speak, and I knew the devil could speak, sometimes we had to just figure who was who. And sometimes we got it wrong by hearing the lie and ignoring the true.

Billy went on to tell me how some great Prophet had prophesied and said that the church would have over 200 people in it and that God was going to bless it abundantly, so I supposed like most of the prophecies I had heard in those places, was most likely made up, or Billy had blown it big time.

Not that I was certain so I just said "I don't know about that, I'm just telling you about the voice I heard". I wasn't going to waste my time and tell him about other voice that I had heard about Brian, and the repercussions of that, because he was too far gone into his defence. In about a minute or so, I was his enemy. But after all the other church madness I'd seen, I wasn't surprised. But it still never felt very good.

Our attendance to that church was put to a halt very quickly. I did see him in the town one day a couple of weeks later and he gave me the evil eye. I was going to say hello but soon changed my mind. But I had nothing against him.

After about three months God had wanted me to go back there. He just kept putting it to me, not in words but in a quiet leading. But I became like Jonah, who did not want to go to Ninevah. I did not want to go to the church. I said to God, "He hates me God, I did what you said, as gently as I could, and he's totally spat the dummy. You saw how he was when I saw him in the street".

That didn't change His mind though. The weight of this task that I needed to do almost became unbearable. Even though there was no other instruction needed, I still had to wrestle with the fear of man. He was an older man, an old hardened Abalone diver. I wasn't fearful of a physical challenge, but I wasn't very good with dealing with other men's tongues. And the taming of my own was far from perfected. It still took me another three months before I decided to go.

On a Saturday night, Poss and I made up our minds to go the next day. She had a weekend off. In the morning I awoke and was singing in my head, "This is the day, this is the day that the Lord has made, that the Lord has made, we will rejoice, we will rejoice and be glad in it and be glad in it…" etc. And I was singing it out loud. Which made Poss smile. Not very often I woke up singing hymns. I knew it was a mission from God, and I had to release the burden.

We walked in and sat down and the first song they played was the one I was singing in bed that same morning. "This is the day' this is the day….." Poss and I looked at each other and knew the mission was underway. This was the day alright. Something was going to happen.

CHAPTER TEN: THE WILDERNESS

But I had no other instructions than to just show up.

We listened to the sermon, which was aimed straight at me, and his glaring eyes told me it was so. Billy was saying how God was to bless his church and every wrong Christian and every witch in the district had cursed him and the place and how he had overcome these and spoke on how he was so righteous and blah, blah, blah. He went on for half an hour really drilling it in.

Instead of the other church being his target, he had a new one. Me. And I was there to see the whole lot. Which in my head was "Wow, you are so in trouble now mate. I am sent here by God for whatever purpose He knows about, and you are attacking me like it's my entire fault. The voice in the dream told me to tell you to forgive, and you are so bitter you can't do it. How do you think you are in any state to run a church"?

So I was starting to give him the idea with my eyes, that his attack was very foolish. When he finished, Poss and I stood up and left that church and never went back. Not that we had to, it was closed two weeks later.

Pastor Billy and his wife had a mission in India. They left St Helens a few days after Billy's rant on how great things were going to be. We heard from those who were attending that church that as he sat on a train in India, a voice spoke to him and said "Your work in St Helens is finished". The church never re-opened again after that.

That showed me the seriousness of the need for forgiveness, because a root of bitterness had begun to spring up in my life also. But the devil is sneaky and rarely knocks on the front door.

So after that, only six months or so, I had just spoken to a friend about Winnaleah church. He said the Pastor and his wife were leaving and they were going to get a man from Launceston to come and preach. This was an hour and a half away.

I was out the side of my house welding up a trailer I was building and I asked God, "What's going to happen to Winnaleah church". And as soon as I asked the question, the answer came. "1 Samuel, chapter 8", the still small voice of the Holy Ghost said.

I knew what that chapter was. I had read it not that long ago and I had recognised how this is affecting the church today. It's amazing what you can see when you step back a bit from a subject and take more in than what is right under one's nose.

It was the Word of God this time. Not a dream or a vision, but a reference for a whole chapter, given to me by the Holy Spirit. And His Word was important to me, as it was important to Him.

> Jer 23:28-29 The prophet that hath a dream, let him tell a dream; and he that hath my word, let him speak my word faithfully. What is the chaff to the wheat? saith the LORD.
>
> Is not my word like as a fire? saith the LORD; and like a hammer that breaketh the rock in pieces?

The last mission I had was to just tell a dream, and the consequences were not good for him who rejected it. What was going to be the outcome of this? It immediately began to burn within me, looking for its release. I totally knew what Jeremiah felt.

> Jer 20:9 Then I said, I will not make mention of him, nor speak any more in his name. But his word was in mine heart as a burning fire shut up in my bones, and I was weary with forbearing, and I could not stay.

After a minute or so of thought, I had recognised what had to happen next. I said out loud, "You want me to go and tell them this don't you", not as a question, but as the answer to Him, what I knew He wanted from me already. After repenting from hiding from the other mission He had for me awhile back now, I wasn't going to fear man anymore. Within another minute or so I had decided to just go the next Sunday and get it over with.

Sunday came and I showed up. Not nervous, not fearful, just intending to do the job that was asked of me and go home. And the perfect opportunity came near the end. The Pastors wife got up and said 'Has anyone got a Word?' I think I had only ever shared something up the front there once before, it was about a Street Preacher who I'd met and he was going to kill his wife before he was saved, and God took him out of his body and showed him Hell. From that time on he was preaching on the street about three to four days a week for the last 30 years. It certainly had an impact on him.

But I don't think the people liked hearing about Hell or street preaching or whatever it was that seemed to upset them. Maybe it was my delivery. But I'll tell you now, if they didn't like that delivery, they were for certain not going to like this.

I put up my hand and she motioned for me to come up the front and also said "I feel that we are going to be encouraged here" and I thought, "Your prophetic utterance is way off track". Not that I had any plan to condemn anyone, I was just going to open my mouth and tell them what I heard.

So I started, "I have heard that the Pastor and his wife are leaving, and also heard that you are planning to get another minister, to travel every Sunday, to run the church. I asked God what was going to happen to this church and this is what He said.

I heard 1 Samuel Chapter 8, which is about Israel wanting a King. It's about them wanting a man instead of God to control them. It says that a King will take your Sons and Daughters and your selves and you will have to serve him. He will take 10% of all you have and take other things also." I then read a couple of the scriptures out.

I went on to say, "All of you people live in this town, you know the people, and you are not young believers. God wants you to run the church. You obviously know enough. Why do you want to bring someone in that will preach to you every Sunday and then leave"?

Then I left them with these exact words, which weren't real holy or politically correct. "If you choose to do this, then God is just going to nick off".

That was it, I returned to my seat and waited until the end and left. Nothing was said about it before I left, but one man did thank me a couple of months later but not before this.

In two weeks the church shut down and they all, about a dozen or more, went to a church about half an hour away. All of them just picked up and plonked down again in another spot. No strength or desire to stand at all. This amazed me.

So now there were hardly any Christians in the whole North East District that wanted anything to do with me. This was God's plan though. I didn't like it but what could I do? All part of the refiners' fire.

CHAPTER ELEVEN
AND THEY OVERCAME HIM

I was out of the box. Out of the four walls where all the religious stuff took place, where all the traditional stuff took place. You could set your watch by the timing of it all. Songs, communion, tithing, sermon, song, cup of tea, home.

The stuff that was taught in the Bible schools was regurgitated and you ate what was dished up and asked no questions. Whatever the theology the group was in, is the way you were steered. If you didn't like the food, then they didn't like you. If you said it wasn't right then look-out. You were told what books to read and what ministries to watch or listen to. Which weren't all bad, but today it is a lot worse.

The same people would preach all the time and some went around and around with a few sermons, chopping and changing them to make people think that they were a wealth of knowledge. With all the things in the Bible to preach on, they seemed to have not much range.

All three of these groups I had been in were much the same. Same program, song, communion, tithing, sermon, song, cup of tea, and home. Except if there was someone to prophesy. They would say amazing things were coming, and of what God was going to do. I hoped they were right, but I have my doubts now. As Jezebel grew stronger, the prophecies came thick and fast. Everyone was doing it.

I didn't seem to have a gift of prophecy that would turn on every Sunday. I was disappointed but in the end, I was glad. It got beyond a joke. With none of them coming true really.

The prosperity and word of faith was preached where Jesus was the fix to everyone's problems and you were meant to be rich and healthy, and if you had some issues then it wasn't discussed. You kept them to yourself, or you went to the doctor to get some pills, if you didn't have enough faith to get through.

Now I can look back and can see what the devil had done in these places, but again, if you don't know your enemy, then basically, you are stuffed!

The hype on the Sundays was sometimes extreme. The jumping up and down and the singing and dancing were at times over the top. But other times there were tears of joy, and feelings of remorse for your sins, and gratefulness to God for saving you and for loving you. This when it happened could be felt by all. It wasn't all bad. When I was only a Babe, the milk tasted good.

Sometimes the Jesus preached wanted everybody rich, with the famous Televangelists flying their own planes around to meetings all over the world, where they would sell their books and videos and fly back to their million dollar mansions, and continually say on TV how God had blessed them, so most believers wanted that.

They would promise the same things in the church. And you had to give 10% or you would get nothing. The witchcraft guilt complex they put on you was enough to make you want to empty your pockets. Or the lust of the flesh in men through the desire to have was preyed upon in vicious style.

But Poss and I tried to give our ten percent until we saw that it wasn't going for souls, most of it was going to those who were preaching this gospel of greed and lust for money. This was at about year three of our walk our eyes were opening to this.

When the Pastor, we'll call him Steve for now, bought the Harley. I tried to tell him that Harleys were owned and ridden by those who were rebellious and I had knocked around with bikers. I knew how rebellious they were, and me too, so there is no judgement here.

I told him that I had seen some men who gt a Harley, become something they weren't previously. I told him I had seen men who would hide behind their mothers' apron, as a figure of speech, but not too distant from the truth, then buy a Harley, get covered in tattoos and their whole demeanour would change in a very short time.

I said that I believed that with every Harley Davidson motorbike made, there was a demon attached, and probably more than one. I tried to warn Steve, but his ears were not open to what I had to say. So I've already told what happened with him, there's no need again.

There was an old wood cutter in the church and he was telling me how people owed him money. I'd been a Christian for a couple of years or so. I said, "Who are the worst payers, what type of people are they" and straight away he said "Christians". I was amazed and confounded here. They are meant to be honest and giving, were my thoughts toward him, and he just gave a bit of a grunt and rolled his eyes. I learnt firsthand about this very soon after this short conversation.

The assistant Pastor (Shaun, is the name I'll use here,) had a lawn mowing business. A man in the church had bought a lawn mower and only used it once and it wouldn't start. So he thought it was dodgy and gave it to the assistant Pastor. He knew little about how they worked and asked me to help fix it.

I had grown up around machinery and motorbikes and had a basic knowledge of motors so went and looked and found that it was only a loose head bolt which was affecting the compression needed to make it run. Within two minutes, it was going, and a minute of that time was used finding the tool I needed.

Now I liked Shaun a lot, and his father. They had a good sense of humour and we did visit his house a lot, for church group stuff and learnt more there than even in church. We got to know people better in this environment also.

To tell the truth, there were people in the main church body of St Helens that we never even knew their last names or where they lived. Even after the three and a half years of attendance, before it all went downhill. And there were only about 40 Adults going. Within the footy club, you learnt this stuff quick. Mainly because of the drinking parties and whatever else was happening but it happened, so it was strange to me that in the church we never got to know people that well. Not much team enthusiasm.

So Shaun was almost jumping up and down with joy. There were Hallelujahs and Praise the Lord's flying about. The mower after all was a Honda. Brand new, except for probably ten minutes work. Or enough time for that head bolt to loosen enough so the spark onto the fuel made no difference. I was watching and wondering what was going to happen. I did get the idea that he was planning to keep it.

Shaun was still thanking God when I said, "Shaun, that's probably a $500 mower and it's basically brand new. Don't you think you should just give it back to Gerry"? Shaun said, "No, God has blessed me, I needed a new mower and it has come, praise the Lord".

My estimation of Shaun was lowered after that. You just didn't do that where I grew up.

CHAPTER ELEVEN: AND THEY OVERCAME HIM

And that was my introduction to the deception of the prosperity gospel. They hear it so much and desire it so much, that they are willing to take from others and say God has blessed them. I saw this so many times.

People saying God wants to bless me and then buying cars and houses they couldn't afford and then struggling to pay it back and then blaming God when they struggled. It was so destructive. They were ten percent worse off than the world and coming under a curse for sowing money where they shouldn't. The doctrine was poison.

So I began to wonder, what else are they teaching that wasn't good, that were doctrines of demons as the Bible spoke about. This definitely made me see that I had to keep my eyes and ears open. All things weren't what they were made out to be.

I was so glad that the Lord had given me a desire to read the Bible and I desperately wanted to know Him and please Him. I owed Him my life, and I was willing to give it to Him.

After about two and a half years of church I was invited up the front to share communion. I spoke about my testimony and basically thanked God for what He had done for me and led people in a prayer to do the same.

There was a man there called John. I had not seen him before and John and his lovely wife introduced themselves to us after church. He said that he absolutely loved my testimony. John had written some books and had been involved with a man called Thomas Varney. Tom was in J Ward in Ararat. This was the maximum security home for the criminally insane. But eventually he was saved and radically changed.

Ararat was only half an hour from Lake Bolac where I grew up. I knew that only the worst of the worst were kept there in J Ward. I did do work experience in Aradale, the mental hospital in Ararat, and had inside understanding of that place. I'll tell you something, if you were too bad for Aradale, and had to go to J Ward, then you were bad.

John and Marion showed Poss and me a lot of love and respect and we got on so well. He knew the Word better than anyone I knew and taught me a lot. Gave me lots of videos of teachings, and although some were prosperity, there was a wide range, and I devoured them. I remember Derek Prince was a good person that I liked to hear.

John loved testimonies. He loaded me up with them and I loved them too. I loved to hear how God could change even the worst sinner, even worse than me, supernaturally. I loved the supernatural of God. It was so clean and had purpose. Not like the devil's. There was little reason in his games and no life.

John would tell me how important it is to glorify God by our testimonies, big and small. He was a wise man. He knew about this scripture below, where I was yet to learn, especially about the last half, of not loving our lives. That was definitely not taught in church.

The him being overcome here below is the devil, and like I already said, I hated the devil. And I was about to learn how to use testimony to overcome him.

> Rev 12:11 And they overcame him by the blood of the Lamb, and by the word of their testimony; and they loved not their lives unto the death.

We loved John and Marion. And we felt loved back. They prayed a different way than what we had heard and Poss got on very well with Marion also. They didn't seem like pretenders, and around 17 years later, I can still say that.

Although John has gone to be with the Lord, Marion is still in touch. Their children were not wicked or rebellious either. It was the most stable family I had ever witnessed being full of love for each other.

One day John asked me for my testimony to put it on his website. I felt honoured. I shared it with him and was amazed to see my story online. He was happy that I was happy and did something else for me. He made five or six copies of it in full colour with pics that I could share with people. And this was so easy to just leave with people and not have to dig around waiting for a door to open.

That definitely has its place though, in learning to hear and know God's leading. A good place to start to listen to the Lord and recognise when one is open or shut, unless you got a quick F#$% off, which was a good sign to back off. Hehehe

I handed one of these testimonies to, we'll call him Sid. Sid worked in a mine. He had been a fisherman and was a hard man. We had fought in the pub before my salvation, but became friends. St Helens only had two pubs and an RSL, so you couldn't dodge each other for ever. Sid was in a cave in and his friend was killed by it when they were working together. Sid was in a bad way. He grabbed his friend by the head and his fingers went into his skull. His head was crushed. Sid was hitting the grog and dope and couldn't sleep and was so tormented.

I felt bad to see him this way and I had my testimony on me that John had given me. Sid could see that I had changed and when I said Jesus helped me, he didn't shy off. Sid told me his Grandmother was a believer, and it sounded as if he had a lot of love for her. Plus he was desperate. And over these years I have come to recognise, that it is the desperate that get delivered. They are willing to give all. It certainly makes life a lot easier for a Deliverance minister.

I handed him the papers and left. In a week or so I saw him again and he said to me, I need this. So I directed Sid to a man who led him to the Lord, and baptised him. I wasn't confident enough to do this, which was a shame. But in the system, the pew warmers were just that. The work was done only by the initiated. How I hated that. I just wanted to get into the battle wherever I could. We weren't to lay hands on anyone either, because we weren't ready. But from what I saw, I think it was just in case someone got healed, and the elders and leaders never got the glory.

When I saw him next, Sid was sleeping well, off the grog and had peace. He knew about what Jesus had done. And told me that he could understand why his Grandmother was a Christian now.

I wish this story had a happy ending, but it doesn't. Sid didn't like the churches and fell away slowly over a few years. He joined an outlaw motorcycle club, and after ten years or more was stabbed to death, trying to protect an abused woman. Sid was never a bad man, and I was so saddened to see this. They did find him kneeling on the kitchen floor dead, with around 16 stab wounds.

In all the time I have been a believer it seems that around 90% fall away. I hadn't seen one as extreme as Sid, but very sad just the same. Just like this below.

> Luk 17:15-18 And one of them, when he saw that he was healed, turned back, and with a loud voice glorified God,
>
> And fell down on his face at his feet, giving him thanks: and he was a Samaritan.
>
> And Jesus answering said, were there not ten cleansed? but where are the nine?
>
> There are not found that returned to give glory to God, save this stranger.

I don't like to think where my old friend Sid ended up, but I'm not God.

So back then when I saw Sid's life change through my testimony, I was excited and planned to do a lot more in this area.

CHAPTER TWELVE
FULL GOSPEL BUSINESS

I had my written testimony which I was now getting printed and handing out like lollies. I had a plan in my mind and I needed to put it into action. I had a purpose, and a reason, for the first time in my life; I wasn't just going with the flow. The Kingdom of God excited me and I wanted more. And I wanted to walk in the place where I knew I was called to, but was seeing little of that at the moment.

> Pro 16:3 Commit thy works unto the LORD, and thy thoughts shall be established.

> Pro 16:9 A man's heart deviseth his way: but the LORD directeth his steps.

I thought if my written testimony is so powerful, what if I get some local testimonies, and spread them around town and really get people talking? I knew some men who had radical testimonies, and some that I had been involved in their salvation. But a video of three or four local testimonies would be excellent I thought.

I went around to the men's places with a video camera, and asked them to share. I was ready for this. I was out of church now but I'm sure some had been warned off me or that is how it felt. Everyone was wary that I asked and said that they would rather do it in the church. So I hung my head and it seemed I was defeated, or so I thought.

When I was going to church we went to a men's meeting and it was called "Full Gospel Business Men's Fellowship International (FGBMFI). They were a group that used testimonies to bring unsaved into the body of Christ. But the body of Christ saw them as the enemy. I couldn't believe how much effort they put in to place new believers in the church, and how ungrateful the church was.

They were purposely standing in the way of this group, saying that the covering was all wrong. It was just more witchcraft mind control happening within the body and fear that everybody was a sheep stealer.

But the FGBMFI was a stepping stone out from under the church control and into a greater freedom to serve God and walk on the path He had for you. Not that all was perfect, but there was freedom here that wasn't in the church. And a lot of that was because it was an all men's group. Which Jezebel absolutely hated.

A man had heard of my testimony and put me in touch with the Australian President of the FGBMFI. This was about 12 months after the asking of the fellas to share their stories, which most of them still hadn't got the offer to do in the church.

I organised a meeting, explaining to Christian men in the area my plan and what was happening. But most weren't interested. I know that there was a lot of control, and there was a fear that this below would happen. Jezebel was nasty, and had neutered a lot of men already.

> Joh 12:42-43 Nevertheless among the chief rulers also many believed on him; but because of the Pharisees they did not confess him, lest they should be put out of the synagogue:
>
> For they loved the praise of men more than the praise of God.

I put a lot of work in though and around 20 came to the first meeting. It was a great day. Bill came from Geelong and while I was expecting somebody like a religious fella, Bill was just like us. He had a testimony too and was thankful to God for his second chance, and there was absolutely no judgement of us in him at all, or his wife.

David the Tasmanian leader came from Burnie and his wife. David was a man's man, a black belt in some Kung Fu stuff but a gentleman. His gift of prophecy was absolutely excellent. I was to receive one from him that was so true. I had trouble believing it, but now I'm walking in it. I'll share later.

I had been led strongly to fast for the meeting. So I started a three dayer. But I broke it in the morning. Then I became really convicted, heavily. So I did the fast and finished it on the day of the testimonies.

Bill shared a bit of his story, then Jezza and Tim gave theirs. It was a great day. There was no worrying if anyone was going to be offended. Poss and Bill's wife and David's also went shopping or somewhere, so we were all men there at the first meeting, and most of us had a past.

CHAPTER TWELVE: FULL GOSPEL BUSINESS

So when they shared things that would shock, we only laughed. That was the attitude through the whole FGB meetings, for a couple of years. The men loved it, and I loved it. I was made President that day and kept this for two or three years or so. And my mother had recently passed away, and left some money, so Poss and I were able to feed them all and bless them also.

The next day after the meeting, Bill and his wife had just left and we were outside and a car pulled up with a man I had met in the pub a few years ago. He said someone told him I had some roosters. I said he could have one so we went and caught a young one.

I think we may have asked him if he wanted a cup of tea and he said "No, my mother is in the car and she is sick so I have to take her home". I said "What's the matter" and he said "She has cancer". Then Poss says without fear or doubt, "Oh we're Christians, we'll pray for her" and this was my thinking that was full of fear and doubt "What are you doing Poss, we will look like idiots here".

But anyway we walked over and asked Evelyn if we could pray for her and she was very happy about this. We put our hands in the window and I said a short prayer. "I rebuke all sickness and cancer and command you to go as well as depression and anxiety also. I bind you all and command you to leave in the name of Jesus Christ, Amen"

We both said our goodbyes and walked off. Funny thing was though; I had no doubt about the prayer. There was no attack of the mind, which comes in to steal, kill and destroy any hope and faith that one has to operate in. Those voices had come in so many times before and I was sick of them and had been shy and fearful to pray for many people. But we just carried on.

Then about a week later Ed rang up. I thought he just wanted to thank me for the rooster, but he said "Thanks for praying for my mother, the cancer is gone, she has been healed". Now they were both unbelievers, but not anymore. Or at least they had begun to believe in miracles. I said "That's God working" and asked him what had happened.

He said they went to the doctors and they could find no trace of the cancer that had been the size of a fist and growing on the heart and into the lung that was inoperable. Two months to live was what they had given her. We praised God, Poss and I ,and were thankful. It was a sure sign that FGB was a go ahead, and that His grace was with us.

The Anglicans in St Helens found out about the healing and asked Evelyn to share at their church, but she denied the offer. Around six months later, Poss saw her buying tobacco in the supermarket.

There was a tumour come into her head after about nine months and she passed away soon after. At I think around 84 years old. Ed did ring us up and we went and prayed for her but nothing happened. And when we wanted to talk about Jesus, she just wanted to talk about the garden and weather and stuff. I don't know how Ed is going now, or where he is at.

After about a year in late summer, a man and woman stopped out the front of the house. His wife was driving him around. They saw our apple tree covered in fruit and asked us if they could have some. We said of course. He was sitting in exactly the same spot Evelyn was. And his wife said her husband had Leukaemia. Poss and I looked at each other and neither of us offered to pray for him. It was the most shameful thing I had ever felt after being saved.

God had delivered to us a man who was almost dead, in the exact same spot as the old lady Evelyn who He healed of Cancer, and I was too gutless to say anything. I am still cringing now and so regretful even as I write this. I repented and repented and said to God "Please don't let that ever happen again".

So he organized some training for me where I would never let fear and doubt block me again.

CHAPTER THIRTEEN
VOICES AND DREAMS

So the FGB meetings went on and we were having a good time, and we had traveled to some conferences on the mainland and were really enjoying it.

Now the dates and times that some things occurred may not be perfectly in alignment but Poss is reminding me of things and I'm trying my best as I recall. But the timing is not that important. What is important is that God speaks. And speak He did. Good and bad, but always the Truth.

I had filmed the boys giving their testimonies, or set the video camera up and pushed record. I placed it on the edge of the mantel piece and stood them in front of the dunny door. So we weren't real organised. But that never mattered. We had a great day and I watched the recordings and they were great ammo to use against the devil.

The small tape in the video recorder ran out when Tim was explaining his Baptism, and it was a really good bit. He kept going and I changed it but missed a minute or so.

This upset me. But God was with us. Tim had actual video of his baptism and it showed him going under and hardly being able to stand when he resurfaced. It was a classic Baptism of his sins, which were many, being washed away. The video showed so much more than what words could. And this was more confirmation of Gods hand on the videos.

We all shared our testimonies and I put the most radical ones on to video and started to copy them. The first thousand were VHS videos. I had no computer then. I made about a thousand of them and handed them out, posting all over the country, which with postage, was very expensive. About ten grands worth of videos were made and posted. A rough estimate of the video ministry costs. I was very busy. But I wasn't worried about that, souls were getting saved.

Everything I had was His, and I knew that He could provide and He always did. Not just financially but with everything I would need. I just believed that, no questions. After what He did for me, the rest was easy for Him

> Ecc 11:1 Cast thy bread upon the waters: for thou shalt find it after many days.
>
> Psa 126:5-6 They that sow in tears shall reap in joy.
>
> He that goeth forth and weepeth, bearing precious seed, shall doubtless come again with rejoicing, bringing his sheaves *with him.*
>
> Gal 6:8-9 For he that soweth to his flesh shall of the flesh reap corruption; but he that soweth to the Spirit shall of the Spirit reap life everlasting.
>
> And let us not be weary in well doing: for in due season we shall reap, if we faint not.

As I was getting out of bed one morning a voice said "Open new doors and new doors will open". I didn't say anything, it seemed clear enough to me. God had just spoken audibly from out of the blue to me and gave me direction. Or it was the same voice that I had heard before, so whether it was Jesus or an Angel, I didn't know. But it was all I needed to hear.

So I started to kick doors down where I saw any cracks and kick doors down that may have needed to stay closed. Not all was fruitful, but I was keen to try anything. I did have the go ahead from the Lord, and I was off and racing.

We started letter boxing small things with a couple of scriptures on them and in the dark so nobody would see us. If a car came, we would walk past the letterbox and not put anything in, for fear of any retaliation from the receivers. This was insane. Here was me, the big star footballer, crazy ex druggy and drunk that lived for the madness of the pub scene and even little old ladies growling because I had stuffed something in their letterbox they didn't want was terrifying to me.

I just had no idea how to deal with this sort of attack. It would feel like it was against the inner most part of me and my knees would go weak. But the attack was against what was inside of me, so I had to get used to it, and although it still hurts, I soon realised that it wasn't personal. I am glad I was beginning to know the Word. It could remove fear and bring much understanding in all situations happening around me.

CHAPTER THIRTEEN: VOICES AND DREAMS

> Luk 21:17 And ye shall be hated of all men for my name's sake.
>
> Joh 15:18 If the world hate you, ye know that it hated me before it hated you.

It was like every barking dog was going to tear your throat out and every door that opened or shut was a murderer with an axe that had been just sharpened up for the job of hacking us to pieces. And in suburbs that were not as well off financially and filled with those struggling a bit, the thoughts were so heavy that would come against us. I was always glad it was all over and we could flee back to our country home and hide away safely. This is no exaggeration. Most physical terrors in front of me through life were never as much of a worry as these. The demonic torments and pictures that the spirits would sow into my mind to try to put us off the job were amazing.

It was here we started to learn about the spiritual resistance and the territorial spirits that were in certain areas. But as we pushed through and overcame, we got stronger and stronger, to do more and more. This had to happen, if any victory was to be won. Hiding in church will get you nowhere in gaining strength and understanding.

We would cut and paste from written materials, with scissors and glue, and then go to printing shops and get thousands of copies made of the things I'd come up with. One was about evolution being a joke.

Evolution had been something in my past that had kept me from believing God so I needed to attack it. So every couple of weeks Poss and I got in our old camper and went letter boxing. We delivered almost 17,000 around Tassie. It was a good exercise to learn how to deal with rejection, because I put my email address on it. And some weren't happy and let me know. And I can't forget to mention the terrifying little old ladies that just wanted my blood and my head on a stick. LOL

By that time I had got a computer and was learning to work it. I didn't mind teaching myself. And I started to learn to make DVDs, CDs, use Photoshop and things. John helped me with Photoshop and I helped him with the DVD stuff, so we could both pump out testimonies and things to hand around. It was a great way to spread the Word. And at last count the Broken Chains testimonies was up to 8000 or more. All given away, except for about four that I sold to a Christian bookshop when the owner wanted to pay for them. God supplied the finances for all these and it was never a struggle.

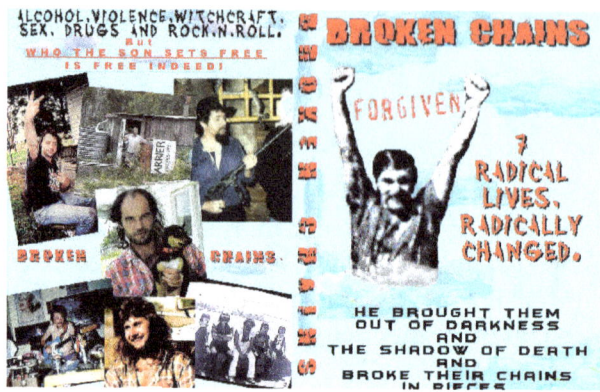
Broken chains DVD cover

I also got an old Caravan and did it up and the Suncoast chapter FGBMFI men went around in it spreading the Word. Some places banned us and others tolerated, but Johnno and his keyboard was a massive advertisement for Jesus. And he was loud. It was fun. But watching some believers at certain places purposely turn away made me sad. Their rejection was hurtful, but I had to get used to it. Sometimes it was hard. I still thought I was badly done by in the churches. And the devil now had sown his plan into me, and from what I know now, it was at the time that the massive snake had bitten me. It had injected me with the poison of a root of bitterness.

> Heb 12:15-16 Looking diligently lest any man fail of the grace of God; lest any root of bitterness springing up trouble *you*, and thereby many be defiled;
>
> Lest there *be* any fornicator, or profane person, as Esau, who for one morsel of meat sold his birthright.

I had a grudge against those that had rejected me and what I thought was very unfair treatment, so I began to speak bitter words about the church. It was general and their rejection of FGBMFI didn't help.

I was seeing no good at all in the church and was letting people know. I really believed that God had shown me all this stuff so I could expose it and keep people away. But God wasn't happy with this. I had been told by a few people that I shouldn't be doing this, but I was on my high horse and thought, they don't understand. This was a time that I had got it wrong.

My heart was starting to play up. I started getting palpitations and skipping and things weren't going good. Then one day I'd been flown to the Hospital, for my heart. It was skipping one beat, and beating two. Beat, beat, miss. Beat, beat, miss. And it was getting worse. But they sent me home without doing anything, praise God.

I was praying to God, "What's happening, what's happening," and He answered this way a week or so later. I was talking to two friends and explaining how bad the church was and God spoke and said loud and clear "I've warned you Peter". That freaked me out. The two mates never heard it but it frightened me so much. I really thought He was going to kill me. He was very angry.

> Heb 12:6-8 For whom the Lord loveth he chasteneth, and scourgeth every son whom he receiveth.
>
> If ye endure chastening, God dealeth with you as with sons; for what son is he whom the father chasteneth not?
>
> But if ye be without chastisement, whereof all are partakers, then are ye bastards, and not sons.

So I went straight home onto my knees. And I knew what He was angry about. I pleaded with Him and said I was so sorry. I told Him that I had tried to forgive the two that I was angry with, that I had prayed for them and tried to ask Him to bless them.

But I said "I can't let go, what do I need to do" and He was listening to my plea and straight away the Holy Ghost said within me, loud and clear, "Fast seven days". I'd never done one of those before but I started immediately, terrified that my days were now numbered.

I fasted seven days on only water and on the seventh day my heart was healed probably three quarters to what it was and the root of bitterness left. There was no way that I was going to break that fast even one minute too early.

I had done that with three day fasts and the devil had stolen them from me before, saying, "You really blew it there, three day fast is three whole days, not a minute less and God won't accept your pathetic effort". So now I make sure I do over the time I set myself. And be aware of this tactic from the enemy when you fast.

After the seven days I could think of the two people that were the cause and there was no resentment towards them at all. So praise God. This chastisement really taught me some things, and about forgiveness also. Which is a must for freedom; spiritual and even physical, which would be vital knowledge to know in the work that was coming.

> Mat 6:14-15 For if ye forgive men their trespasses, your heavenly Father will also forgive you:
>
> But if ye forgive not men their trespasses, neither will your Father forgive your trespasses.

This also showed me the seriousness of this next parable, and the truth of it. Here is the end of the parable of the unforgiving servant, which is a major cause of unbelievers, and believers' sicknesses.

> Mat 18:33-35 Shouldest not thou also have had compassion on thy fellow servant, even as I had pity on thee?
>
> And his lord was wroth, and delivered him to the tormentors, till he should pay all that was due unto him.
>
> So likewise shall my heavenly Father do also unto you, if ye from your hearts forgive not everyone his brother their trespasses.

I did wonder too if I had of died with this root of bitterness, if I would have made it to Heaven, and my conclusion, according to the Word of God, was "NO". Remember this also, get people to forgive their enemies out loud before praying and you will see a lot more miracles.

I did go and see the people who I was upset with and found I had truly forgiven them, and asked for forgiveness also. And it was so much easier to do than the devil was telling me it would be. I also noticed that my bitterness had not affected them one bit. All its weight was on me. This was a good thing to learn. Now I'm quick to forgive. REAL QUICK!!!

I was to learn about this scripture below, not of flagellation with whips like some crazy Catholics do, or beating myself up over my sins and errors, but to make my disobedience cost me. I found that this really hastens the work of repentance, which we take too lightly.

> 2Co 10:6 And having in a readiness to revenge all disobedience, when your obedience is fulfilled.

A day's fast after a willing mistake will certainly put you in a place to think twice next time the temptation arises. I know it does me.

FGBMFI came and went and we were still in the wilderness. I was wondering what we were to do now and still opening doors to forward the gospel.

CHAPTER THIRTEEN: VOICES AND DREAMS

I had made a website and it was getting some hits, people were watching the videos, that were now DVDs and contacting me, but nothing ever came about really that was to put me where I thought I should be or wanted to be or whatever. It seemed I always wanted the blessed door of ministry to open and I could say I've arrived. But it never came.

There were some spirits that I had picked up in church, and from generations past that were making me think like this. And now as I think, they were a form of torment, but I didn't know enough to recognise them or come out of agreement with them. But they did come out eventually, by prayer and fasting. 40 days of it. But we are not up to that bit yet.

I was getting out of bed again and an audible voice again spoke and said, "I have anointed you". Then all sorts of things started swirling in my head. Some confusion on what that meant. Some vain imagination, or maybe a lot, and many high things that most likely exalted themselves above the knowledge of God were trying to enter my mind.

I was learning and training myself to take my thoughts captive. To watch what comes into my mind, then discern who it was from. And I could cut thoughts off very quick, that I deemed to be poisonous. No doubt I cut a few of Gods thoughts off too. But He is gracious. I know I did cut His thoughts off as well actually with hindsight.

> 2Co 10:4-5 (For the weapons of our warfare *are* not carnal, but mighty through God to the pulling down of strong holds;)
>
> Casting down imaginations, and every high thing that exalteth itself against the knowledge of God, and bringing into captivity every thought to the obedience of Christ;

So many problems start when we can't shut our thoughts down. This is so vital for a Christian, because our enemy is real. And he always attacks our weakest points. He's a dirty fighter and kicks us when we are down. But he can also lift us up and fill us with pride and all sorts of filthy self-centred junk. When we are full of self and our ears are blocked from true humility and repentance, we are an easy target. And be aware, the enemy never sleeps.

> 1Pe 5:8 Be sober, be vigilant; because your adversary the devil, as a roaring lion, walketh about, seeking whom he may devour:

Another audible voice said, again when I was lying in bed reading my Bible, "Hello Pastor". This was another cryptic comment or statement that I wasn't sure what it meant. Or it was obvious what it meant but I would say out loud, "If I'm a Pastor, where's my flock?" And "If I'm anointed, then how do I activate it, and what am I anointed to do?" because nothing much had changed yet.

I still had to get up on the cold frosty mornings and go and milk the farmers' cows, which I didn't mind doing too much. My temperament was good now. There was no depression at all. I would milk in the mornings and evenings and have all day reading my Bible and listening to audio sermons, which I did a lot. Hours every day of audio sermons and talks, some good and some bad, I was starving for the truth and the Word of God.

I'd left far behind the diet of prosperity, once saved always saved and Christians can't have demons, and the mind control cloning spirits that were rife in the religious system. I was free to pick and choose how and what I wanted. And by reading the Bible so much, I was getting discernment on who was real and who was not.

And now I have gone through thousands of hours of audio. And have a massive library of the best audios on deliverance and other things, to do with who knows what.

One audible voice I did hear that threw me off was "You will experience dread and an unexpected end". It sounded like the voice I knew so much, being calm but with authority. And that brought all sorts of things to the surface. First was, "What did you tell me that for"? "What do I do with that?" Is that you God or what"? I knew the scripture that was contrary to that voice though,

> Jer 29:11 For I know the thoughts that I think toward you, saith the LORD, thoughts of peace, and not of evil, to give you an expected end.

That made me very confused. So I thought, this voice does not add up with the Word of God. But it was the voice I thought I had recognised. Has the voices all along been the devil, or has he impersonated the voice to bring fear.

I contacted two of my Street Preacher friends who knew the Word also and both gave me the scripture above. So I decided to treat it as a curse, break it and move on. And so I did and here I am years later and no dread or unexpected end.

The devil will try and sow the seed, and if we agree with it in our minds, then it can put down root and grow. Be careful the thoughts you follow. These seeds can also be sown at night.

> Mat 13:25 But while men slept, his enemy came and sowed tares among the wheat, and went his way.

And that happened so many times, that I just stopped jotting down all my dreams. It is a good thing to keep them, but lots are only one off warnings or guidance or instruction, so I only put down the ones that I feel are very important now. God will bring to remembrance the things that are His, when we need them.

> Joh 14:26 But the Comforter, which is the Holy Ghost, whom the Father will send in my name, he shall teach you all things, and bring all things to your remembrance, whatsoever I have said unto you.

And through the fire I went, with trials and testing, ups and downs. But the roller coaster of life and Christianity was starting to level out. With the highs I was learning to not let them get too high, because the devil can exalt too, just to knock you down, and the lows, I could lift up by encouraging myself about the victories I had seen and experienced. And they would become larger and more often, as time went by.

> Isa 40:4 Every valley shall be exalted, and every mountain and hill shall be made low: and the crooked shall be made straight, and the rough places plain:

CHAPTER FOURTEEN
TIME TO PICK A FIGHT

"Awww God, you know what they do, they'll come looking, no doubt about it". But I knew He wanted me to expose the Rosicrucians, there was no mistake. "God they're gonna astral project and come in at night and cause trouble, but if you can protect me then I'll do it". And how could I think he couldn't.

By now I'd had lots of skirmishes, some in the natural and some in the spiritual, but most inspired by the devil. Some when he was working in others and some when he was working in me. But I was learning all the time. I had made so many mistakes, but now they were coming a bit slower and not so painful. I uploaded a portion of a video I had made a couple of years, give or take a bit, earlier, when I'd heard the "Open new doors" word. I had shown selective people the video, to show them an exposure of the plans and tactics of the enemy.

I revealed the oaths, the rituals and the occult techniques of deep meditation and divinations and things that were to help you listen to, or hear your inner voice or your higher you, or the god within, or whatever they called it to soften the truth. Which was to put it bluntly, the demon you get in you when you do the ritual with the mirrors and the candles, and invite the divine essence of the cosmos to come in and infuse your being. Cosmos being the Greek word for World, so it meant, god of this world. The Bible calls him "Satan".

If they told the truth you could put it exactly like that. But they didn't. Satan's a liar. They made it sound like you were a super being who could understand all wisdom and with their way of illumination, you would become a mini god. What a load of crap. Again, Satan's a liar. It was a dangerous trap, and I fell into it.

> Joh 8:44 Ye are of your father the devil, and the lusts of your father ye will do. He was a murderer from the beginning, and abode not in the truth, because there is no

> truth in him. When he speaketh a lie, he speaketh of his own: for he is a liar, and the father of it.

In the video I tied it all into the same beliefs of Aleister Crowley and Anton Lavey. And other occult teachers and new age preachers that I was following before I was saved. All this is still in the videos I put up on the internet.

When the thing that I invited in was screaming in my head back in the church, because Jesus Christ was entering my spirit and it had to go, I figured out quick that these beings and this organisation is so dangerous to humans, and run by high level witches that knew what they were doing. So then the fun began, almost immediately.

Within probably two days there were comments coming that were attacking me, full of slander and malice, and that I had to block for a bit. And there were emails that threatened, and weird cryptic stuff coming at me, because the rejection from the past was still working on me and I would retaliate with words straight back. Until I learnt to walk away and calm down and wait for a bit to reply.

I did discover though, a few years later, that as soon as I stopped acting in anger to the comments on my videos and looked at them as more of an opportunity to witness and shed light on the truth, 90% of them just stopped. It was incredible and gave me full understanding of how the devil uses our own weaknesses against us.

Look inside when the trouble is all around, and ask God "Is this something I need to deal with that is within me?" Because mostly the answer is yes, you do.

There were curses being hurled through the spirit realm fairly regular and in bed I was pinned to the bed and couldn't move more than once. The world calls it "sleep paralysis" but I knew better. It was the witches or the demons they were assigning to me through their curses, to come and harass, or kill if they could, no doubt about it. But everything that was let through was for my learning and for my spiritual growth. I know now that it was my pre-season training and I'm still going through it. Like the saying goes, new levels, new devils. How true that is.

The name of Jesus was the best defence. When these things had me pinned, (and this has happened five times now over the years, and three times to Poss), I couldn't move. It was like you are frozen. You can't breathe or speak, so I could only think "Help me Jesus" then a whisper, "Help me Jesus", then with a normal voice "Help me Jesus".

In about half a minute or less the bogey man, devil, demon, wicked witches of the west or whatever you wanted to call them, were gone.

First time it was a worry, second I was not quite so fearful, and third time when I could speak I said, I rebuke you in the name of Jesus Christ. There was no fear, I went on the attack. And I felt this thing get ripped off me and it actually hit the steel flu on the chimney and made it rattle. That was interesting. There must have been a physical aspect to it somewhere. All this was opening my eyes, and I was being trained in our weapons, our defences, and in keeping my peace amongst the chaos.

Fourth time I never panicked and started to rebuke but must have been too cocky and it took a bit of moving. I realised that I could not do it alone. And I can do nothing alone. That is true!

So not just were the demons manifesting as sleep paralysis, they were coming in my dreams and the voices and the animals and ugly critters. Not that it was happening every night. It was about once a week or so that God would pull back His hand and let me face another hit, to toughen me up a bit.

I had false brethren come when I was FGB president. One wannabe, who was a member of a different chapter, came from a few hours away to my house and told me that I had to stop handing out certain tracts, with some imagined authority he obviously thought he had. He said "Those tracts are too heavy and will turn people off". I said "I think they are good" and didn't agree. They were Jack Chick tracts. "This Was Your Life"

And while they were heavy there were many testimonies of people who were affected by this certain tract. So I had a few of them in my back room. I said to him "Come here and look at this", and took him in and showed him boxes full of them, about nine and a half thousand, and said, "Sorry mate I can't do that".

He was deflated immediately when he realized that I was seriously in the game. Same bloke came again about six months later and said, "You have to step down as President, you don't know what you are doing", and bought a mate with him, for back up.

I gave them a cup of tea and told him I agree, that I didn't really know what I was doing, and then told him that "I was voted in and you two never got to vote on this because you aren't even members so why do you think you have any say at all". And some other better ammo I had was this. A couple of members told me that he had been to their house

CHAPTER FOURTEEN: TIME TO PICK A FIGHT

and were slandering me. So I put that on him and told him that while he was acting high and mighty, his actions didn't agree with his words.

I was so grateful to God also that he warned me in a dream the night before, that trouble was coming that day. I didn't know what, until I see these blokes pull up. And I had been expectant of some sort of strife and as prepared as I could be. And that definitely lessened the blow and readied me for the conflict.

I was so glad also that I restrained myself from, how can I put it nicely; err…..man handling them a bit. I hadn't been affected by that since I'd been saved, except for when I had the elder around the throat, but that was about three years before this. (Although I did have a wrestle with my brother when he was abusing my father and me, a few years ago, but not sure if that counts, does it? There were no punches thrown so I never felt bad). I did get a dream later that I was punching him in the head and his mouth was still hurling out abuse, so I realised that it was a waste of time to try to force righteousness into him, which is obviously fair enough. But families can be hard work at times. I know most of you will agree here.

> Mar 6:4 But Jesus said unto them, A prophet is not without honour, but in his own country, and among his own kin, and in his own house.

So the devil failed there mostly, and I held myself together and I think even the fellas friend was shocked when I mentioned about the slander. Both of these men are having troubles today. Tasmania is a small place, and it's easy to follow others' lives, whether you want to know or not. Everyone knows someone who knows something. Be sure, your sin will find you out soon enough in Tassie.

It was amazing though, how when they left I was feeling dirty, or covered in muck, or something wasn't right at all. I was wondering what it was. It lasted all day and into the next day. Like I was sick but it was a spiritual sickness.

About 24 hours later I was still suffering and I said to God, "Aww God, what's going on". And immediately the Holy Spirit said "A power is vindictive of your work". I never even knew what vindictive meant. So I grabbed the dictionary and looked it up. It read "Resentful, Revengeful". I thought, Hmmm….Demons came in with the bloke who visited and his mate and they stayed. So straight away I said, "I rebuke you vindictive power in the name of Jesus and command you to leave now". And straight away it felt like a dirty coat was ripped off me and they left.

It was another lesson in testing all things. Just because someone acts like a believer, doesn't mean they are. They may be full of demons, and used by the devil to share them around. This is why I don't like people I don't know laying hands on me, and reader, you shouldn't either. Giving them more time than I should, when things are not moving right is also something that I have grown to discern too. The devil will send all the time wasters under the sun. Or you could call them Vampires. They will drain you to feel good and it will take you a couple of days to recover. And with these vampires, the Rosary beads are useless. LOL

> Mat 7:20 Wherefore by their fruits ye shall know them.

Also I realised that a power was a group of demons. And now I just learned that I could move them in groups, not just one at a time. This was a good thing to recognise for the future battles. It made me start to understand the Power and Authority that believers have. So a bigger sense of strength came after it.

But I was grateful to God for everything I went through. Well, now with hindsight anyway.

I used to do this a lot below. And it would make me laugh. And the problems would become so much smaller almost straight away. Try it, it works.

> Luk 6:22-23 Blessed are ye, when men shall hate you, and when they shall separate you from their company, and shall reproach you, and cast out your name as evil, for the Son of man's sake.
>
> Rejoice ye in that day, and leap for joy: for, behold, your reward is great in heaven: for in the like manner did their fathers unto the prophets.

Many times I leaped around the lounge room, and prophetically knocking dust of my feet, and brushing myself down and whatever. But leaping for joy, actually gave you joy. As I moved forwards in the Kingdom of God, my enemies were increasing. I had to keep watch and pray. This Christianity was a dangerous game.

With the Rosicrucians troubles, I was getting sick of it. Once the bed was shaking and I woke up Poss, and said, "Is the bed shaking"? And it was for sure, I just wasn't sure if I was dreaming, and I said, I rebuke you bed shaking demon, leave now in Jesus name" and it slowed down and then stopped. Then we both just went back to sleep.

CHAPTER FOURTEEN: TIME TO PICK A FIGHT

Things like this were becoming common.

But this was with another mob from Canberra who picked a fight with me when we drove through there. I dreamed that I was hung up by my ankles upside down and about six inches from my nose were hundreds of rats and mice. Then God gave me the strongman's name in a voice in the dream when He said "Lilith" who I knew could be a principality.

Next day I saw her big statue in the middle of town and knew it was her, right outside the Canberra Legislative Assembly office near the art gallery. I waited until I got home to Tassie before attacking it, and the bed shook the same night.

The next night I had a dream and a real spooky bloke with an eye patch in a big black coat, was walking by about 15 meters away, and I looked away thinking, "Wow, he's really creepy, I'll just put my head down and wait until he walks by". Then I thought, "OK, he would have to be gone now I'll look up" and bang! There he was. If it wasn't a dream I may have crapped myself. He was looking straight into my eyes with his one eye from about two feet away. It was freaky and woke me up straight away.

I did get on the internet and typed in, one eyed man in astral plane, and Odin came up. That was him. Odin swapped his eye with three witches for wisdom. But guess what else. He was Lilith's brother, or so some mythology said. So that freaked me out, showed me a glimpse of the networks in the second heaven but most of all I realized that my Prayers were getting more powerful, and I was starting to affect principalities more and more.

But I still hadn't learnt to do warfare and see it out; I was operating more like a sniper. Hit and move to next target, but the bigger kills weren't happening yet. I needed to learn to pray until the release felt in my spirit. I did give Odin a good whack anyway of whatever I could throw at him too. And he never came back.

A lot of the people subscribing to my videos on YouTube were definitely satanists, and the fear that the devil was trying to put on me was intense. So I started to cry out to God. It felt like it was about to overwhelm me. He gave me something that took a lot of my worries away. It made me know that He was watching and allowing the measure of the strife that was coming. Not giving me more than I could handle, but keeping me on my toes. He had to get me to the place where He wanted me to be.

I guess that was the "Anointed Pastor" place, which I felt still miles and miles away from. So I'd had a bit of a sook to God, as we all do, but this was probably the last time I would seriously moan in his ear. I opened the Bible straight after this whinge and this scripture jumped out at me and hit me right between the eyes.

> Jer 12:5 If thou hast run with the footmen, and they have wearied thee, then how canst thou contend with horses? and *if* in the land of peace, wherein thou trustedst, *they wearied thee*, then how wilt thou do in the swelling of Jordan?

A lot of times this happened, that God would speak by his Word. But I knew that I was not to use His Word as a divination tool. He would give me what I needed; it was foolish to force it. Deception was waiting there in that place for an opening. This is my interpretation of what I felt God saying. Or what I knew He wanted to tell me. I had been moaning for a while about all my troubles.

"You want to whinge and moan about all your troubles. Look what troubles I faced for you. They may come in the night, they may write nasty emails, but if you can't stomach these, then how will you be able to handle the real fighting because it's coming if you want it. But if you don't then I'll find someone else who will".

So that really shut me up and I repented and said to God, "You have delivered me, healed me, protected and provided for me, I do trust you and I do want to be a mighty man of God. I owe you my life and I give it all to you. Forgive me for my whinging and carrying on, I won't do it anymore".

And that was that. That is how the Word of God can work. So mightily, when the Spirit transfers the Word to our spirit, right down to the bottom of our souls, where it becomes unmoveable, and part of the strength we need to stand. And the more of the Word you read, the more of this Light can enter. The Light redeems the darkness as the Holy Ghost once told me.

> Heb 4:12 For the word of God *is* quick, and powerful, and sharper than any twoedged sword, piercing even to the dividing asunder of soul and spirit, and of the joints and marrow, and is a discerner of the thoughts and intents of the heart.

CHAPTER FIFTEEN
THE MOUNTAIN BECKONS

I used to compare the Kingdom of God to an Aussie rules football match. You could do all the running around and jumping up and down and think you are dressed to kill, but if you never handled the ball before then, your legs will be worth nothing.

The ball is shaped strangely. It takes years to get an understanding of its movement, to kick, to mark, to bounce, to handball. It all had to be practiced, or used over and over. And after many years you would get to be able to see how its strange shape was going to bounce, even before it hit the ground. So you could run at full pace and be where it was going to be even before it got there. A lot of times you missed, but when it payed off, it looked good and felt good, and was very good for the team.

It was always the one percenter actions that would win the close match. How much you wanted it meant everything. And you had to back your own judgement, in the split seconds of the intensity of the game there was no place for double mindedness. It also depended on the surface of the ground. Every ground played a little different. So you had to read the game, depending on the arena.

And the opponents were different, every time. Different strengths and tactics and some bigger blokes were a lot harder to get around and bring down. And some little blokes were on your heels all the time. All had to be worked out and percentages weighed constantly to win the game, or to do your part at least, without regrets. If there was a blockage, then you had to rely on team mates to be in position to hand the ball on, or try and get around those walls. And with my size and weight, straight through was the shortest way home for me.

To compare Christianity with this game that I had played for most of my life was a fun pastime for me. Because God was putting me in His game, but I think I was probably still in C grade or so. But I was praying hard to go up a level. Then I received an email from somebody. It just said "Thanks for putting your testimony online. It was very encouraging". That was it and it had a name, Eric Geoffrey Okello. So I replied and asked "Where are you at?" and the email conversation worked back and forth.

I found out he was in Uganda and he told me that his parents were killed by Joseph Kony, who was the rebel leader and high level witchdoctor in North Uganda and South Sudan. Eric said that he was just living in Kampala where he could. So I sent him $50.

He was very grateful and he said he bought some tracts and handed them out in a nightclub and some people got saved. I was a bit suspect on this but he sounded sincere. So I sent him a Bible and stashed 50 bucks in the binding. I waited for his response and it was thankful. And he passed the test so I told him where to find the money.

Now I warn you who are looking to sow without knowledge. Africa and India are full of liars. I took a risk, but God was leading. Many give to those who cry over social media and the phone and they may as well burn the money. There are many white groups ripping off people also. Ask God where to give and let Him show you. Try to have a bit more of a say in the process and see what God will do. God will direct, and you will learn to hear His voice through it. I have noticed that those who won't give don't get far. And it is so much better to give where God is leading.

> Luk 6:38 Give, and it shall be given unto you; good measure, pressed down, and shaken together, and running over, shall men give into your bosom. For with the same measure that ye mete withal it shall be measured to you again.

Don't give to the wrong place because someone tells you too. That can bring a curse. And a lot of the church is under this curse.

> Pro 22:16 He that oppresseth the poor to increase his *riches, and* he that giveth to the rich, *shall* surely *come* to want.

If you desire to see the Kingdom of God grow, He will begin to use you. Jesus told His followers to pray this prayer. Most don't bother, but those who do will see it for themselves. They will be the ones who are sent out. I prayed it many times, hoping for God to send out those who I thought better equipped and slicker and smarter than me, but in the end it was me that was being sent. Will it be you? Do you even want to go?

CHAPTER FIFTEEN: THE MOUNTAIN BECKONS

Mat 9:37-38 Then saith he unto his disciples, The harvest truly is plenteous, but the labourers are few;

Pray ye therefore the Lord of the harvest, that he will send forth labourers into his harvest.

So I was helping Eric to know the Word and began to support financially. This was to some foolishness. They said I trusted too easy. But Eric was hungry. He was asking the right questions and I was teaching him the things I already knew, about life in the Kingdom of God.

With email exchanges daily, we were becoming good friends. I told him to fast if he is going to pray for people and it will help in other areas also. So righto, I never said how long. He had read in the Bible Jesus, Moses, and Elijah, fasted 40 days. So after about 12 months or less, Eric started a 40 day fast. I thought, "Wow, that's a bit extreme" but didn't want to put him off. If God was leading, then Eric would be right. Then a couple of months later he's done another one.

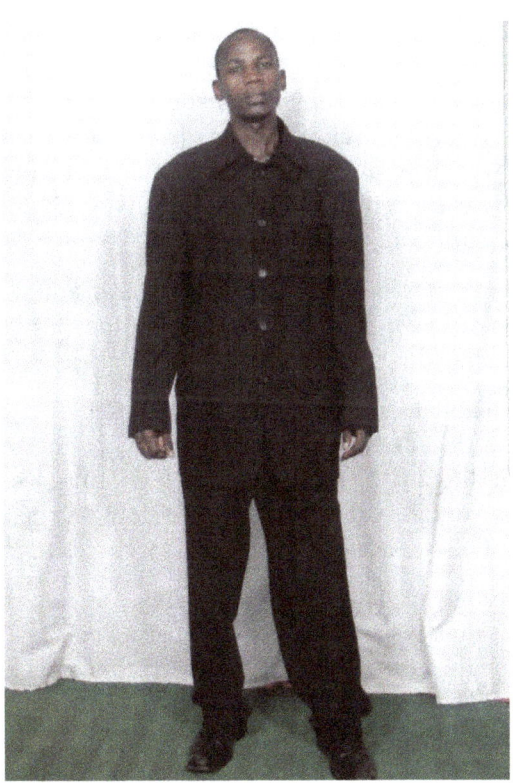

Eric after his first 40 day fast

He sent me a picture of himself afterwards, in a suit we sent him that was just like a small school kid that was dressed in his father's clothes. But I never wanted to warn him off. Even when he said he was fainting in the hot overcrowded taxis and saying that he was speaking prophecies over people when not even conscious, and they were amazed.

When he finished the fast he said he was praying for people and the blind were seeing, the lame were walking and demons were coming out, and a dead boy was raised back to life. I was so excited. But the voice of doubt in the back of my head kept saying, this is all fakery, he's a scammer. And I had trusted those who pretended to be men of God in the past. I was hoping and praying that this was real.

Eric was sending me dreams and visions to interpret almost every day. The Lord was certainly speaking to him and through him. Some of the words were for me also, through him. And Eric was speaking to others that I had given his email to.

Once I had an argument with my Daughter, that I had little to do with. I met her when she was 14, just after I was saved. I had went out with her mother for around three months and then moved away. I was frustrated with her and not happy after something happened. Eric sent an email the next day and said, "I saw a vision Daddy, (he called me Daddy, which was nice, and I had never heard that before) where there was a girl about 25 and you were arguing with her. God is telling you to give her a bit more of a go".

I knew that I had not told him about my daughter, and this was a confirmation to me, even though I didn't need one. But I used this example for others who thought I was sowing into a lie.

Now I had been able to interpret most dreams. Some were harder than others though and some were not able to be finished. I could just give some understanding on the symbology used and that was it. But Eric was appreciative and he was starting to see more here also. I did get the gift more fully after a 21 day fast. And it was a lot clearer.

The amazing thing was, after a couple of days, Poss was reading Eric's emails and she could see the interpretation also and we would get exactly the same thing, even apart from each other, which I tested her a lot and it was obvious. I had fasted 21 days, not for anything but to crucify flesh and got a gift, and Poss got the same gift. I thought, "Ripped off, 21 days fasting and Poss did zero, and she gets the gift too".

CHAPTER FIFTEEN: THE MOUNTAIN BECKONS

We would laugh about this. It was a blessing though as our ministry together was taking shape.

> Mar 10:8 And they twain shall be one flesh: so then they are no more twain, but one flesh.

After seeing how God was blessing Eric, I did want to do a 40 day fast. I was working though milking cows, so I did an 80 day fast with not eating every second day for 24 hours. It wasn't too hard and didn't affect my work. But I did eat like a horse every second day and lost no weight. And 80 days is a long time. But it was the most disciplined thing I had ever done and I felt like I had achieved a lot.

Then I organized a two week break from milking cows. I started a 21 day fast a couple of days before knock off and finished it just after. I was pretty weak when I went back to work but just paced myself and pushed through. This is when the dream interpretation came. And also gave up coffee and sugar, and lost almost 20 kgs.

I did go to the mainland during this break and I shouldn't have. My father saw me not eat for about ten days and was saying if sheep don't eat for a few days they die. I kept telling him, "I'm not a sheep", and if a sheep's not eating then it's probably old and toothless and dying anyway".

He was a good farmer and didn't starve his animals though, so it was a tactic from the devil. My little sister was spinning out too and carrying on. If you fast, stay away from family if you can. Or say nothing.

> Mat 10:16 Behold, I send you forth as sheep in the midst of wolves: be ye therefore wise as serpents, and harmless as doves.

I did have this dream not long after meeting Eric. I was having lots of dreams and lots of fights in them, and so was Eric. But there were many other dreams that were prophetic or words of knowledge, revelations and warnings, guidance and instruction also. And these have increased as time goes on. Some were obvious and easy to understand, and others took more time to unravel, even years.

I will tell you this one, it went like this. Poss and I walked into a big hall where there were heaps of people in sleeping bags and under doonas, singles and families. We had our dog with us and someone woke up and said "What are you doing here?" as if we didn't belong. I just ignored them and went to a dinner table in the back corner because I was so hungry.

I got there and wanted a feed of meat but all there was were sauces, and salt and pepper, condiments, and every additive in the world it seemed, but no real food. I kept looking "Where's the meat, where's the meat" but nothing to eat at all.

I could see a huge mountain through the wall somehow and knew that the mountain was Africa and a voice spoke and said "You will have a lot to do with this mountain". There were African men in this building in another corner of the building who were handing out really strong coffee. I wasn't ready for it though as I said "It's too strong for me, can you water it down a bit." So I think it's obvious what is happening here. Many believers are asleep but not knowing this and do not realise.

I was starving for meat that the church didn't have to give but only programs and offer memberships and promotions and so forth that are useless without the real food. So God was calling me to Africa, but I wasn't ready yet. But I was puzzled about the dog. Why was she with us, and God said, "That's how they see you, as out of church Christians". This was no surprise to me.

So Hallelujah, we were going to Africa. I waited a few weeks, then a few months and then a few years and after about four or five years of helping Eric's ministry, and sowing into it, which was on another level entirely, we got to go to Africa.

But the dream had shown I wasn't ready for the strong wake up stuff yet. So I organized a forty day fast. The first one I did.

CHAPTER SIXTEEN
THE FOUR LETTER F WORD

Fast, the four letter F word that believers steered clear of.

Early on before I started on this spiritual exercise, I did hear of some doing this for three days or so, or even more, but it was rare. And from what I seen, they wouldn't do it without eating broth, which was watery soup. Some may have, but I hadn't been as a young Christian, taught anything on fasting. And I thought, did Jesus take soup out in the wilderness with him? I knew the answer already.

> Mat 4:1-2 Then was Jesus led up of the Spirit into the wilderness to be tempted of the devil.
>
> And when he had fasted forty days and forty nights, he was afterward an hungred.

I got the idea that He did it rough. Not just fasting TV or chocolate and ice cream, which seemed acceptable to some. And to some, that was the extent of the sacrifice they were willing to give. People can be their own worst enemies, and laziness and apathy, definitely promotes lukewarm believers.

So how hard can it be? The 21 day fast I'd done wasn't too bad, so I started, and a friend Andrew also started on a 40 dayer. I got to three days. That's the hardest. That's when the devil tempted Jesus to turn the stone into bread. All I thought about was food. Then the food craving went but weakness came, as the body started to feed of its fat supply. And I had plenty in store. I was almost 25 kg over my football playing weight, which was 95kg. It started coming off though, quickly. First four or so kilos in the first three days then a bit over half a kilo per day, and the stomach emptied out, then the stored fat was being used up.

I remember the first few three day fasts, as it got to around two days and the stored food in the stomach was almost gone, and the body started on the stored excess in the fat supply. It was like I had injured my back and I never knew that I didn't. The pain was so bad. I couldn't get comfortable at all and even in the fetal position on the lounge room floor was no good.

What was happening here? Then I found this out after about three or four three day fasts, that the toxins in the body will come out and it will be painful as the poisons stored in the fat would filter through the kidneys. So after I found this out, when I did a three dayer, I would take some panadol, to ease the pain. I thought it better to get through the time and get rid of the toxins than cut short the fast and they remained.

Also the headaches from what I learnt, was from the caffeine withdrawals and they were really bad too. This is another reason why I gave up coffee. It made it hard to fast. The urine colour was very dark and you know it's got to be a good thing.

I did get to the point after a few three dayers that no painkillers were needed. Then I felt like it was done properly. Just totally on water. Except for a couple of dry fasts where there was no water either. But God had to help here. I actually never even got thirsty, and received really good things for these. They were a spiritual cleansing and strength that I needed.

After about ten days into the 40 day fast I started to get strong again, or could do more than just sit around. And it was amazing how long a day drags out when there is no food to break it up. On the 15th day I collapsed because I got out of bed too quick. I hit my head on the doorway on the way down and was bleeding. "Wow, I have to be more careful there".

My breath stunk until about the 20th day and my tongue was like the bottom of a cockies cage. It was a weird feeling too. Food was always in your mind but you weren't hungry. There were dreams and things, but spiritual things were an effort. It was hard to read and pray. My friend was struggling with stomach pains but he was determined to get through. I'm not sure our motives agreed with each other's but we pushed on.

At around the 18th day I visited a friend and he had some blueberry muffins in his house. He was eating one. He waved it under my nose to tease me, which just reminded me. When I was a six year old kid I teased my Sisters pony and ate an ice cream in front of it and waved it under its nose, going, "Mmmm, Mmmmm, Nice, Nice" and was really exaggerating how good this Ice Cream cone was.

CHAPTER SIXTEEN: THE FOUR LETTER F WORD

And every time it went to bite it I would move it away, and didn't give it one lick. Then I climbed over the fence where it was for some reason and it let loose on me with both barrels. Kicked me in the head right in the eye socket with one foot but missed with the other.

Mum was watching out the kitchen window and she ran out screaming, and I was covered in blood and had to go to hospital for a bit. I had to wear an eye patch for a little time. Never did like horses after that. I have got a bit of a phobia still.

The temptation was too much and I decided to break the fast after 21 days for one of those blueberry muffins. But, remember the scripture I put back a bit, how Esau sold his birthright for a morsel? So many times we take the path of least resistance and miss the opportunities that God is trying to lead us into, and still keep asking God, "Where are you God, Where are you"? Luckily my friend Andrew was determined to get through, and gave me some wisdom, and said, "You'll be over half way soon. If you break it, then you will have to cover all this ground again".

So I resisted the blueberry muffin and decided to push on. Like pushing through a pre-season of football training, I resigned to the fact; it just had to be done.

20 to 30 days and we were in cruise mode. You couldn't do much but you could pace yourself and weren't really tired unless you over did it. Remember this was just on water. That's what a proper fast is. Even Daniels fast of 21 days, people say he ate. But He got massive answers to prayer that doing a half-hearted effort won't bring. Believers are so quick to make excuses about crucifying their flesh through fasting. There are so many excuses. All by those who refuse to do it. And they may never get to their highest potential.

I have one go at this life and I desired not to waste it anymore, like my past. Jesus fasted in the wilderness. We were in our own homes, hot and cold running water, electric blankets on the beds and nice pillows to lay our heads on.

> Mar 1:13 And he was there in the wilderness forty days, tempted of Satan; and was with the wild beasts; and the angels ministered unto him.

I wasn't doing this to get anything; I was doing it to see what was on the other side. But it was the least I could do. Like I just said, I have one shot at this salvation while I'm on this planet, and I wanted to know what was available. And I believed that things would change.

> Eph 3:20 Now unto him that is able to do exceeding abundantly above all that we ask or think, according to the power that worketh in us,

After 35 days I was looking like I had AIDS and so was Andrew. I visited him in Hobart and he was looking for something to help with his stomach cramps. He did have more trouble than I but a lot less weight to lose also. But he made it through, which I was glad for him and him for me.

The last five days I just stayed inside. I became very weak and couldn't do much. But the days were counting down so I hung in there. 40th day came and went and I broke it.

I wasn't very disciplined in the days I fasted. Not that I ate anything or drank anything but water. But could have done a better job I thought. I told God about this and just the last couple of minutes I heard a voice clear say, "Do another day". I thought, 40 days is all Jesus had done, so that's all I'm doing devil. I really didn't try to discern the voice. Thinking back I should have done another day, but I never.

But I made up for that with the next 40 day fast I did. And it was more disciplined this time, with really good results. While going through this there were temptations. The devil was trying to distract and get you to cut it short. Jesus was first tempted with food.

> Luk 4:3 And the devil said unto him, If thou be the Son of God, command this stone that it be made bread.

Then I was offered two good jobs or doors open to ministry, but I would have to stop the fast to comply, around half way through, and something like this happened in almost all my long fasts, of two 40 dayers and four or five 21 dayers, I can't remember how many now. The season was for a few years and I did it a lot. No doubt the offers were going to be dead ends, but the devil was desperate and I realised this. I wanted God more that I wanted money.

> Luk 4:5-7 And the devil, taking him up into an high mountain, shewed unto him all the kingdoms of the world in a moment of time.
>
> And the devil said unto him, All this power will I give thee, and the glory of them: for that is delivered unto me; and to whomsoever I will I give it.
>
> If thou therefore wilt worship me, all shall be thine.

CHAPTER SIXTEEN: THE FOUR LETTER F WORD

Then the last temptation, which I seen another friend fall for. He had done two 40 day fasts and went to 45 in one and I think 46 in another. But it was for bragging rights in the end. He was convinced now he was Gods man and fell into a massive trap, and paid dearly for it. And still isn't out of the ditch. This was his trap.

> Luk 4:9-11 And he brought him to Jerusalem, and set him on a pinnacle of the temple, and said unto him, If thou be the Son of God, cast thyself down from hence:
>
> For it is written, He shall give his angels charge over thee, to keep thee:
>
> And in *their* hands they shall bear thee up, lest at any time thou dash thy foot against a stone.

The enemy snared him in Pride and tore things apart around him.

> 1Ti 3:6 Not a novice, lest being lifted up with pride he fall into the condemnation of the devil.

I finished and had lost almost 30 kgs. I felt ten years younger and was going well. Now maybe we were ready for Africa? A fast will crucify the flesh. It will get rid of fears and anxieties, depressions doubts and all sorts of problems. The stomach shuts down and gets a rest and all toxins disappear. Plaque will leave the arteries and everything feels brand new. Best thing out. Although hard work, the rewards are greater than the cost. The church has been stolen from severely, and anyone who says to not fast, run away from.

The second 40 dayer I was determined to do a better job. This was just after we got back from Africa the two times we went, and I was ready for take-off. I wanted all I could get and needed to get into shape. There was no reason except to get closer to God. Africa really stirred us up, which I will get to.

I was milking cows in the morning and evening through this fast, only on water. No food at all again. I got to around the 20th day or so and I hadn't had a dream or a vision or any leading from God in His Word and I was wondering why. I was putting more effort into praying and reading, and although hard, I was trying harder. I said to God, "God. What's going on? I've been fasting now for a few weeks and haven't got anything from you". Then He spoke by the Holy Spirit and said "After 35 days".

So that was my target at least. I had to get there and was determined to make it, now being excited to see what was coming. I had read my

Bible and had opened it up on a story about Absalom many times. He was a good looking bloke who wanted to be King. I did have a show off mentality and there were struggles in the flesh with pride. I had recognised before about my need to repent for this, and they were thought patterns that I didn't agree with, and I had repented, and renounced, and had tried to command the spirits out, but I couldn't even dent them.

So I just thought it was a thought pattern that I had to put up with, a thorn in the flesh. I milked through it, and asked for the last week off. It wasn't too hard the milking, all done by machine. But it was getting harder. Then the 35th day came. I woke up and opened the Bible. It opened on the story of Absalom. I was amazed at how many times the Word had opened here and I read it again.

This time I had insight into Absalom's pride and arrogance, and self-righteousness, self-love, self-promotion, and his desire to be first with all others under his feet. I saw my sin clearly now and how filthy it was in the eyes of God, and although I had partially recognized it in the past, I needed this uncovering in a big way.

I burst into tears and was fully repentant, and as soon as I repented I began to cough. Deep coughs from the bottom of my lungs and stomach, and when it seemed that every bit of air had come out of my lungs, some more would come out. I ended up on all fours on the bedroom floor and coughing and snot and spit flying about. And then it finished. I knew something major had come out. Because we were doing some deliverance by now on others, not to mention myself, and deep coughing was always a good sign.

So it was the 35th day of no food, only water, and that water was tank water, from rainfall. Every impurity even in bottled water could be tasted like it had poison in it. Town water was impossible to drink. And on that same day, I went to the toilet and my bowels moved. Sorry to be graphic, but it was a putrid mess that came out. I thought I was going to need and angle grinder to remove it off the toilet bowl.

I am positive that it was something that had been inside me, that demon or demons had been living in for decades. It was too much of a coincidence. And after doing deliverance a little, and learning lots about it, I knew that all sorts of things could be rejected by the body when the demonic entities were being expelled. They love the filthiness of the flesh.

CHAPTER SIXTEEN: THE FOUR LETTER F WORD

After that I was, and still am free, never to suffer those thoughts again. Or if they tried then the thought taken captive and they could be rejected.

The next couple of days other spirits came out. I'm sure one was a Simon the Sorcerer spirit among others. I believe these were picked up in the church and Absalom was strengthened by the worship I seen the Pastor getting. Everyone wanted to climb the ladder and get to that place, and I was no different. So the opened doors were there. I am so glad God got me out of the religious system.

So 40th day came and I had to milk the cows. It was some emergency though. I was meant to have it off and I wasn't looking forward to it. I went up and was a walking zombie. I struggled through and at the end told the farmer, "Wow, I'm glad I got through that, I'm knackered". I had barely enough energy left to even speak, but I did get back to the house and went and slept through a few hours of the last day which shortened it a bit.

He hadn't noticed that I'd lost almost 30 kg in just less than 6 weeks. And I looked like I had AIDS. He was surprised and so were my friends. They saw me the first time and thought I was dying, then to see me do it to myself a second time, was just crazy to them. Not that I advertised it, sometimes you were just seen. I'm glad I never went near my father after this. He'd have rung up the insane asylum.

> Mat 6:16-18 Moreover when ye fast, be not, as the hypocrites, of a sad countenance: for they disfigure their faces, that they may appear unto men to fast. Verily I say unto you, They have their reward.
>
> But thou, when thou fastest, anoint thine head, and wash thy face;
>
> That thou appear not unto men to fast, but unto thy Father which is in secret: and thy Father, which seeth in secret, shall reward thee openly.

But so much freedom came and I was ready now for something new. In between all this I had done many three day fasts with so many answers to prayer and blessings that I would have to write another book to tell all. And maybe I will. There definitely aren't too many about the Christians dreaded four letter F Word.

The result for Jesus after His 40 dayer was this. If you make it through, many doors for ministry will be available, because you are now stronger, cleaner and your temple is cleansed and the footholds the enemy uses are destroyed.

Are you willing?

> Luk 4:13-14 And when the devil had ended all the temptation, he departed from him for a season.
>
> And Jesus returned in the power of the Spirit into Galilee: and there went out a fame of him through all the region round about.

CHAPTER SEVENTEEN
THE SPIRITUAL KINGDOM

So back to earlier on, before the long fasting season I went through. The Rosicrucian witches were still harassing me but only on and off. And one night I had the worst nightmare I'd ever had. And I had a few over my years, but this one did definitely win the prize.

Here is the email I sent out two days afterwards, below. Exactly as I had written it, apart from a couple of spelling corrections and an old dead link taken off. I think I said two years or so that the witches here were harassing me earlier, but I see now that it was only about 16 months since I put the video up on YouTube. But it certainly felt like two years.

Now I have to add before you get to the email, the spiritual world is very had to explain. I will try to do this in a fashion after you get through the email. I don't remember anyone replying to the email except Eric. And I had around 30 on my email list.

No doubt some thought I was mad, and some still do. I was learning to keep things to myself after this. Eric had a vision of two men coming after me, just before I had the nightmare, and he lives in Uganda, Africa. I opened his email the next morning after my dream and this is what it said. There are no corrections here, but some other unconnected things, I removed.

> ----- *Original Message* -----
> From: Eric Geoffrey
> To: Peter McMaster
> Sent: Saturday, April 17, 2010 6:34 PM
> Subject: Re: Prayers Request for Jimmy.
>
> *I believe in God, yesterday I saw a vision of two white men and had wanted to write to you, however I have forgotten one was putting on novae blue (dark) shirt and another white but driving at high speed. Am believing God for this vision to come back again and monitor it well in Jesus mighty name.*

Its just a matter of time you will be completely delever Peter

So Eric had seen the two men coming to do their worst, but I had opened the email too late to pray against the warning. But God knew this. It had to happen for the deliverance to take place. And this also was more confirmation that Eric was yoked with us for a season.

I did write back and tell him that the thing had already happened, and this below is what I sent out to my email list. The scripture was what I received when I asked God, what the weapon was that he had me use.

And when I was using it, I was looking out my eyes, but something was animating my body, and using the weapon like a mighty man. I destroyed about 80 of 120 or so was my rough estimate of whatever they were.

----- Original Message -----
From: "Peter McMaster"
Subject: death threat
Date: Sunday, 18 April 2010 3:33 PM

G'day friends

I have been getting nasty emails about my videos on Youtube and on Friday night I had a death threat in a dream in the middle of the night. I will tell you about it.

First a fella walked up smiling with a knife and then cut my throat with it but I never died and I went and found a bit of a waddy, (it wasn't big enough though to do the damage I wanted to do) and started beating him and his mate around the heads with it. I woke up and prayed for a bigger weapon and then went back to sleep. Then I was in the middle of a human sacrifice where the people all turned into demons and were after me but this time I had some sort of nunchuka thing with wild blades on the end that just carved em up but there were too many so I left and in the middle of it all a voice spoke to me and said " Take your videos off Youtube if you value your life".

I woke up and prayed and rebuked everything I could think of, had a bit of a coughing fit, (I think it was something that entered in my dream, maybe from the knife cut. I know when I have still felt pain from snake bites or crocodile bites after I have woken up, there has always been some sort of demon gain entry and it has taken awhile to get over them) so I feel fine and I think I coughed it up. After the 40 day fast I did I find it very easy to expel any demon from myself that's looking for a home. Praise God.)

CHAPTER SEVENTEEN: THE SPIRITUAL KINGDOM

It was the worst nightmare I have had for years, maybe ever and remember, I had nightmares every night for about 2 or 3 years before I was saved, and when I say every night, it was EVERY NIGHT.

My new friends never came back last night, did a bit of praying before I went to sleep though, I tell ya. So praise God. People say you shouldn't send things back like this but I do and always will. When these things have a go, they have a go, but to send them back dumps it on them and reveals the power of the Word of God and the Name of Jesus. The name above all names. (I definitely didn't want them hanging around home!!!)

It's not the first time I have been visited in the night, 3 times I have been pinned to the bed and couldn't breathe or speak or move and all I could do was think "help me Jesus" and the grip loosened, then whisper the same and it became looser still, then speak it out "help me Jesus" and the thing has left, but the last time I rebuked this thing and it shot off me and actually hit our steel flu on the fire and made it rattle (that was freaky).

But now it's the Rosicrucian mob. I've upset them a little. But I'm not taking the videos down, that's for sure.

The enemy hates to be exposed. I was praying against masonry and stuff that it would be exposed only about a month after I was saved cause I knew that they were dishing out demons, and it was in the night, It was warm so I had the curtains open just laying on my bed, and a flash of lightning flashed across the sky but the night was clear as anything, not one cloud. There was no thunder but just an amazing bolt of lightning. I actually hid under the doona thinking, WOW, what have I done? So this is part of that prayer being answered I suppose.

Eph 5:11 And have no fellowship with the unfruitful works of darkness, but rather reprove them.

You may be encouraged a little by what I have wrote hopefully but do not ever be fearful or intimidated. If you slow down or start to back up when these things have a go then they will pour the pressure on and grind you down.

Isa 41:8 But thou, Israel, art my servant, Jacob whom I have chosen, the seed of Abraham my friend.

Isa 41:9 Thou whom I have taken from the ends of the earth, and called thee from the chief men thereof, and said unto thee, Thou art my servant; I have chosen thee, and not cast thee away.

Isa 41:10 Fear thou not; for I am with thee: be not dismayed; for I am thy God: I will strengthen thee; yea, I will help thee; yea, I will uphold thee with the right hand of my righteousness.

Isa 41:11 Behold, all they that were incensed against thee shall be ashamed and confounded: they shall be as nothing; and they that strive with thee shall perish.

Isa 41:12 Thou shalt seek them, and shalt not find them, even them that contended with thee: they that war against thee shall be as nothing, and as a thing of nought.

Isa 41:13 For I the LORD thy God will hold thy right hand, saying unto thee, Fear not; I will help thee.

Isa 41:14 Fear not, thou worm Jacob, and ye men of Israel; I will help thee, saith the LORD, and thy redeemer, the Holy One of Israel.

Isa 41:15 Behold, I will make thee a new sharp threshing instrument having teeth: thou shalt thresh the mountains, and beat them small, and shalt make the hills as chaff.

Isa 41:16 Thou shalt fan them, and the wind shall carry them away, and the whirlwind shall scatter them: and thou shalt rejoice in the LORD, and shalt glory in the Holy One of Israel.

Isa 41:17 When the poor and needy seek water, and there is none, and their tongue faileth for thirst, I the LORD will hear them, I the God of Israel will not forsake them.

Isa 41:18 I will open rivers in high places, and fountains in the midst of the valleys: I will make the wilderness a pool of water, and the dry land springs of water.

Isa 41:19 I will plant in the wilderness the cedar, the shittah tree, and the myrtle, and the oil tree; I will set in the desert the fir tree, and the pine, and the box tree together:

Isa 41:20 That they may see, and know, and consider, and understand together, that the hand of the LORD hath done this, and the Holy One of Israel hath created it.

Praise the Lord.

Pete

So that was what I sent my email list.

But the western world is unaware of this reality, and the church sadly is willingly ignorant to a large degree. If they did want to fight the bigger battles for the souls of men then the Lord would train them. But to be looking for an advantage in life from God and not worried about the state of men's souls is not beneficial for any blessings or favour to come to us from God. Also little insight or discernment, wisdom or understanding, or any true gifting. Why would we need them? This is the will of God for men.

> 2Pe 3:9 The Lord is not slack concerning his promise, as some men count slackness; but is longsuffering to us-ward, not willing that any should perish, but that all should come to repentance.

And this is the reason Jesus came. This is what He was anointed for. This was His ministry and what the Holy Ghost entered Him for. This is where the Holy Spirit will activate us and use us mightily, when we start to desire these same things.

It becomes an exciting walk when we shift our focus from ourselves, to others.

> Luk 4:18-19 The Spirit of the Lord *is* upon me, because he hath anointed me to preach the gospel to the poor; he hath sent me to heal the brokenhearted, to preach deliverance to the captives, and recovering of sight to the blind, to set at liberty them that are bruised,
>
> To preach the acceptable year of the Lord.

So God will equip you to fight. He will not send you to a war untrained. He will give us as much as we can bear and no more. If it's too heavy, cry out. I know I did many times. But the more you allow yourself to carry at times, the quicker the training works to strengthen, and the quicker the things we need for ministry will appear, whatever they are.

There are many talents and many gifts and many works that are waiting for every believer, to walk in. But the majority of believers are missing them and walking straight past or around or through without recognising them. If you start to come into agreement and pray for souls and desire to walk in the Luke 4:18 ministry of Jesus Christ, then things will really start to move. But there is another sure thing also; the devil will begin to move against you also. Do not doubt this for a minute.

So there are three Heavens. Sky and stars are the First. Astral plane is the Second Heaven. Satan was cast down to here. And these spirits can affect our world, and move through the veil into this dimension. They are fallen angels and demons. And they operate through opening doors to sin in humans for them to gain access to and enter, and also they use witches to operate in two dimensions, the physical and the spiritual, and use them to get their wicked works done.

Then there is the third Heaven, where God is. God can use us to bring His Heaven to Earth. There was a war in the third Heaven and this happened.

> Rev 12:7-9 And there was war in heaven: Michael and his angels fought against the dragon; and the dragon fought and his angels,
>
> And prevailed not; neither was their place found any more in heaven.
>
> And the great dragon was cast out, that old serpent, called the devil, and Satan, which deceiveth the whole world: he was cast out into the earth, and his angels were cast out with him.

So now he's in the second Heaven because they are spirits, invisible to most.

But witches can astral project and meet with these spirits in the astral plane. And do their dirty work for promises of ruling and reigning with Satan in Hell for ever, and for worldly fame and fortune, spiritual powers like divination, insight and secret knowledge that the devil gives, by infesting these people with spirits of the same.

And all the while the deceived think they are gaining advantage, their souls are slowly being suppressed within them, and they are losing all of the self-control they once had.

The devils will take over, and can to the point where those who have fallen to the deception are totally possessed, and can become reprobate, with no chance of salvation. Then the demons just live on the surface, and animate the body, while the soul is down low, sometimes screaming for help. It is a very sad truth here, and maybe this is part of why Solomon said this.

> Ecc 1:18 For in much wisdom is much grief: and he that increaseth knowledge increaseth sorrow.

But there is also Angels working for us, and things they can use. The Bible talks about Angels binding with chains and having swords and armour and even Angels eating with men and all sorts of things that are hard to comprehend. Paul said they can look just like us.

> Heb 13:2 Be not forgetful to entertain strangers: for thereby some have entertained angels unawares.

And just as there are streets in Heaven, gates and mansions that are mentioned in the Bible, also there is also a counterfeit set up by the devil and his Angels, in the second Heaven. There are kingdoms under the water and in the air and other places.

When I was doing the Rosicrucian stuff, they gave me a picture of the "Celestial Sanctum". It's a magical looking castle where they said to meet at when it appears, obviously when I was out of my body and in the astral plane. And it looked a lot like Disneyland. Funny about that, hint, hint. The devil likes to advertise and brag to those who can read his signs, the spiritual wickedness in high places.

And there are other Kingdoms. Most Africans have heard of the underwater kingdom, where the Witches all meet and plan to work their wickedness against humans. Now I hope I haven't lost you at this time. I do have some evidence of this coming up, about this kingdom underwater, that is the devils counterfeit, that even some people running churches are attending.

This info fell into my lap and I will share it very soon in the following pages. It will open your eyes to the real war that is raging all around. When things are happening down here, they have already happened in the Heavenlies. But most are unaware. And even when we try to understand, it is very difficult.

Jesus said this...

> Joh 3:12 If I have told you earthly things, and ye believe not, how shall ye believe, if I tell you *of* heavenly things?

When we are ready for the understanding, then God will give it. I am just hoping through this book that any closed doors to knowledge to these things, may be prised open a little. And that it is the work of God that will do this for you. He knows who is ripe for this. But also, all you have to do is ask.

The devil has weapons also and a massive army. I have seen all sorts of things and animals attack me, or try to. And some get through and some don't. It is very active out there. Especially when you have upset the Enemy of mankind and He wants you dead. But the ministry that God has given me here is something I do not share with anyone really.

I have met others that He is using in this area, but very rare. And they keep it quiet as well, because of ridicule or rejection or things that people throw at you in unbelief.

I have seen all sorts of weapons and defences and vehicles in my dreams. Used by the demons and the witches, and there are many that God has had me use. I have used guns and knives and swords and even flamethrowers and sticks and fists and feet and you name it, it is a war. I believe that God uses me in the astral plane to fight the things that need to be defeated and destroyed. Actually, I know He does!

The thing is, I'm just looking through my eyes at the work He has me doing, and I use some weapons like an expert even when I have never touched one ever. It amazes me every time. And if there is a struggle in my life then I pray and a lot of times God shows me the enemy, whether it's an animal, or demon, or just looks like men and women. And after it is defeated it in the spirit realm, or dream state mostly, then the problem is solved. Or slowed down at least, and the assigned curses are broken and scattered.

Also if I warfare in prayer on a subject, God gives me confirmation of my hitting the mark by seeing things torn down in the spirit realm and enemies defeated. This happens a lot. But there is no glory in this work, most don't believe, so it is trench warfare, and lots of intercession alone.

My wife has many dreams too, although she is not in the fight that I am. She is a massive support, and I'm very grateful to the Lord for her.

I will give two examples of an attack and the results here.

One night early in my walk a large bear came up and bit me on the finger. It hurt in the dream, and I woke up wondering what it meant. That same morning God had given me a scripture also to beware of men, and not to wish "God Speed" on the wicked. I thought about this a lot that morning and had to go to work in the afternoon. As soon as I got there, a very tall man nicknamed Bear, was at work. And he welcomed me with "God Speed". I knew something was up but didn't know how to neutralize these things yet in prayer.

Anyway, Bear did the wrong thing by me and it hurt me a little and caused strife with other believers, because Bear was a believer, although lukewarm. And I wasn't really expecting the trouble from another Christian. Since then I am very wary of everyone.

There is no doubt, if I had broken that curse, neutralised the bite, and crushed that demonic seed that was sown that night in my dream,

CHAPTER SEVENTEEN: THE SPIRITUAL KINGDOM

there would have been no trouble or strife for any of us. The enemy planned the trouble in the astral plane, sowed the seed, and I walked into what was waiting for me. It's simple now to see it. I hope you can too.

Another thing was not that long ago, even though I battle things a couple of times a week in my dreams, and usually win, and God has blessed us with this, and kept us ahead of the enemy of our souls, there are things that I must go through to learn, or doors I need to shut from the enemies access.

There was a low feeling, or dullness that I was in for a couple of weeks. I couldn't shake it. I was praying and it wouldn't leave. But one night I had this dream. I was coasting down a slight hill on a small pushbike, and I saw a policeman down the bottom, with a gun. I looked behind and there was a massive male lion chasing me, and gaining ground in a hurry. So I tried to outrun it. I weighed the speed I was travelling and the distance to the bottom to the man with the gun, who I was hoping would shoot the lion and kill it. But the lion was far too quick, and I started to panic.

I thought, "I'm gone, this lion is going to get me, no worries". And as soon as I knew that nobody could help me, I had decided to turn and fight what a few seconds ago I thought was an enemy that was too great for me. So I stopped the bike and said angrily" Lion, I rebuke you in the name of Jesus Christ and I command you to go. Leave me and never come back". And guess what, it stopped and left.

I woke up and that was another plan or attack of the enemy even defeated in my dream. And the heaviness was gone that I had and the oppression also. So I obviously had defeated something in my life that was making me think that the problem was too big for me to handle and I was trying to escape.

And the pushbike meant that although I was getting help from God in travelling forward, on a downhill slope, I was still trying to move in my own strength, like pushbikes take to move them. And the policeman with the gun was an out of reach reliance on other men to help fight my battles. But to conquer the fear here was a victory. And no doubt an enemy was defeated in the second heaven.

There is still fear in my dreams at times though. But the more you defeat fear in your life and begin to trust God, the more He can do greater things with you, because you are stronger to hang in there without fleeing, and you will see so much more get done within, around and for you. And I'm not saying not to have other people pray for us, it doesn't happen enough, but there is a weakness where a lot only want others to fight their battles. These people will never get anywhere. I prayed and broke the curses of the weakness of fleeing from the Lion then coughed up a bit after self-deliverance, and then asked God to fill me with His Holy Spirit, in the void of what had come out, and all was well. Praise the Lord.

Also many times witches and warlocks show up, trying to feed food and stick things into you and steal things and whatever they do. God lets me see them and deal with them. Not just for myself, but for others. The devil likes to hide, and work in darkness, but God puts light on some things for us, so we can see to be equipped for the battle and have understanding of what is coming against us. To know what to pray, even if it's just praying about the symbology in the dream, is a massive advantage, and the problem can still be defeated.

We need to trust God to do it for us. All we need to do is initiate some sort of faith and He fills in the holes and covers our mistakes. To pray a one sentence warfare prayer is so much more powerful than praying nothing.

God promises this.

> Mat 6:10 Thy kingdom come. Thy will be done in earth, as *it is* in heaven.

And He gives us what we need.

> Jas 1:17 Every good gift and every perfect gift is from above, and cometh down from the Father of lights, with whom is no variableness, neither shadow of turning.

We need things done in Heaven before they can come to Earth. But the second Heaven Astral dimension tries to block and hinder these things coming.

If you start to pray warfare against the devil and his demons, then things will certainly pick up for you and things that are broken in your life will begin to be restored. I must add that without obedience to God and repentance and forgiveness, you will be mostly wasting your time. Or even worse, if you stir up the devil with open doors then you will get yourself into BIG TROUBLE.

Also the believer believes that others are praying for them, but probably not as much as they think, and most likely, not at all. If we are relying on prayers from others to get us through, we are not going to make it. Pray for yourself. If you are struggling in everything, how can you help anyone else with any consistency?

Also there are times when I am at places in my sleep that I don't know, praying for the sick, preaching to people and rebuking men and women for wickedness. I know this is hard to fathom for many, but it's real to me. And because I see the results manifest in the physical a lot, I know it's real. So if God could translate Phillip in his body away to another place, after preaching to the Ethiopian Eunuch with no trouble, then to use people like this when they sleep is no great thing to me. He is God and I am not.

> Act 8:39 And when they were come up out of the water, the Spirit of the Lord caught away Philip, that the eunuch saw him no more: and he went on his way rejoicing.

And also this happened to Peter.

> Act 12:5-11 Peter therefore was kept in prison: but prayer was made without ceasing of the church unto God for him.
>
> And when Herod would have brought him forth, the same night Peter was sleeping between two soldiers, bound with two chains: and the keepers before the door kept the prison.
>
> And, behold, the angel of the Lord came upon him, and a light shined in the prison: and he smote Peter on the side, and raised him up, saying, Arise up quickly. And his chains fell off from his hands.
>
> And the angel said unto him, Gird thyself, and bind on thy sandals. And so he did. And he saith unto him, Cast thy garment about thee, and follow me.
>
> And he went out, and followed him; and wist not that it was true which was done by the angel; but thought he saw a vision.
>
> When they were past the first and the second ward, they came unto the iron gate that leadeth unto the city; which opened to them of his own accord: and they went out, and passed on through one street; and forthwith the angel departed from him.

> And when Peter was come to himself, he said, Now I know of a surety, that the Lord hath sent his angel, and hath delivered me out of the hand of Herod, and from all the expectation of the people of the Jews.

Never limit God. And when He starts to use you in this way, and nobody wants to believe, then don't worry. It's the commendation from God is what we need, not from man.

> 2Co 10:18 For not he that commendeth himself is approved, but whom the Lord commendeth.

CHAPTER EIGHTEEN
AFRICA, HERE WE COME!

It got to the point where we were thinking our Africa trip will never come. So when Poss took her long service leave we thought, this is the best and maybe only chance we will get financially to go. I wasn't rolling in dough and Poss was working three days a week.

Although we were far from poor, with enough to do whatever we wanted in Tassie, we did not save money. If we got extra we would give it out, every time. And every time we needed something then somebody would knock on the door or ring us and offer me work.

In the almost 20 years I lived at Pyengana, I only once asked for a job, and got it, but then knocked it back because of other's advice. And I'm glad. I didn't want to work full time. No way. How could I fast and pray and read the Bible when I'm working. I couldn't. And with full time work in the past, all I wanted to do was get home, have a wash and sit on my bum until bed time. To put extra energy into anything spiritual after that was difficult. It was an effort that I didn't want to do. Why bother. I trusted God for money and work and He sorted out the rest. And gave ample time in between to read, fast pray, make tracts, DVDs, work on my website and other things I could do for Him.

I would rather be poor and happy than rich and miserable, a slave to the system, and always looking for more. I'd been without money so many times in the past; it didn't scare me at all.

But God promises this.

> Psa 37:25 I have been young, and now am old; yet have I not seen the righteous forsaken, nor his seed begging bread.

We bought the tickets to Uganda. Got a good deal and were set to go. Around five grand return. And we were excited. God wasn't saying much and I had got to the stage where this didn't make me anxious. If we are doing the right thing and He is quiet then this is no reason to fear. It can show us that we are on the right track.

This is where people need to calm down and wait. Instead of running to man to do this thing "Have you got a Word for me, can you give me a Word". This so easily can bring wrong advice and have false prophecy sown into their hearts. If we would just learn to wait then God would show them the things they need to know. I know it. I went for years without any man's direction, but got plenty from God.

And the devil can see the blessings coming to us sometimes, and can drive us into that place to get us to run ahead, and destroy the plan of God for us. God has made me wait to the last minute almost every time, loads of times. This builds character and inner strength by trusting Him for everything.

> Isa 40:31 But they that wait upon the LORD shall renew *their* strength; they shall mount up with wings as eagles; they shall run, and not be weary; *and* they shall walk, and not faint.

Also to go through the wait, and past the anxiety, will bring reward into your life.

> Heb 11:6 But without faith *it is* impossible to please *him*: for he that cometh to God must believe that he is, and *that* he is a rewarder of them that diligently seek him.

I was working for a farmer for a short time, feeding his cattle and doing cowboy stuff, for a few weeks. I had got my fortnights pay and our house insurance came in, also two car regos, the power bill and rates. Every bill you could think of it seemed. And two weeks before we were leaving the work was over and I had two hundred dollars in the bank.

I was starting to worry. And even though Poss had some stashed away and was going to have a small wage come in for the two months we were going for, I still wanted some cash to do some things over there, whatever they were, and not just survive on her hard earned money.

So I prayed, "God, you know we are going to Africa. You told us awhile back. I don't feel like I've made a mistake but You know, err…. You know, I've only got 200 bucks in the bank. And umm… am thinking this may not be enough. But I trust you and know you won't let us down." And straight away I got a vision. It was of a stone wall and an old door. And beside that door were two large guards, covered

CHAPTER EIGHTEEN: AFRICA, HERE WE COME

in ancient armour and helmets and holding spears. And straight away I knew that what I needed was behind that door. I prayed something like, "I strip all weapons and armour off those guards in Jesus name and pick up the Word of God and smash down all those walls that hinder my finances, and kick down the door also and take what is needed", all the while, doing the actions prophetically.

And that's about all it was. The word of knowledge was given by the vision and the prayer was prayed. Two days later we were given fourteen thousand dollars. We couldn't believe it. God had come though and blessed us abundantly. And I said, "Wow God. What do we do with all that?"

And I heard a voice from within say, "Have fun". I thought, "That can't be right, that voice had to be mine" so I asked again. "What do you want us to do with all this money"? We knew it was His, not ours to splurge on junky stuff with or whatever. I heard again, "Have fun". And I thought again, "Surely Gods not just saying have fun. That's gotta be coming from me".

So I waited for a few hours and wondering what we were to do and then thought I better just ask one more time, "What do we do with this money God"? And the answer was the same, "Have fun". That was it.

No matter how much fear people around us were trying to lay on us, from the Doctor who was a Nigerian Catholic, where we had to get the required shots and told us we were very unwise, and then told the nurses at the hospital that we would probably lose everything, even our lives, and the workmates and friends and family all putting in their two bobs worth. They made it sound like Africa was full of cannibals who would put us in the pot as soon as we got off the plane.

But God told us to have fun, so I was going to have fun. And there was not the slightest bit of fear in us at all. And we had enough cash to do it properly.

We sent Eric enough to rent a house in the suburbs for six months, which was still cheaper than a motel. While we were only to be there two months, he and his family who we were supporting could stay there the rest. Which had gone from Eric, to wife and child and two other children, one each, from previous relationships, (no birth control in Africa, babies everywhere) and six others, four were orphans and a couple were very young men who were being discipled by Eric.

The plane landed at Entebbe and we went to get our luggage and it wasn't there. And neither was Eric.

And the devil was saying "It's all been a mistake. No Eric, no luggage, just turn around and go home, you've been conned".

But Eric wasn't allowed in the Airport because of the paranoia in Uganda of terrorists. It wasn't long before that over 200 people were blown up at a soccer game, so there were armed guards everywhere. Even in the supermarkets. It actually made you feel a bit safer.

First thing Eric organised was a ten day crusade in a Kampala suburb called Mutungo. It was at a school right on the main road. People were coming and going and sick people were being prayed for and we were seeing healings. I prayed for a woman with bad eyes and they were healed and a lame woman who hadn't walked for months came on the back of a motorbike, and walked away.

Demons were manifesting and a snake came from nowhere in the middle of the crowd. It was trampled by one of the young men whom we had just bought a pair of boots for a couple of days before. It was fantastic. No fear, just fun. We had an old rented sound system that was turned up as loud as it could go and so crackly that you could understand little of what was said and the music that was belted through it was unrecognizable to us.

But this was Africa and we were straight into it. We were under no instructions from anyone or guidance through the madness. No carefully crafted formulas for soul winning or drawing a crowd. Just crank up the volume and preach, yell and scream through the microphone and see what happens next. I loved the chaos of that environment. It was so exciting.

The devil was always trying, but the Word of "Have fun" that I had heard over rode all that the devil was going on with, and forced his voice out of my mind, time and time again. And I'm sure this upset him totally. Hehehe. He was watching though.

We walked out of the crusade late one night and we saw a very abnormally large dog peeking around the corner of the front gates to the school that went out onto the street. It was staring straight at me with what seemed to be a human glare. There was Poss and I and Eric and his wife and maybe some of the children, all going to walk up the street about the one kilometre to the house.

It was around 11 PM but the people were as numerous in the street at this time, as any time in the day. And on weekends even more. It seemed to me that Africa never slept.

CHAPTER EIGHTEEN: AFRICA, HERE WE COME

After the years at Pyengana with the population of eighty or ninety odd, and it even hit near 100 once after a quick count one sleepy evening. All depending on how many were renting the old farm houses at the time. It was the most extreme contrast one could imagine, unless you lived in a cave on a mountain top. That would widen the gap a bit more, but not much.

Anyway this extremely ugly mangy dog made a big arc around us about three or four meters away, looking at me straight in the eye. The hairs on my back of my neck stood up and I knew what was looking at me wasn't a dog. It was a witch inside the dog or maybe they had shapeshifted into that mongrel looking thing. It certainly made me wonder. Then when it had gone the 180 arc, it walked off still looking at me over its shoulder. It was a wakeup call that Africa is the land of witchcraft. I was going to enjoy this, and learn so much.

I had no fear of the devil, now that I had been doing self-deliverance and warfare for a while now. I knew the power in the name of Jesus; the name above all names, and was not intimidated in the spirit much at all. This was tested one night after we went around the streets handing out tracts. There was Poss and I and five Africans. I had taken a heap of tracts and DVDs to hand out. I didn't know that DVD players were rare, but tracts were devoured. We handed out about 500 in a little over 150 meters. People would come to see what the white man had, and they would read them on the spot. Many souls were being won.

One night in the house Eric rented for us and him and his extended family, which had a lock up gate and fence and lots of broken bottles cemented in the top of it for security, the dogs came, to cause a bit of stir. The house had bars on the door and windows, which was best, I'm sure.

Eric liked the security and after seeing his parents get killed by Kony, I'm sure he felt more secure with his family too.

At night they would pray, all of them, and thank God for getting them through the day, and in the morning, first thing, which was five every morning, the whole family would get up "Thank you God for getting us through the night" and then pray for an hour about whatever they were led to do.

This took us out of our comfort zone for sure. But this is where I learned to pray, with the Africans, who cannot rely on money for anything really. They need God and you could see that and understand it too.

I did start asking them what they were dreaming and they were all having dreams so I taught them a little about looking into them. And this excited them. We were getting much insight into lots of things in and around us all.

Broken bottle fence security

We had been out on the street and praying for people and at a little after midnight, or later, the dogs came to the front gate, which was not far from our barred up but open window. We had the malaria pills and had mozzie spray, so in the heat, we let in some cool night air. Then they started. "HOOOWWWLLL, OWWUURRR, ARROOOOO". Right at the gate, ten meters from our window. Not one would bark however, at all.

I grew up on a sheep farm and we had dogs all the time. I estimated that there were about five of them. It was so freaky. And what I had seen in the big mangy mongrel one a few days before, I realised immediately what was happening.

CHAPTER EIGHTEEN: AFRICA, HERE WE COME

So I said, "In the name of Jesus Christ, I rebuke you". And it was just like somebody flicked off a switch. It was amazing. Not one whimper after that. Next night they came, same thing. "In the name of Jesus Christ I rebuke you, and bang, instant reaction. Cut them off mid howl. Third night, they came and I thought, "Ahh, here's those idiots back again, I'll fix them". And said the same, but this time they only quietened down a bit but kept trying to howl. So I had to put a bit of effort in this time and they wound down and stopped their noise.

I soon figured out that when we think we have a formula worked out then God is not in our prayers or commands to the extent that we need him. And it can become us trying to do the work in our own power, not His. This happens in Christianity so much.

And to think we have arrived is a bad place to be.

> 1Co 4:7 For who maketh thee to differ *from another?* and what hast thou that thou didst not receive? now if thou didst receive *it*, why dost thou glory, as if thou hadst not received *it?*

We had a TV that we would watch the world news on and we saw this. Uganda had in 2012 a death penalty for homosexuals, and the American Luciferians, Obama and Clinton were trying to cancel this law. But all the Ugandan government would do was lower the punishment to life in prison. While this was being reported on the news, a flash came across the bottom of the screen that said, "Uganda politicians still undecided on punishment for child sacrifice".

I couldn't believe it. Homos got life; Witchdoctors got sometimes fame and fortune. Because from what we heard, they were all involved, and child sacrifice brought much advantage to them. This is why a lot of African parents put ear rings in their young girls to mark them and add a blemish, to put off those who would kidnap them to sacrifice. And it seemed to be common knowledge that all in foundations of every big building were victims of sacrifice. But that was Africa. Any advantage was to be taken if it would help ease the suffering in one's life.

So witchcraft was their national religion and even at the soccer games they were taking chickens and sacrificing them. It was no wonder that in the Museum, about one-fifth of the displays or more were glorifying this. They had all sorts of spooky masks and ritual items and the guides would tell you straight out that people were the victims as well as animals.

Two of the displays were famous witchdoctors who could astral project in times of war with other tribes or countries and rain down death and destruction on their enemies from the astral plane.

It fascinated me to know the deeper things, because with the war that was coming my way, I would need some of this info very much.

CHAPTER NINETEEN
KONY COUNTRY

The Crusade on the Mutungo Primary School property was over and we had been in Uganda about 5 weeks or so. Eric wanted to hold a Crusade in his old village of Otwal in the North. About six hours away from where we were. He went up and organized people who were interested to help and gave them a date. We paid the rent on a house there too for the choir, and some of the preachers who were not local.

Eric organized the sound system and the marquees and chairs for oldies and posters and all the stuff he thought was needed. We had the cash and this was the fun I was looking for. More organized chaos of an African Crusade.

The crusade had been going for about a week when we showed up. There were many that came to it. Six or seven hundred was a fair estimate once, most after dark. The Catholics were told they would be banished if they came and so they and others came but stood in the distance, wondering what this witchcraft was.

A few days before it started, there were Catholic Priests there who were obviously worried about their congregation being lost to the Life that Jesus Christ could offer and spread rumours that the white man preaches a gospel of men can marry men. Which I thought was funny, considering the law in Uganda at the time. I guess it was the worst rumour they could think of.

These men, the day before we got there, who realized that their lies weren't working, apparently had another plan. They got on a motorbike and were going the 60 minutes by bike to the main town of Lira, to put in a formal complaint in the big police station there. Well we found out they never made it. They ran under a truck and that was the end of that, and the end of them. Africa is a serious place we discovered, and we saw more than once, that those who block the work of God there sometimes don't get another chance.

And God was working mightily in Uganda.

> 2Ti 4:14-15 Alexander the coppersmith did me much evil: the Lord reward him according to his works:
>
> Of whom be thou ware also; for he hath greatly withstood our words.

So we got to Lira and then out to Otwal. The road was out so we had to go on a 4 wheel drive track that only humans and bikes and goats used by the looks. The potholes were massive and full of water and we had to get out a few times to lighten the load to allow the driver to get through them. But it was all an adventure. This was no drama to me. I was used to muddy tracks and getting bogged on the farms I was working on and the one I grew up on.

Road to Otwal

We get to Otwal and it was the market day. There were thousands of people there and Eric led us down the main street, to show us off I suppose, because they did look hard. He showed us the large posters that we had made up, that were splattered here and there. It was a surreal feeling all this. But we just kept moving forward, wondering what was next. Because in Africa, I don't think anybody knows. Stability was hard to find, especially in amongst the villages.

Otwal was where the Ugandan Army was situated and it was a camp for refugees in the Kony war. People were driven off their land and put in camps. Three Thousand of them got AIDS and there was a lot of sickness and disease. When we got there, people were coming back and setting up again. And they were happy to get on their land and work the soil, with their hand tools, and not have to worry about looking over their shoulders.

CHAPTER NINETEEN: KONY COUNTRY

A few years before, Kony, who was a high level witchdoctor, was creating the child soldiers after murdering the parents and kidnapping kids. Eric was taken by him, but he said that he was only used to carry items through the bush.

Now Joseph Kony was a rebel for 22 years that could not be removed by the Ugandan army. His witchcraft was too powerful. I remember there was a video called Kony 2012 that was made by a man that was not a Christian. It got a lot of coverage by the world press. The maker lasted two weeks before he went insane and started running up and down the street masturbating and jumping on cars. This was obviously a curse that came at him. And it hit him hard.

Eric said he had seen him create storms to come against the army and flood them out and he also said that he could command bees to attack the soldiers as well. Now I didn't doubt, but I wanted more proof. And it came. A witchdoctor called Jimmy came to the crusade to test our power, but could feel the Spirit of the Lord. He came up to me and asked how he could get saved. He could speak English a bit more than most, and an interpreter was needed only a little but also for me because my old farming Aussie slang was hard for them to interpret. Even Poss was doing this for me at times.

So I got Jimmy to repent and forgive and renounce all witchcraft and something happened. He said he felt a wind blow through him and clean him out. So he was born again, and also filled with joy. Jimmy wrote to me when I was home again a little. I did like Jimmy.

Here are a couple of emails that he sent. And I put these up for evidence that I'm not a raving lunatic, as some may be thinking. And if not now, then hopefully this will help hold back those thoughts later on, when things get really wound up. There are so many emails I kept over years of what was going on in Africa.

And maybe those stories may be told one day also.

> ----- *Original Message* -----
> *From: Eric Geoffrey Okello*
> *To: Peter McMaster*
> *Sent: Thursday, January 10, 2013 7:30 PM*
> *Subject: Even bees hears the word of God!*
>
> *Hey, daddy we had a good time yesterday at James home; i went to his home for prayers and found out that he had bees that has refused to leave his home! He tried many ways after coming to salvation but could not leave his house. Immediately I entered I saw bees flying all*

over and i asked him! He said the bees have been in his house for the last 8 years and they normally get honey out of it yearly. They were part of the things keeping his home before he confesses the Lord and something things he used to wear them. I just entered into his house and i spoke few words by the Help of the Holy Spirit, i said every connection, alter of the devil or of the Evil spirit in the house must leave in Jesus mighty name. We entered into warfare only five of us. And bees began making noise; i do not know what has happened with the bees. In about 40 minutes later we discovered that the bees were few numbers and after some time they all left James house. The man is happy and he may write to you within the week

----- Original Message -----
From: Odongo James Jimmy
To: Peter McMaster
Sent: Thursday, January 17, 2013 8:54 PM
Subject: Good Morning Pastor

Good Morning Pastor Pete, hope you are fine. When are you coming to Uganda? we are missing the kind of church you started with eric in Otwal. Eric came to my home and i have joy, peace and i have testimonies!! Eric is called by god, he prayed for my family and bees left my house up to to-date, i brought only one bee in tin few years back for protection and something that would update me when i was still in the bush i was a Soldier!! I was deep in witchcraft and i have done many things. Eric entered into my house and he refused to speak nor to sit, but he just began praying and we too joined him. minutes later eric reminded me of all i have done, i don't know how he got to know them but he spoke everything about me after wards he called me and asked me to repent. i did everything he told me and bees left my house, i burnt these bees, they became many from one, thousand of bees from the one i brought from the bush, i do not know how the number increased since i brought only one in my house and locked my house, went back for work.

Sometimes the emails were not that easy to follow but sometimes they were straight forward. No doubt prayer had rid the bees from Jimmy's house. There were other things Jimmy had confessed earlier to me and here is one more of them. This was the first email contact I had with him.

CHAPTER NINETEEN: KONY COUNTRY

----- Original Message -----
From: Odongo James Jimmy
To: Peter McMaster
Sent: Saturday, 10 November 2012 5:44 PM
Subject: Pastor pray for me

Good Morning Pastor Peter how is Kampala? I came to Lira town to buy some stocks for my small business I am been willing and planning to write to you but we have no internet in our home village and we have no power connection. I want to appreciate you for your effort to come for crusade in Otwal Rail way station we were blessed I use to drink and spent a lot of my income drinking and on women, I met you personally and you prayed for me, and I removed the chain that I was given when I was still in the army for protection if you can remember me! I had peace for about three weeks I could sleep well after throwing my chain and some stuffs at my home I dumped them in toilet.

Few days ago things changed Pastor, I dream my wife has miscarriage she was pregnant four months; after two days the baby came out. In the same night I dream when my chain came back in my house and the man ordered me to put on my chain or he will kill me but I refused and said Jesus and he disappeared. I used to have beautiful women in the dream especially in the night and when Pastor Eric was preaching he called people with such problems and I went up. The thing disappeared, I used to sleep with these ladies daily and I only used to meet my wife day time in the night I told her I need to rest and we used to sleep in two different beds in one room. I was free and delivered, but now thing have changed these ladies has started coming again! When I was a soldier we used to sleep with some ladies especially when you feel you need a woman, we were given egg and we light candle in the middle of the night to come a woman. And we could sleep with any woman as long as you know the name.

I was sent away from my former church, because I made a mistake and told them I am born again and god has delivered me. What can I do, can you come back again to otwal; I spoke to past Eric six time to come and pray for us even before my wife got miscarriage but he only promise me he will be coming but now things are hard on me. Yesterday I called him I got his phone number from the poster he said he is coming on Monday. Help me if possible come with him, we stay at home full time.

I will be grateful if you consider me and put me in your program, I want you to pray for my home, please come before these things kill me,

I am suffering too much. I went last week to a orthodox church in bar anyalo but the priest said I have got demons from the crusade and yet I was free for about three weeks. They prayed for me but I don't see any change I had the same problem last night. your testimony its too good for me and i have done many things but i feel god will set me free again; i was free for three weeks but now in bondage again

Yours

Odongo James Jimmy.

The solution was as easy as this. I sent Jimmy a warfare prayer and he prayed it and the things left that were tormenting him. The desperate get delivered. Jimmy was willing to lay down his past and follow the Lord as closely as he could and He was obedient. And in the name of Jesus Christ, Jimmy won a victory.

Religious people have no understanding of these things and have done massive damage to true Christianity. And in Africa, this religious stuff is everywhere.

> Mat 23:4-6 For they bind heavy burdens and grievous to be borne, and lay *them* on men's shoulders; but they *themselves* will not move them with one of their fingers.
>
> But all their works they do for to be seen of men: they make broad their phylacteries, and enlarge the borders of their garments,
>
> And love the uppermost rooms at feasts, and the chief seats in the synagogues,

Jesus said this to the religious ones.

> Mat 23:27 Woe unto you, scribes and Pharisees, hypocrites! for ye are like unto whited sepulchres, which indeed appear beautiful outward, but are within full of dead *men's* bones, and of all uncleanness.

We were getting ready for the last night, the Grand Finale. Eric and I were to preach and neither had any idea what was going to happen. But it blew me away and everyone who was there too. It was the best thing I had ever been involved in. And I had played in six winning football Grand finals and I would swap everyone for another night like this.

But first I need to tell you about the training I had received to be ready for this. There was a man and his wife called William and Lucille Lau. And he came to Melbourne to teach, so I went over from Tassie. They had been missionaries in Borneo. He went there as a very young Christian after wanting more from God. Left everything and went to Borneo with his wife.

The natives were not interested in Christianity because the witchdoctors could give them what they wanted. So William fasted and prayed and the Lord showed him how to pray for people to be more effective. That was the same way that Jesus and his disciples prayed, with a command. With faith and the name of Jesus behind the activation of the power and authority that we all have when we are Born Again, the sickness and disease, and demonic entities have to flee.

William also taught to persist. If nothing happens, keep commanding. The dam will eventually burst and the brick wall will, with enough hits from the hammer, collapse. And just as the Word of God was showing, the miracles would happen to the followers of the Lord Jesus Christ.

> Mat 10:7-8 And as ye go, preach, saying, The kingdom of heaven is at hand.
>
> Heal the sick, cleanse the lepers, raise the dead, cast out devils: freely ye have received, freely give.

I still wasn't too confident so I needed some more training and understanding. I didn't want to go straight into this work without being prepared. Part was that I didn't want to damage those who were tormented, any more than they were damaged already, and part of it was that deliverance was dealing with demons. I still wasn't real sure about how best to confront them and deal with them. So I devoured everything I could, to be ready to rumble.

I heard about a man called Win Worley. He was a Deliverance worker who did group Exorcisms or Mass Deliverance as he called it. He would run the people through repentance and forgiveness prayers and get them to renounce all sorts of witchcrafts and break all their curses and then he would let rip. He would call out demon names and functions and the battle was on. There would be screaming and cursing and rolling around on the floor, and all sorts of manifestations, large and small, noisy and not so noisy.

I learned a lot from a radio show called Omegaman radio with Shannon Davis. It was based solely on deliverance, and had the best deliverance ministers on, giving away all their testimonies, tactics and strategies for free, and doing deliverances over the phone and mass deliverances also. I listened to thousands of hours and got myself equipped for the fight.

I was so encouraged by this that I wanted to try this out one day, a mass Deliverance, but I needed somewhere and someone to experiment on. And this time had come.

> Mat 8:16 When the even was come, they brought unto him many that were possessed with devils: and he cast out the spirits with *his* word, and healed all that were sick:

CHAPTER TWENTY
THE CRUSADERS

I am really going to enjoy recalling this part of my life, and how much of a blessing and encouragement it was in my life. It was definitely the pinnacle of the first trip to Uganda and also the second. All of it was good though, but this stood out a long way apart from the rest. Like I just said before, I have played in six winning football grand finals, which were the high points of my life in the world. Although only country footy, they were great fun to be involved with and the men who played also.

There were footballers in my family and my uncle, Captain coached Geelong in a grand final. It was my most enjoyable past time. And I was good at it. I had represented country sides for Collingwood.

But the drugs and alcohol took effect and I only stayed in the country sides, playing up and getting a little money. Only enough for a couple of days on the grog was all I wanted. It was not too serious and I liked that.

Also the best fishing trips, and the best dirt bike rides, screaming through the bush, pushing it to the max, was nowhere near close to this. All the worldly stuff and pastimes had nothing on this. And I do pray that it will happen again, and again, and again. And while I'm still kicking then there is hope.

We were into the last night of the crusade at Otwal railway station. The largest crowd we had and most were so loving the music, blaring at top volume, with so much distortion that is was hard to handle in my ears. Coming from the world where everything is FM Stereo quality, neat and clean, and all the rough edges tucked away out of sight, to the torn apart villages of northern Uganda, filled with the sick and diseased, the downtrodden, poor and desperate.

Wikipedia says that 66,000 children became child soldiers, and 2 million were displaced internally from 1986-2009. Joseph Kony was doing things I don't want to mention here.

But the people didn't care how much of a racket came out of the speakers. With the kids and the adults moving to the music, it was interesting to see the men were dancing more than the women.

You could imagine the tribal meetings where they would dance for whatever reason they had. Like the Aboriginals here in Oz holding their corroborees, and the men get right into it, it seemed that the Ugandans all had different styles, and would even have dance offs. Or trying to out-do each other without saying as much.

The boys and young men who were in the house with us would be saying that they were the best dancers, and singers. And they loved it. The women would dance more in unison with each other, like the back-up singers in the music videos here. They loved it very much and it was a big part of their lives.

With the smoky, noisy generators cranked up to pump out the volume of the worn out speakers, everyone could join in. And they did. They even got me dancing up there looking like an idiot, but I didn't care. We were all laughing and dancing like little kids, something that would never be done here in Oz.

There were smiles all through the crowd, except a handful or two of most likely religious priests looking for the disobedient; who showed up at the crusade, when they were warned not to. We heard afterwards, that many were told not to come back to those churches, when the priests found out. But we also heard that they didn't care that they were banished, like in Jimmy's earlier email.

The resurrected Jesus that they had found was so much more filled with abundant life, than the cold dead Jesus of the religious, who was still hanging on the cross.

CHAPTER TWENTY: THE CRUSADERS

There were a few witchdoctors that came to test their stuff. They never looked happy either. But we were not there to worry about their games. God was winding things right up so they would have to scatter or fall, which some of them did. The first seven people who fell were the children of the local witchdoctor, who had just been buried.

Jimmy got saved earlier, so he just watched, amazed. As did everyone else and myself. I couldn't believe what was happening. And words will never suffice for the action of the night. It was absolutely amazing. So I better tell the story.

The crusade numbers were getting bigger and bigger over the three days we were there. The theme was Luke 4:18. Set the captives free. And with the posters put up in the prime places in the village, there were many in the area no doubt, who desired this.

The war had taken its toll. The witchcraft had taken its toll. The disease had taken its toll. The poverty and the hunger had taken its toll. People had come back to their land but were still carrying a lot of baggage. So it was time for God to do something for all of them. With God, when we initiate an action, there is always some reaction. Sometimes the thing that looks the hardest is actually the easiest.

There would have had to have been 600 to 700 in attendance at least and when you live in a town of only 80 people, that's a lot. More would always come after dark when the eyes of the unjust judges could not see them as easily, and the fear of being excommunicated was not the battle in the mind that it was in the daylight.

The choir had done their thing. Jumping around on and off for hours. Bit of preaching, and a bit of singing, all afternoon. Then it was fairly late afternoon. Eric invited me up to share my testimony, with an interpreter. Which you had to speak in short sentences to let them keep up.

Apparently some interpreters would do their own thing and add and subtract as they liked. Especially if not many knew the other language. It was an act of self-promotion. Draw the attention to yourself. Also they would take selfies with their phones with the crowd behind to use as advertising for other crusades that would need a big man, ready for the job. It was funny to watch. No different here really. Like I said before, any advantage to gain ground in life, was never missed in Africa.

They loved my testimony. I got a massive picture made of me before salvation and after and I would use that to show the contrast of before and after Jesus. And they could see it. It made them hungry. And when I said I got shot in the guts and survived, and that God had warned me twice before that it was going to happen, their ears were open. If you get shot in Uganda you are dead.

I actually had people say to me, "We want to know your God". This was so different to how things worked in Oz. If that happened here in Australia, most wouldn't know what to do. They would be looking for the front man who did all the religious stuff in the church. And without him about then, "Sorry mate, you'll have to wait, Pastors on holidays", which is very sad. The devil loves to shut open doors almost immediately after opening. But some doors are opened and are there waiting for us to come along and do the work.

> Rev 3:7 And to the angel of the church in Philadelphia write; These things saith he that is holy, he that is true, he that hath the key of David, he that openeth, and no man shutteth; and shutteth, and no man openeth;

Do not procrastinate in the Kingdom of God. This is very important. It can mean life or death. I have regrets here also.

CHAPTER TWENTY: THE CRUSADERS

The Africans believed in spirits, demons, devils, angels, curses, spells, and they understood so much more about it that we in the western world do. They knew if sickness came then it is an act of the devil and a witchcraft curse could destroy many people. So when I said that Jesus could bring righteousness, peace and joy then they wanted it.

> Rom 14:17 For the kingdom of God is not meat and drink; but righteousness, and peace, and joy, in the Holy Ghost.

He could bring healing, freedom and deliverance from the demons and ancestor spirits, and all sorts of entities that plague them at night. Many were tormented by witchcrafts. Instead of going to the doctors for money, that most never had, they could go to the witchdoctor and get the job done for the price of a chicken or a goat or a pig or whatever. Not that it would be a final answer, Satan never trades down. But can transfer spirits for a time, for his wicked purposes.

> Mar 3:26 And if Satan rise up against himself, and be divided, he cannot stand, but hath an end.

I did hear of a study once between the western world of Psych drugs and the hocus pocus of the African witchdoctors, and the witchdoctors got a larger percentage of better results than the highly paid so called professionals here. I will add, if you have emotional trouble or psychological trouble, try a deliverance minister, instead of the meds, because, once on the psych meds, deliverance won't work. You have turned yourself over to the world.

> Isa 30:1-2 Woe to the rebellious children, saith the LORD, that take counsel, but not of me; and that cover with a covering, but not of my spirit, that they may add sin to sin:

> That walk to go down into Egypt, and have not asked at my mouth; to strengthen themselves in the strength of Pharaoh, and to trust in the shadow of Egypt!

Anyway Eric had really blown up the night. This was the Grand Finale. He had a vision of people getting prayed for in the rain the night before and many came up front and it rained. "If people will stay through the rain then God will rain down His blessings", he said. And many were healed. Though it was only a small warm up to what was coming. He said many will be healed tonight; many will be set free tonight. Demons will flee and Jesus will bless all. This is your chance. The God of the Holy Bible wants to free you from the tormentors and break your chains and bondages.

It was getting dark. The Africans were hard to see in the dark unless they smiled. Or you could only see the whites of their eyes too. That's because there were only two 100 watt globes, maybe less, to cover the size of an Aussie rules oval. I am amazed at how Africans could walk anywhere in the dark. Although, they did use their mobile phones as torches a lot. I still haven't worked that out, how they all had phones. But making a call in Uganda was very cheap.

We tried to get video at night but that was impossible. But when the Holy Ghost and the unquenchable fire fell, we were all a bit busy, or a lot busy would be a better way to describe it, to go around filming anything. African people dressed so well, all full of colour and very excellent. It was always amazing to see how much effort they put in to dress, especially for church.

That was Gods day, and an extra effort was needed. I felt a bit lacking in that department. But it was hot near the equatorial line in middle of Africa, especially for a pair of Tasmanians in September. But despite all the effort they put in, a lot of them were going to end up filthy dirty. Hehehe, and I also.

I finished my testimony and led them in prayer. The kids at the front were keen and a lot of the adults also. I said just pray this. "Help me Jesus". A lot knew who Jesus was. He was the one who was being preached about for days, plus there were a lot of Catholics around, just not born again believers.

But Mary was the Catholic's god, a lot more than Jesus. And there were so many with rosary beads on as well. That's the advantage thing again, but it's actually a curse, being in agreement with idols and doctrines of demons. They believed the white men who were building

Poss has a preach.

the schools and the churches because they were doing this work. But the devil isn't stupid. He loves to steal men's souls.

> 2Co 11:12-15 But what I do, that I will do, that I may cut off occasion from them which desire occasion; that wherein they glory, they may be found even as we.
>
> For such *are* false apostles, deceitful workers, transforming themselves into the apostles of Christ.
>
> And no marvel; for Satan himself is transformed into an angel of light.
>
> Therefore *it is* no great thing if his ministers also be transformed as the ministers of righteousness; whose end shall be according to their works.

At a large Catholic Church in the larger town we were staying in there was a stall out the front with hundreds of rosary beads for sale, Idols and images of Jesus, Mary and the saints and posters of all sorts of religious stuff. I noticed a poster of the Ten Commandments. But I noticed that the second commandment was removed.

> Exo 20:4-5 Thou shalt not make unto thee any graven image, or any likeness *of any thing* that *is* in heaven above, or that *is* in the earth beneath, or that *is* in the water under the earth:
>
> Thou shalt not bow down thyself to them, nor serve them: for I the LORD thy God am a jealous God, visiting the iniquity of the fathers upon the children unto the third and fourth *generation* of them that hate me;

And the last one was split in two, so this below instead of being the tenth commandment, was now, ninth and tenth.

> Exo 20:17 Thou shalt not covet thy neighbour's house, thou shalt not covet thy neighbour's wife, nor his manservant, nor his maidservant, nor his ox, nor his ass, nor any thing that *is* thy neighbour's.

And this demonic trick was used regularly and the people were told that this word below in the scripture was statues, or idols. And you had to keep them.

So the con men priests were making a killing on the worthless junk that was held in high regard in people's homes here.

Lev 20:7-8 Sanctify yourselves therefore, and be ye holy: for I am the LORD your God.

And ye shall keep my statutes, and do them: I *am* the LORD which sanctify you.

But it's statutes, with an extra t, or laws and commandments. You may laugh, but some things in the West that are told to gullible believers are so stupidly followed also. Africa has a shortage of Bibles, but our laziness in the West to read ours is a big problem. Anyway back to the Crusade business.

Rosaries for sale and the Commandment Con

"Repeat after me, forgive me Jesus" I said. And the interpreter would repeat in the Luo language, and then the crowd would have their go.

"Deliver me Jesus"

"Wash me Jesus"

"Heal me Jesus"

"Set me free Jesus".

And they all repeated them with much joy. Then I just got them to say, "Repeat after me, I forgive all my enemies" which they did easily. It was the right time. Then I said, "Repeat after me, I renounce the devil and all his works," and they did. Then came the biggie. "I renounce all witchcrafts."

Whoa, very few would say that. In fact from the front, up on the side of a small embankment I could see some start to walk off. I didn't expect that reaction. With witchcraft playing a large part in even daily life, some were fearful, whether a fear of lack, or retaliation by the

CHAPTER TWENTY: THE CRUSADERS

spirits, or rebellion, or for whatever reason, they wouldn't repeat that prayer, and about almost 100 walked away. I started praying under my breath, "Help us God." I had no idea what to do. I said it like I meant it, and I did, "God can bless you more than witchcraft" and tried them again. Repeat, "I repent of all witchcrafts"

And it seemed to me like a lot said in their minds "Stuff it, let's try it" and a good half said it. Then I started breaking witchcraft curses and magic and generational curses and remitting sins and you name it. It was a mass deliverance with no direction, no knowledge of what result would come about, or the chaos that was coming.

With me not wanting to stop and wait for the interpreter, I told Eric to take over. Our words were just a jumbled mess. And again, the speakers weren't helping, LOL. There were around 20 or 30 came up the bank onto the flat piece about as big as a tennis court. I walked among them laying hands on them quickly and praying to break witchcraft curses, and generational curses, down to the tenth generation. I walked down the line quickly and back again.

As Eric and the interpreter were going full bore into whatever they were saying, through the distorted speakers, who knows what??? I can't compare this to anything here in the West. It was like nothing before ever that I had ever been involved with. It was the beginning stages of a mass deliverance. Which we were hoping for and we had watched a couple of mass deliverances by Win Worley, so we knew it was possible.

But it was nothing like the program in the churches here. Even the Pentecostal church always had a sense of order, music, communion, tithes, announcements, preaching, praying and more music. Then a cup of tea, talk about the weather and go home. You could set your clock by the structured set ups. And they all did things the same way. Like that was the rule book and that's how it works.

But this was nothing like the churchy happy clappy Sunday session. This was the most exciting thing………..err, I think I've already told you that.

The Bible is the rule book, and that's all we need. The Lord must have been in control, because I definitely wasn't.

The first one went down in the crowd of who know how many, manifesting, and rolling around in the dust. That went on for about a minute or so. But he went off like a rocket and looked like he was break dancing. Instantly people backed away as far as they could, like three or four meters away until the crowd stopped their retreat.

Then others who wanted to see would push forwards and those on the inside of the circle were being forced back towards the demon. Some had turned tail and ducked into the advancing crowd of interested onlookers, while others I think were worried but a few meters seemed safe enough for them.

I could see all this from the vantage point of the flat part on the embankment. It was a perfect place to view, about four or five foot above the crowd. I went down and picked him up and prayed for him. He was like a fully drunk man who could not keep his balance and his head thrashing about. So I rebuked the devil and he calmed down a little. I thought, "Thank God for that," as I had no plan of attack.

Then he pulled away and was screaming out, back in the dirt and rolling around. So I knelt on top of him and rebuked the demon until he stopped, which didn't take long, Thank God!

And Eric's screaming through the speakers, "God is here, repent, and be saved. Do not go to Hell. All devils leave now in Jesus name. Death and destruction leave and witchcrafts leave and sicknesses leave and………….."

And the interpreter was going a mile a minute as well with no gaps and no rests and all through the crackly distorted over rented speakers that should have been thrown on the tip years ago. They were big and loud though, that's all they wanted. I climbed back up the front and another went down, and another, and another, and the screaming started.

Apparently the first seven were the dead and buried witchdoctors' kids. The locals said that he died a week before and was buried with a lot of the family stuff. No doubt put the satanic blessing on his kids, who now couldn't stand under the power that God was doing, way out in the wilderness, of northern Uganda.

Then some more went down onto the ground. Some were standing screaming and others would fall straight over. By now, a lot of the 20 or 30 people involved in the choir were into it, casting out demons. Some of the more timid women like Poss were grabbing the babies off the mothers who were about to explode in wild manifestations.

When witchcraft demons are cast out, they really bung on an act. Or they did this night at Otwal railway station, way out in the whoop whoop, where they never even had electrical power, and only a goat track as a road. How much fun could a bloke have? Probably a good thing there was no trains coming through. They had ceased long ago.

We had no idea what was going on back there about 80 meters away in the dark where the track was and where the imaginary boundary was for those who would not step any closer. Let alone the whole village that could hear the warfare and deliverance prayers of the young Africans yelling into the microphones. I'm sure the devil got a kicking for miles around.

So the show was on for young and old. The choir, preachers and interpreters were wrestling and yelling and were rolling on the ground in the dirt, screaming at demons as they screamed back from the possessed and demonized. And with the dim lights flickering; and the dust flying; and the demons carrying on like they were terrified of going to Hell for Eternity, and maybe they were.

I had no idea what was being said by the majority of the Africans screaming out at the ones who were thrashing wildly about and what was being screamed back. It was like a scene out of the Exorcist, times about 50. I could hear demons that I was casting out speaking some English when most people there couldn't speak it. The main thing they were yelling was "NO, NO, NOOOO……." as they would leave with a scream or a shudder or deep coughing and throwing up. How much fun, you ask? Sorry, already said that. But heaps is my answer!!!

"GET OUT DEMON IN JESUS NAME". There was no time to stop and think. Just keep at em!!! Didn't matter who they were or how big they were. God was behind the Power and Authority that the born again believers were operating in. No time for stupid questions, or no need for words of knowledge to get to a root cause or some knowledge needed to dislodge the enemy.

It was as easy as, "LEAVE NOW IN JESUS CHRISTS NAME AND NEVER RETURN". And it was surprising how quickly some were subdued and others just went down and some just screamed and it was over. I often wondered what was happening in the spirit realm and how many Angels were fighting with us. Like this with Elisha.

> 2Ki 6:14-17 Therefore sent he thither horses, and chariots, and a great host: and they came by night, and compassed the city about.
>
> And when the servant of the man of God was risen early, and gone forth, behold, an host compassed the city both

> with horses and chariots. And his servant said unto him, Alas, my master! how shall we do?
>
> And he answered, Fear not: for they that *be* with us *are* more than they that *be* with them.
>
> And Elisha prayed, and said, LORD, I pray thee, open his eyes, that he may see. And the LORD opened the eyes of the young man; and he saw: and, behold, the mountain *was* full of horses and chariots of fire round about Elisha.

And the Lord was definitely there, directing his troops.

> Mat 18:20 For where two or three are gathered together in my name, there am I in the midst of them.

God was revealing the truth of his Word, and it was amazing Sometimes it seems you can struggle for hours on one person just to get a few demons out, but here it was a free for all. A massive war in the Heavenlies, and the devil was coppin one hell of a flogging, if I can say that? Too late, just did. It was made easier to understand the place in the Bible where the severely possessed man was set free and the demons went into the pigs, a couple of thousand of them.

> Mat 8:31-32 So the devils besought him, saying, If thou cast us out, suffer us to go away into the herd of swine.
>
> And he said unto them, Go. And when they were come out, they went into the herd of swine: and, behold, the whole herd of swine ran violently down a steep place into the sea, and perished in the waters.

With a Word they were banished and with a few words, even the apprentices were casting them out. And it was giving much Joy. Reader, the Bible is true.

> Act 8:7-8 For unclean spirits, crying with loud voice, came out of many that were possessed *with them*: and many taken with palsies, and that were lame, were healed.
>
> And there was great joy in that city.
>
> Luk 10:17 And the seventy returned again with joy, saying, Lord, even the devils are subject unto us through thy name.

CHAPTER TWENTY: THE CRUSADERS

We were novices doing the good work that the Lord had ordained for this time, and they were coming out so easily. I wish it was always the same. I think the witchcraft demons were ordered to explode first or just couldn't stand the Holy Ghost Fire, which was there. I'm sure for this small instant in time, we were connected to the throne room of God Himself and He was watching everything that was occurring. And I know He would be smiling and at times laughing, because I sure was.

I was walking around helping others who seemed a bit overwhelmed, and some of the helpers that seemed a bit cautious, but now the seriousness of it was calming down. Many were not violent now, just falling down and screaming. So they got a bit of a spiritual kick into a demon or two as they felt to do safely. But the workers did not flee. Even those who had never been in a deliverance before. It would be a lot difference in the West here, I am positive of that. The doors wouldn't be wide enough for the mass exodus.

I have no idea how much time went past. It was dark at about 6:30 and we didn't got back to the place we were staying until 11:30 after the one and a half hour return trip, first on the goat track, then the gravel, then the main road. So the fun must have lasted almost three hours.

The sweat, the dirt, and the whites of the Africans wide open eyes during the screams and the yelling, and the glint of the pearly whites, whether in smiles, screams or a demonic growl is hard to describe, all under the dull glow of the incandescent globes. Not to mention the screaming over the microphones.

Everybody on the choir wanted a go, to speak in a mic at a Crusade was high up on every believers bucket list, and I have no idea of what they were saying, but it all added to the atmosphere that was the most super charged environment I have ever been in. Did I say that before? LOL.

I am now reliving it and asking God to let me see that again. This was the definitely part of the fun He told me to have. This was where a lot of the money we had, went to. And instead of going to watch the mountain Gorillas in the mist or whatever tourism was going that cost an absolute fortune, we decided to do this instead.

I think God was happy with our decision, because He sent us back seven months later. And we still had coin left over from the first trip to pay our way and return with a little left over.

CHAPTER TWENTY ONE
KAMPALA, THE RETURN

We arrived back in Kampala, the six hours south on the roughest bitumen roads I have ever seen. This was the Main Hwy through the middle of Uganda with potholes as round and large as a car and deeper than your ankles and strewn everywhere. You could see the larger buses and trucks that had hit them, crabbing their way along the road with obvious damage to the chassis underneath. But with a few extra dollars the drivers take for the journey, the police would look the other way. We saw money exchange hands many times.

There were deep edges that would roll vehicles I'm sure. And the evidence was in the crashed cars and trucks on the sides of the main roads. There were smashes from head on collisions and lots of carnage. But no wonder; with the adults and kids sitting on the deep edges to have a rest, with no regard for their own safety, and goats and chooks and motorbikes and cars and people. And even baboons in one place that would run up and you could feed them bananas from your hand. No wonder there was 3000 deaths a year on Ugandan roads.

Then we arrived back in the Kampala suburbs. Not like suburbs here though, I'll tell you that. Where we stayed was 200 meters from where there was what I would call a slum. Not the worst in Kampala, but far from clean and healthy, where kids would play in the drains, full of crap and everything else. And it was right at the bottom of a big hill where the King of Uganda lived in his massive mansion on the top, a huge contrast.

There was a church about two doors down from us that was a tin shed about 20 meters long and 15 wide. The man's name was Kafeero. They would have services often but not many went. He didn't like us for a start because we were handing out hundreds of tracts and things, not far from his church. But after a couple of weeks we talked to him and he asked me to preach. So I went and preached on repentance and forgiveness and forsaking witchcrafts and idols. Things that Africans

Kampala city kids.

desperately need to hear. Instead of the prosperity junk that has invaded the planet, and has been making the believers poorer and more frustrated. Jesus is not Santa Claus. Or the one I know isn't.

I slipped a 50,000 shilling note in the money bag on its way past, to encourage Kafeero. It was about 20 bucks in Oz. There weren't many attending and I thought I'd bless him a bit. And I got an invite back next Sunday, which to me the reason was obvious. I thought, he didn't like us but now he loves us. 20 bucks in the bag every week and I'd have been on that pulpit forever. I think it works a bit like that here too sometimes.

I preached on the USA Dollar bill witchcraft symbols and said that there is a bigger witchcraft in the world than the localized stuff in Africa. And it's advertised on the money. And Kafeero was amazed. Like most who have never seen it there. But most here don't care. Just want, want, want, gimme, gimme, gimme, me, me, me. But in the land where witchcraft is the national religion, their ears were wide open.

Then Kafeero organized a meeting for me to preach this at the Pastors gathering they had every Wednesday Arvo. Our friend Peter who was a young man being discipled by Eric, who left West Africa when he was 17, after hearing a voice from God to go, and had fasted 40 days already at 19 years old was not allowed to attend. He was told to go home by Kafeero. A bit like this parable it was.

> Luk 18:10-14 Two men went up into the temple to pray; the one a Pharisee, and the other a publican.
>
> The Pharisee stood and prayed thus with himself, God, I thank thee, that I am not as other men are, extortioners, unjust, adulterers, or even as this publican.

> I fast twice in the week, I give tithes of all that I possess.
>
> And the publican, standing afar off, would not lift up so much as *his* eyes unto heaven, but smote upon his breast, saying, God be merciful to me a sinner.
>
> I tell you, this man went down to his house justified *rather* than the other: for every one that exalteth himself shall be abased; and he that humbleth himself shall be exalted.

I saw his sadness and was about to say "If Peters not allowed then I don't want to go either". But I felt I had to. It must have been important. And it was.

We arrived and Eric had already instructed us do not take anything from them. No food and no drink. And make no agreements with them. Not that Kafeero was the enemy. But Eric knew who was who in town, and he knew that in the group Kafeero was involved with, some were not good men. Eric had been bashed and robbed and houses we were helping him with to rent were bought out from underneath him or he was kicked out. He had been locked up several times by false accusations. And now we were going into the midst of the unknown for me. But God had said "Have fun" and this was just another adventure.

I have often thought afterwards what a difference it would have made to not have that assurance of His safety and protection, and how fear would have hindered the work that He had for us. Although what most of the people who knew us thought was stupid, as in just going to Africa by ourselves, just to see what would happen, we did take a bit of responsibility in our actions. But with a lot less than we would have needed without Gods' blessing, I am sure.

So we were welcomed and the leader of the group said we will pray for half an hour before we start. And the whole time was basically, "God, give us money. Make us rich God so we can spread your word. So people can see we are men of God. We need this and we need that". It was unbelievable. Without money they seemed to think they were nothing. And that's probably because they were. There was no power in their prayers. Eric used to say, "Look at Moses, he only had a stick!!!

These men were so greedy and self-centred; it was hard to respect any of them. If I knew then what I know now, and was not as intimidated as I was in front of those men who thought they were something, I would have just said, "Go home you wicked and greedy men and

CHAPTER TWENTY ONE: KAMPALA, THE RETURN

leave the business of God to others more righteous than you". But I stayed, and was really going to give them a message they wouldn't forget.

I spoke about the dollar bill again and made it clear that the most powerful of all witchcraft in the world revolved around the money. And greed and lust and mind control, and deceptions and delusions.

> 1Ti 6:9-10 But they that will be rich fall into temptation and a snare, and *into* many foolish and hurtful lusts, which drown men in destruction and perdition.
>
> For the love of money is the root of all evil: which while some coveted after, they have erred from the faith, and pierced themselves through with many sorrows.

This scripture became so clear to me after this. These men had no shame in their begging from God, and using the hard earned money from their congregation to make themselves fat. They were never going to receive anything from God. Almost half of the 20 or so men that were there at this high flyers greedy man meeting were giving me the evil eye. They were not happy at all with the message I gave. But others looked amazed and even ashamed, and they that had ears to hear heard.

I finished up and some left straight away and a couple of them came and said "Thanks, you opened our eyes to our error. The exact thing we were praying for could have brought destruction to us". And they were genuinely repentant, which made me encouraged. As we left Eric told us that some of the men there had been the ones that had given him trouble. They were involved with Samuel Kakande, the big man minister in all Uganda. A warlock who uses witchcraft and mind control to con the people to give him much respect and adoration, all the while leading people to use daily water sprays and to drink highly demonized "Anointed Water" to keep evil away and to bring salvation into people's lives.

Eric had told us that these men are high level satanists who were even running churches now. And sending out many to infiltrate the smaller ones and curse the believers. We already knew that they go underwater to meeting places to plan church attacks and to destroy Christianity. Not straight out and bringing in obvious deception, but to lead into idolatry and delusion to lead people from the Truth and draw them toward themselves.

It was amazing how many true African Christians know about this and believe it. And because of what I had experienced already and the little I knew, I believed it too. We already knew how true it was. I will dedicate a chapter to that; with email evidence of those involved confessing to me. Amazing how it fell into my lap. God wanted me to expose it and I was ready for the next fight.

After two months we left Uganda. It was enough. No hot water and no steak sandwiches, and the beans and rice and constant heat and dust were wearing thin. Not that we had a bad time, we loved it, and the people, but it was time to go.

When we arrived back in Pyengana it was such a change. The Africans can pray all night and they really are on fire, and that fire had moved into us. We were excited about it too and knew it. But we saw the attitude of the people in Africa who have nothing and are joyful, to the attitude of some here in Oz who have so much more than they need and are miserable and complaining constantly. It was depressing.

It looked very pathetic to us now we had seen the contrast in cultures. But Australia was built on Christian principles and values and we are definitely blessed. But that is fading fast. Too fast.

> Ecc 5:10 He that loveth silver shall not be satisfied with silver; nor he that loveth abundance with increase: this is also vanity.

CHAPTER TWENTY TWO
AFRICA, THE RETURN

The day before we left Uganda we looked for some gifts we could give to our friends and family. There were lots of carved animals out of extremely hard wood that were black as the Ace of Spades and they grabbed my attention. And a Rhino looked a good gift for my Father. It was about 18 inches long by 10 inches high, just a good size. I bartered with the seller as you do in Africa and got it for 50 bucks. Which I thought was a fair price.

Now I figured I had been careful. There were obvious demonic images and masks and weapons and all sorts of ugly junk that I thought, "If there's going to be a demon on anything, it would be on that stuff". I thought I knew enough about things like this, after the experience I already had, to not fall into a snare of bringing home a cursed object. The man who sold it said "I will go and wrap it up for you." "OK mate" I said. And he was gone for about half an hour.

As we had finished all the looking around and were ready to go we had to wait. And it was a long half hour which never made me suspicious then, because that was an Africans 5 minutes. Little did I know then, but now with hindsight, I do believe that the man did more than just wrap it.

I sent it off to my father when I returned home. And the day after he got it I rang him and he said it arrived and he put it on top of the fridge for all to see. He also told me that he had a really bad pain in the ear, or in his jaw. A couple of days later he said the pain was worse and more constant. And I also had a little pain in my ear, or jaw or somewhere up there, but didn't add things up.

After about six days my father said that his pain was unbearable and he had gone to the doctors and they diagnosed him with a disease called, Trigeminal neuralgia, or the basic name was, "The Suicide disease". He said that his brother had it and he had strong medication to stop it so he resigned to the fact that it was a generational thing and he would have it forever. He was a pessimist mostly. The doctors put him on some sort of epilepsy medication. My ear was getting worse as well and more constant and the devils saying "You got it too, how are you going to live with this pain constantly".

And I'd heard similar things a few times already. So I knew exactly what it was and said to my father, "It's the Rhino I brought back from Africa. The things cursed. Destroy it". And he just thought I was crazy and said much the same.

But my brother who lived nearby was a believer and I told him and he could see the connection clearly. I said to him over the phone "Destroy that thing, it's cursed, cut it up and burn it and do what you can. Forget what the old man will say, just get it out of the house".

So he took to it with the chainsaw and said "It wouldn't cut". I know the wood was so dense and my brother was not good at sharpening the saw, so I didn't relate anything spooky to it, although that may have been there too. Then he chucked it in a fire and burnt it.

And two days later my father's ear was back to normal and the sharp stabbing pains that I had in mine went away to. And this was another good lesson learned without too much damage associated with it.

So please take note. This world is not a game and there are all sorts of dangers and snares out there that many of the unwary fall into. Even the church is unwise in this area, and some will argue the point blindly. But when it says this in the Bible, to not bring cursed items into our house it means it. And my uncle with the problem has a house full of elephants from all over the place. I still wonder if……??? But many do not have eyes to see.

We did go back to Africa a second time around seven months later for seven weeks, and built a building for the people in Otwal who were saved in the crusade. And there were many. There were lots of healing and deliverance after the last crusade that the Lord had done for the people there, and they wanted to know more about the God who had set them free.

With enough money for fares and other savings, we went on a different adventure, staying in another rented house in the North Ugandan town of Lira. We did buy a 100 cc Indian made Yamaha motor cycle to get around on which was fun. It wasn't much stronger than a pushbike, although it was better than walking. But with the road rules more like a pecking order, you had to keep both eyes open. Once a mad cow charged out of the bush at us, and if I hadn't had some skill from riding dirt bikes for a good part of my life, I would never had evaded it and we'd have come a real good gutsa. And Eric and I did both agree that the cow had demons. You could see them in its eyes, poor cow.

Also same trip back from the village a massive lizard goanna thing ran right in front of us with us just running over its tail. And with Eric just smiling on the back of this tiny motorbike, loaded with me at 115 kgs, him at about 65, and a bag of mangoes and 2 or 3 chooks hanging off the handlebars, it was a fun adventure again.

YAMAHAHA

We built the church building after many people were banished from their religious meetings, and they wanted a place to meet instead of under the big tree in the middle of Otwal village. Although OK from the sun it wasn't really sufficient in the heavy rains and the massive thunderstorms that came in Uganda.

So we bought the land and put up a basic post and beam structure to keep the rain off. It was good size though. And they were very happy and joyous at the opening. Lots of singing and dancing at the opening crusade and I'm sure the same dodgy sound system was used that had been around for yonks.

There were many came and enjoyed the celebration, but many stood on the boundary of the block, not wanting to step foot on the property. Just like the other crusade. Whether by fear of the strange witchcraft or because of their own demons warning them off, or what they may have thought to be their ancestral spirit voices in their heads telling them not to. Or possibly the witchcraft mind control that was operation though the Catholic churches of fear of banishment and Hell for Eternity if they set one toe on that property of the wicked African and his white Man and Woman friends and their unreligious and untraditional meetings.

Early in the day and people lined up on road and would not come on the property.

But most didn't care. Even the drunks were dancing around and the town drunk was there too. Eric had befriended him and told us a bit about him.

A man was caught thieving in the village. It was law that if you got caught stealing food from the garden of another, then people were allowed to kill you. I don't know what he stole, I didn't ask. The story got to the end quickly and those details were not even thought about then. So the elders in Otwal charged this man and the punishment was getting his ears cut off. Which is a bit better and lighter a judgement than death, that's for sure. But nobody wanted to do the job. The pay

CHAPTER TWENTY TWO: AFRICA, THE RETURN

was $20. So this fella, drunk, got the knife and cut off the man's ears, and went back to drinking. I thought that it would take a special person to do that job and here he was. Happy as Larry, thank God!

The speakers were cranked to full bore, and this time there were 3 wireless microphones. Three young African men praying on them warfare and whatever else they thought of. And they were all calling for "HOLY GHOST FIRE, HOLY GHOST FIRE".

And believe it or not, one of the speakers caught fire. And there was nobody near it. The ones who were running the large system, (which could be heard for miles I'm sure), ran over and poured water on it.

Of course one would think a short or something, and I thought, "Oh no, they've cranked it up that loud that it's all going to burst into

Holy Ghost Fire

flames and be destroyed. It was the front of the speaker that burst into flames, the thin cover over the big woofer that was way past its use by date.

There were whispers of "Witchcraft, Witchcraft" by the Africans from Otwal, who never had power on at the village, so I thought, they don't understand electricity and the dangers, which was obvious by the unbelievable power supplies about that I did see in Uganda. It was like they were strung up by school kids in a hurry to get somewhere else. But maybe they knew more than I gave them credit for at the time.

The speaker was still working and even after they doused the flames with water. Which made the owners and controllers of the system scratch their heads. They'd never seen anything like it.

So we just decided that it was Holy Ghost fire that lit up the speaker. It was the obvious choice, because the atmosphere was definitely being super charged again in a good way, this time full of joy and hope and love and freedom. And the young African men were calling for the fire of God to fall.

The Spirit of the Lord did come and people were moved to confess. There was a bigger man there who had been born again but backslid and he got up and testified of his life. He said he went to the Congo (which was the country next to Uganda) to a witchdoctor, and he did a ritual to get rich. And he did get extremely rich. But he said in about six months intervals he would get extremely poor. And this went on for a couple of years. And with a public repentance in front of the few hundred at the crusade, and by his remorse, we could understand the price that someone innocent had paid for that satanic blessing.

So into the night we went, and I'm sure Eric had used the same two dim flickering lightbulbs used those months ago at the train station Crusade, for illumination again. But this was different to that meeting. It was so joyful. We did try another mini deliverance session but nothing much happened. It obviously was a different season here and now a time for celebration.

I will recount this story before this chapter ends, and it will get you wiser to the working of the enemy that is in full swing in deep dark Africa. It totally blew me away. But for Africans, it just seemed to be almost normal. Which made the situation even more extreme in my mind. If this can happen and be seen as not too out of the ordinary, what are the depths of wickedness on the planet, that are operating, that we are just ignoring? That is affecting our everyday lives. Although I knew that it was a war, I gained a little more respect for the devil, and his workers, and their power, at this time. And I'll tell you something, I was going to need it badly in the near future!!! God had already planned another battle for me to enter, and I had to be wised up.

A woman came to a Sunday meeting we had a week after the opening. She wore a dress that just covered her knees and a T-shirt. She wanted some prayer. I did notice that she had scars on her forehead and was covered in little scars on her arms and legs, and some of them were healing still and some were more recent.

Eric had gone walked down the town a bit on a mission for something so an interpreter helped us. Their English wasn't too bad, but I thought

CHAPTER TWENTY TWO: AFRICA, THE RETURN

when they were explaining this problem that it wasn't too good. They said the woman was blamed for a cow dying, and a witchdoctor cursed her, and now pins and needles and razorblades were coming out of her body, pointing to all the cuts and slices on her body. Also she said that the woman had epilepsy and had fallen on her face a lot, and pointed to the big scars on her forehead. Now I could understand that.

I thought the interpreter must mean that she's a cutter and doing self-mutilation on herself. But she checked and both of them shook their heads and she repeated, "pins and needles and razorblades are coming out of her body". No different than if the woman had an ingrown toenail or something.

What I was hearing and the attitude of the interpreter, and the woman who was suffering, didn't show any panic, or any strange exclamations of high weirdness, or anything even close to it. While I was still trying to understand what was happening, Eric came back. So I said, "What's happening here Eric"? So he questioned the woman and I thought "Wow, the interpreter was telling the truth", relaying the story.

With no show of surprise or 100 questions to get a straight answer, really showed me the extent of the darkness that these people were living under and used to in their part of the world.

So Eric told me. There was a cow that died in the village mysteriously. And a powerful witchdoctor was called in. He cut a chicken in two, longways, and filled it with pins and needles and razorblades. And said, whoever killed the cow, pins and needles and razorblades would come out from that person". All said as matter of fact, and with no great surprise, like one would think anybody would or should have.

While I'm standing there looking at Eric, looking at the interpreter and the woman who was afflicted, and thinking, "Have I just entered the twilight zone here or what"??? While they just were retelling the story like a nice little family BBQ outing story about the kids or the pets or whatever, I'm thinking. "Fair dinkum, have we all just gone insane here or what's the story."

So I asked her straight out, "Do you have pins, needles and razorblades coming out of you. Not cutting yourself with them, but actually coming out of your skin"? And Eric relayed the message, with a nod from the woman and pointing to her many cuts and fresh marks.

I said" How long ago did the last one come out"? And she said through the interpreter, "Just this morning" and pointed to a fresh bloody mark low on her leg.

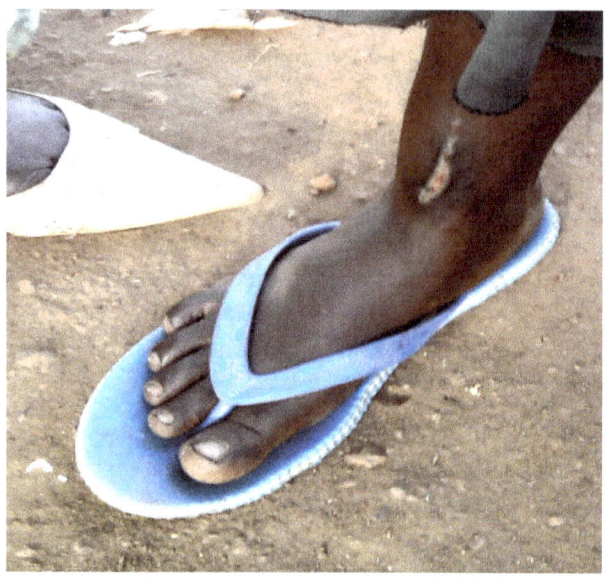
A week after the cut healed from the witchdoctors curse.

So we broke the curses and prayed healing and Life into her and she wandered off happy. Next Sunday came and the woman was back. Although the wounds that were open had healed. But she was complaining that she had a pin coming out of her inner thigh, high up.

I really wanted to see this happen but because of the place she was pointing to, I didn't want to look. Some watching might have thought I was a pervert or something. So I just had to believe her. Then Eric said bluntly, in Luo, but told me afterwards "We prayed for you on Sunday, did they stop coming out" and she nodded. Then he said "How long were you better for"? And she replied "Until Friday". Then without asking any more questions he put it to her "You went to a witchdoctor didn't you". And she hung her head and just nodded and then Eric rebuked her a little and told her to have faith. Then we prayed again and that was the last time I saw her. This was the most full on witchcraft thing that I had ever witnessed.

I was a bit interested in the devices of the devil, but I wasn't hunting them down constantly to get a buzz by the horrors of it all. I did know that the devil never sleeps but I wasn't really doing deliverance constantly to come across this stuff. I did pray to God to show me if this was all real or an imagined attack by the woman. But the other Africans seemed to believe without any trouble whatsoever.

CHAPTER TWENTY TWO: AFRICA, THE RETURN

And God showed me the truth. I came across a small booklet about one month later called *Blumhardts' Battle*, a testimony written by a German Lutheran in the late 1800s that did deliverance on a really bad case. It was his first ever deliverance too and knew little about it. The woman was so severely possessed that there were rusty nails and coins and pins and stuff coming out of her head and eyes and tongue and lots of other stuff going on. He battled for 2 years straight, a massive battle.

So God had ordained this little meeting for us to open our eyes to the reality of the enemy; to do things that the normal person would not and could not believe. And all this understanding was to be needed, a few years from now.

My eyes were being opened to the spiritual realms and wisdom and understanding and knowledge were increasing all the time. Not that I could see it. But with hindsight, these revelations that we received, helped to strengthen the foundation on which I was standing on by the Holy Bible and the Lord Jesus Christ. And the knowledge of this scripture was beginning to operate through me. Not just for me but for others as well.

> Rom 8:11 But if the Spirit of him that raised up Jesus from the dead dwell in you, he that raised up Christ from the dead shall also quicken your mortal bodies by his Spirit that dwelleth in you.

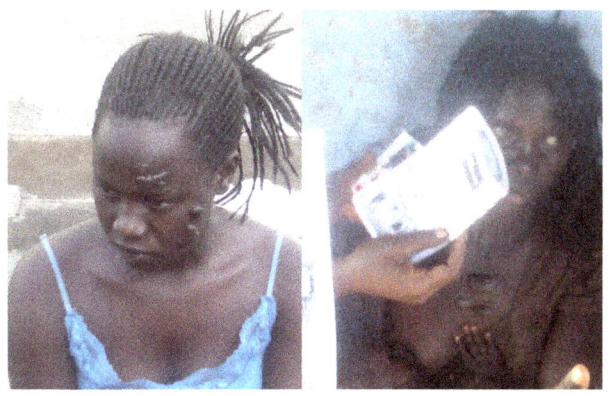

Witchdoctor marks. They cut to insert objects for whatever purposes. Many Ugandans had these scars.

CHAPTER TWENTY THREE
THE UNDERWATER MEN

The next two chapters are excerpts from my website of the exposure of the wicked imposters of Christianity in Africa, and the world. They have millions of followers. I have removed some of my replies to shorten the chapter. It is a lot to read. But if you are still with me then I'm sure you will find it very interesting. I know the spelling is bad in the emails but this is how they came to me.

All this is true and real. It all happened and continues to happen. If you seek, you will find. God will put you on the path you are to tread. I pray your eyes are opened here in Jesus name. The real Jesus Christ, King of Kings and Lord of Lords.

Eric at the church

One day a demon manifested in a woman in a church Eric was preaching at, but she was delivered and born again. She was a witch sent to infiltrate and curse and get to Eric, but the power of God overcame her. She was sent by the men who go underwater, the false Apostles who appear as angels of light, but were wolves in sheep's clothing. In her pocket were two pictures, she said this was the Jesus

CHAPTER TWENTY THREE: THE UNDERWATER MEN

they follow and who they serve. These are their gods. She spoke of men going underwater, (learning to astral project, soul travel, when I was involved in the Rosicrucians, I had no questions about this possibility.) Eric questioned her and she said she was sent by these men and she named certain lakes that the men were using for the satanic meetings and to get their power.

Eric went and prayed at the lakes, the local fishermen at these lakes knew of the place they went in. He anointed with oil and destroyed some of the power bases.

So they needed to try to curse our little friend again. This time they used an old acquaintance of Eric's, James Umzing. James wrote to me after trying to kill Eric and was surprised at my reply?!?! Obviously I was a little upset. Here are most of the emails that passed between us. When they talk $$$ they are talking US Dollar amounts. I place the emails in the order I received them from those involved. Mainly Eric, James and myself.

----- *Original Message* -----
From: *Pastor james Umzing*
To: *Peter McMaster*
Sent: *Friday, September 02, 2011 11:31 PM*
Subject: *Paster pete, praise the Lord*

Good morning Pastor Peter,

Greetings to you all in the name above every name in Jesus mighty name, Amen. we have not met before and this is my first time to write to you; however i saw your picture and your wife hang in Eric house in the wall frame; Eric has been a good friend to me and a young man with the love to serve God. of late i admit the devil trying to use me to destroy my own future and i wrote to Richard about it few days back. Richard said you are too close to Eric and he gave me your Email address; i have been sick with the entire family for about a week. after failing to get treatment and my children we prayed and i saw a vision of what the devil deceive me to do about this young man. Eric is a good friend to me and i know most of his plan and secrets but in 2009, devil entered my house in my ministry; had wanted to build a church and a certain man of God, whom am not going to give you his name for security gave me $200,000, he has connections with some pastors in USA and UK, we build a big church and God has blessed our ministry we have aver 5000 members in the church. in the middle on 2009, Eric is my closet friend; this man arrested Eric and put him in prison but after two days he won the case and was set free. since this man is also my friend; he called me and told me Eric is a young man but spoiling his name and the name of his church. He gave me $30,000 to poison Eric. i went to his home, but immediately i entered Eric's room my eyes closed and i could only see darkness. had wanted to take Eric out to get time and to sponsor our meal and drink and believing God to get the opportunity to put poision in his drink.

We had made plan to allow someone to call him and move out to pick his phone; i went with Eric but i had fear that i will kill my friend but i had the money and this man of God love me he connected me and got money to build my church. when his phone rang, Eric move out and received his call, but he came back and order for another drink and i paid i do not know what happened up to now.

Last year Eric went to Kenya and prayed for a certain lake, my boss was so annoyed with him and again he gave me money and promised to buy me BMW car if i poison Eric, or to talk to him and change his ministry and get for him open door for his church. he had money to

CHAPTER TWENTY THREE: THE UNDERWATER MEN

built for Eric church but Eric refused. since then i have been trying this young man but have failed.

recently i even tried to block his wedding but few days later i felt sick and i saw a vision taht reminded me i was doing the wrong things. He was using me, ask Eric to forgive me but do not tell him about this message i only want God to forgive me.

i even have fear for my own life now!

Thank

James Umzings boss. Samuel Kakande.

From: Peter McMaster
To: Pastor james Umzing
Sent: Friday, September 2, 2011 11:32 AM
Subject: Re: Paster pete, praise the Lord

It is God that needs to forgive you James, not Eric. It is God you have come against,

(I wrote a lot more here and gave him lots of scripture. Obviously I wasn't happy with him. And James spat the dummy).

From: Pastor james Umzing
To: Peter McMaster
Sent: Tuesday, September 06, 2011 11:41 PM
Subject: Re: Paster pete, praise the Lord

I think God forgive people! I do not need anything from you and not asking any assistant but you talking as if I asked for help. I am sorry but this is not how servants of God should write to children of God. I never wanted to reply this kind of words but my friends allowed me to write too. Eric has nothing and we are sure he won't go through with his wedding if he continues with such words to people; we want to help him but behaving like a boy. I will never get any closer to him anymore. I wanted to help him and gave him free motorcar which he can not afford to buy, I was ready to clear off his problem of $13,000 for his wedding budget but he refused my free money and the motorcar! I need nothing from Eric I have many friends, there are over 5000 people in my church how about Eric.

You can tell him I am not his friend now, there are millions people out there, what is he doing and why he can not stay in one church, what benefit dose he get from burning stuffs, he fear just water, something that has no breath, he has burnt decorations that was bought at 6,000,000= (about $2400) but only went and destroyed what he dose not know its cost. So many people are not happy with him and to be honest he made a mistake to go to Kenya, the water Eric went too and did bad thing there he will pay the prize! that water had power. Its a living water and we used to baptist new pastors and our ministers in there but now we have got another place for water baptism, again he went to k yoga lake, Eric must face what is ahead of him but not people, we had meetings ......

Thank

From: Peter McMaster
To: Pastor james Umzing
Sent: Tuesday, September 6, 2011 11:38 PM
Subject: Re: Paster pete, praise the Lord

You have sold out to Satan James and your end has already been determined.

(This bloke had tried to kill our little friend and I was very angry with his response in trying to justify his actions. I couldn't believe it really. This bloke actually thought he was a righteous man. So I was praying much about this group)

CHAPTER TWENTY THREE: THE UNDERWATER MEN

----- Original Message -----
From: Pastor james Umzing
To: Peter McMaster
Sent: Wednesday, September 28, 2011 6:14 PM
Subject: May God bless you all

Praise God, i am sorry, am sorry, all you wrote to me its happening in my life now. i am sorry and requesting you all to forgive me Peter, Eric, Richard forgive me. i have lost what i had because of my bad friends. They have supported me but now i have no peace i have money in my account but i cant even eat food now, i had no strengthen to write but today i have strength i cant even drive my own cars now, i have lost my properties, i am sick, am the first to run mad in my family because of money, i went under water, under ground looking for money but now it cant not help me. i have already disconnected myself from my bad friends and willing to start new friends.

My Friend Eric i am sorry for all i have done to you, its because had wanted money, i have build two big houses through the money i have got from my friends to finish you up but now i cant even sleep in my own house forgive me. i am ready and willing to take back all the money i have in my account and hand back the houses i have build using the money they gave me.

i want to become a new christian today, Eric come and pray for me and lead me afresh to salvation with all my family. My church was build by my friends, through their connection in USA and UK, i think they all do the same thing. i am ready to stop ministry in that church and hope to start praying in a new church let someone take over my church now.

I am sorry forgive me friends

From: Peter McMaster
To: Pastor james Umzing
Cc: Richard Emyedu Eric Okello
Sent: Wednesday, September 28, 2011 1:27 PM
Subject: Re: May God bless you all

You are playing a dangerous game James. You have read these scriptures before in my last email. They are THE WORD OF GOD!!!

Heb 10:26-31 For if we sin wilfully after that we have received the knowledge of the truth, there remaineth no more sacrifice for sins,

But a certain fearful looking for of judgement and fiery indignation, which shall devour the adversaries.

He that despised Moses' law died without mercy under two or three witnesses:

Of how much sorer punishment, suppose ye, shall he be thought worthy, who hath trodden under foot the Son of God, and hath counted the blood of the covenant, wherewith he was sanctified, an unholy thing, and hath done despite unto the Spirit of grace?

For we know him that hath said, Vengeance belongeth unto me, I will recompense, saith the Lord. And again, The Lord shall judge his people.

It is a fearful thing to fall into the hands of the living God.

Mat 3:8-10 Bring forth therefore fruits meet for repentance:

And think not to say within yourselves, We have Abraham to our father: for I say unto you, that God is able of these stones to raise up children unto Abraham.

And now also the axe is laid unto the root of the trees: therefore every tree which bringeth not forth good fruit is hewn down, and cast into the fire.

What are the names of the other ministries in Kenya, The two in Uganda, and Tanzania, India, UK and USA that you are connected to?

The Lord is the one striking you. No man is doing this. So you need to repent to Him alone. It is He who you need to ask forgiveness from. Ask God to tell you what you must do.

Pro 16:18 Pride goeth before destruction, and an haughty spirit before a fall.

Peter McMaster

From: Eric geoffrey Okello
To: Peter McMaster
Sent: Wednesday, September 28, 2011 7:50 PM
Subject: Re: May God bless you all

i have just got this message from you. however i have received a called from James wife that i should go and visit them at their home and i never responded to her, two days ago James spoke to me and said i should go and pray for his family and asked about my wedding; i had no answer for him and i only said all is well with me. this morning James wrote to me and told me about five different places they have been going under water with some people...... but all of them are in different countries, one in Kenya, two in Uganda, another in Tanzania and in India. He said i should forgive him over phone but i fear he is pretending so i couldn't meet him and i heard he is mental disturbed. If he has come back to his mind then its ok. He wanted to take me to all these places any way but instructed me not to tell his wife about. i think if God want me there i will go alone since i know the place by God's garce

(I did some research and had to ask this question.)

*From: Peter McMaster
To: Richard Emyedu Eric geoffrey Okello
Sent: Wednesday, September 28, 2011 1:43 PM
Subject: Re: May God bless you all*

Hello Eric and Richard.

*Is a man called T.B Joshua in Nigeria connected with Kakande??? Do you know or have you heard of him? He runs Synangogue, Church of all nations. Is he going underwater also?
Pete*

*From: Eric geoffrey Okello
To: Peter McMaster
Sent: Wednesday, September 28, 2011 11:35 PM
Subject: Re: May God bless you all*

Hey, daddy its very difficult to know exactly the people these people are connected to, however in Uganda here i know them and many false churches in Uganda here. we have a church just open close to our fellowship place. its now three months old but they don't allow water baptism and they said Jesus finished everything on the Cross no repentance, no giving offertory and thitn. in their church, they claim God dose no need money. This kind of churches are too many in Uganda here because their leader has money and using young men to have many branches. most struggling young ministers and some struggling ministers of God and people looking for miracles, healing, power run to them and they get the money to set up churches but controlled by those who gave them money. they have a main branches in Nigeria and most of their sponsor are from Nigeria, they are normally called Synangogue Church of all nations, they preach using even TV's all over the coner. some are now starting ministry with different names but connected to them. i am not sure about those outside but they normally comes to Synangogue, Church of all nations Ugandausing their plain. Etc

From: Peter McMaster
To: Eric geoffrey Okello
Sent: Wednesday, September 28, 2011 5:34 PM
Subject: Re: May God bless you all

They are the ones Eric. I was just attacked in a dream by three men and a very large demon dog. (It was so ugly) I would be careful. James has wrote, i will forward his email.
Pete

From: Pastor James Umzing
To: Peter McMaster
Sent: Thursday, September 29, 2011 1:01 AM
Subject: Re: May God bless you all

The churches I know are Synagogue Church of All Nations and one man in Nigeria sent me $30,000 for my ministry I called him prophet TB , all support I get from Kakande ministries. kakande is the one supporting my ministry I aaaaam not talking about the names but I will talk to Eric, I feared but I want to be a new Christian now. he gets support from his sponsors and he only support us to expand the church. i am talking about the blessing water we go in uganda not churches etc

From: Eric geoffrey Okello
To: Peter McMaster
Sent: Friday, September 30, 2011 10:40 PM
Subject: Re: thanks, daddy, greetings from my wife Jackie

Hey, daddy I am sure Pastor James is willing to come back to his God, today he went and prayed in our fellowship and he was actually very humble but monitoring him daddy! He has three smooth stones round and black. And a black Bible at his home, he called it deliverance Bible and was given to him by Prophet Tb I do not know him but Kakande connected him. Its seems his time has comes to return back to God now. He has actually spoken to me about his boss and what he dose but when I get transport I will disappeared and pure anointing oil in those places By God's grace and they will remember one day.

CHAPTER TWENTY THREE: THE UNDERWATER MEN

----- Original Message -----
From: Eric geoffrey Okello
To: Peter McMaster
Sent: Saturday, October 01, 2011 6:52 PM
Subject: James is back daddy

Praise Jesus Daddy,

God is faithful yesterday we went for a prayers overnight and we normal go for this prayer every last Friday of the month and every other Friday's night we prayer in our fellowship prayer room. This time Pastor James and his wife came and we sat in the same taxi that takes 32 of us for prayers overnight. Five of our ministers led prayers and I was went alone praying with James and Pastor James spoke to me a lot of things and the covenant he has entered into he drank blood but its not clear of what kind of blood. James has really entered into a covenant but I believed yesterday demons left him in Jesus mighty name. He told me about three different lakes where they get power and we prayed about it together.

We came back home at 6am this morning and I rested but that's when the Lord spoke to me, God instructed me to go to Lake Tanganyika on 7th and manyanra, I am sure I will find a way to go there daddy. The Lord has won back James he has stopped using his vehicles and now planning to rent a house and start staying when waiting from God, he wanted short cut but he is paying for it.

----- Original Message -----
From: Pastor james Umzing
To: Peter McMaster
Cc: ***@yahoo.com
Sent: Saturday, October 01, 2011 9:03 PM
Subject: Pray for my family and god to forgive me

Dear Pastor Pete, Brother Richard and Pastor Eric, i am sorry and will never allow Satan to sue me again. I didn't know that i was following a wrong man, he has blessed me and i was blind but now i am seeing. Yesterday my eyes open more in prayers over nite, i admitted i am sins and have done so many bad and evil things but i didn't know but what Pastor pete wrote to me opened my eyes and i knew i was in the wrong hand. i have prayed and repented i am willing to be apart of you people; Eric was my good friends but Satan deceived me. i am ready to tell you all my testimonies and what i went through. We were instructed not to repent but yesterday was my first time to repent again after four years. For over three years we drink water from church, we were served with water and distributed every weekly service and Sunday service the water we keep in the fridge and you only add unto tap water but the one we bought are called living and clean water got from Lakes. we were all distributed three small dark stones and a black Bibles, we go together with our stones and Bible, every time we go under water we are instructed to go deep and pick three stones for the next journey and you throw the three stones into the water to open way to go through before jumping into the water. the places we go under water so many people are there and we also pray to god. He normally comes and instruct us, and we present our prayers request to him. there is a woman called queen wealth, she only drink blood not water. We have a lot of money but my life is more than money, i had no peace for two months and My wife is not a wear of all these things. i go alone every months on 11, these stones allow us to go at any time but from 11 day of the month. i have burnt some of my things given but i fear some of my friends will kill me now and queen wealth pray for me.

I need a new Bible, Eric buy for me a new bible if you still love me and pray about it

From: Peter McMaster
To: Pastor james Umzing
Sent: Tuesday, October 4, 2011 12:20 PM
Subject: Re: Pray for my family and god to forgive me

Hello James

It is a good thing that you are repenting. Repenting is not a one off thing, it is an ongoing process. A daily event. We can upset the Holy Spirit and He will leave us. So we are given this warning.

Eph 4:30 And grieve not the holy Spirit of God, whereby ye are sealed unto the day of redemption.

Some have given up of repentance and their conscience is seared.

1Ti 4:1 Now the Spirit speaketh expressly, that in the latter times some shall depart from the faith, giving heed to seducing spirits, and doctrines of devils;

1Ti 4:2 Speaking lies in hypocrisy; having their conscience seared with a hot iron;

So if you have truly repented then it would be good to expose the workings of the enemy. The Word of God tells us to do this.

Eph 5:11 And have no fellowship with the unfruitful works of darkness, but rather reprove (expose) them.

CHAPTER TWENTY THREE: THE UNDERWATER MEN

These devilish things you were part of is destroying many people, who will end up in Hell (which is the ultimate plan) for Eternity. (You have been part of this)

The road is narrow James and I know my letters are hard but they seem to have brought some correction so Praise the Lord for that.

I don't care if you don't like me much, but I do care where you will spend Eternity. I want it to be in Heaven with the Lord Jesus Christ.

If you do want to tell me more of what you have been up to I am listening. There are true Christians who are interested and they will pray about these things. And we will pray for you also. The Lord will protect you if you are serious. And if you are not then

Gal 6:7 Be not deceived; God is not mocked: for whatsoever a man soweth, that shall he also reap.

Peter McMaster

From: Pastor james Umzing
To: Peter McMaster
Sent: Wednesday, October 05, 2011 4:00 PM
Subject: Re: Pray for my family and god to forgive me

Thanks man of God, i want to start new life with new friends, i also want to wed my wife next month now, after many years but i believed its the right thing to do so. Continue praying for my family we were all lost! by the grace of God we shall still come back and do greater things.I have one big challenged now my other friends are on my neck. I was invited by one of my friend and kind of refused to make it. We normally go to Kenya at the beginning of every month to get water for blessing and miracles water but this time i couldn't make it and my friends are asking what has happened? one of my friend wanted to give me but i refused and reported me to my pastor and now we are not in good term pray for me.

From: Peter McMaster
To: Pastor james Umzing
Sent: Wednesday, October 5, 2011 11:59 AM
Subject: Re: Pray for my family and god to forgive me

Well done for resisting your old friends James. that is excellent. You will find that they will become enemies once you decide to follow Christ.
Praise the Lord.
Pete

From: Pastor james Umzing
To: Peter McMaster
Sent: Friday, October 07, 2011 1:52 AM
Subject: Re: Pray for my family and god to forgive me

Man of God i am sorry for all i have done, my friends do come to my home daily and asking me many questions but i have decided to stay focus and taking care of my family, i suffered for about three months non of my friends help me now i am fine and i know the cause of my suffering. i have made have up my mind never to go under water to look for power or blessing in the first place we used to go for others because you want people to see you moving in power and miracles but at the end of it death will come, either i preach in power or not i will die one day so i am ready to wait on God's power not under ground or water power. i really want Eric to start trusting me, he has been a good friend to me for so long but now he fear me!

From: Peter McMaster
To: Pastor james Umzing
Sent: Thursday, October 6, 2011 10:50 PM (7 hr time difference)
Subject: Re: Pray for my family and god to forgive me

James, you must understand that you never went under the water for others, it was for your own self. Your own pride, Your own ego, Your own vanity, and for your own glory. Just like Simon the Sorcerer wanted power, you did too, and sold your soul to the devil. Your motives were wrong.

I had a dream James that the 3 stones were tied around your neck still. You must totally renounce this because if you fall again you will probably not recover.

Isa 66:1 Thus saith the LORD, The heaven is my throne, and the earth is my footstool: where is the house that ye build unto me? and where is the place of my rest?

Isa 66:2 For all those things hath mine hand made, and all those things have been, saith the LORD: but to this man will I look, even to him that is poor and of a contrite spirit, and trembleth at my word.

Eric Okello knows the way.

CHAPTER TWENTY THREE: THE UNDERWATER MEN

From: Pastor james Umzing
To: Peter McMaster
Sent: Sunday, October 09, 2011 6:37 AM
Subject: Re: Pray for my family and god to forgive me

Man of God, i read your message and so encouraging, i am ready to start new life, if there is away i can repent then help me and do so. i have changed my phone number with fear not to communicate to some of my friends. Yesterday something beats me up, burnt and i got out of sleep and discovered my body burnt with fire! i do not know how. i know all i have done but for the last three weeks i haven't torch anything and asking for forgiveness i have burnt every things that i have got for blessing, i bought it at $17000 an image of queen wealth, now i have burnt it and i do not what it any more. i am not sure if this is the caused because i am too been burnt in the night.

Continue writing to me and if you have some Christian books, help me i want to be strong.

From: Peter McMaster
To: Pastor james Umzing
Sent: Saturday, October 8, 2011, 1:11 PM (7 hr time difference)
Subject: Re: Pray for my family and god to forgive me

Hello James. That is very good that you are destroying all that was involved with the devil. There may be backlash from the enemy after destroying his stuff but

Rom 8:31 What shall we then say to these things? If God be for us, who can be against us?

We all have battles in the Spirit. All true believers do. But we can not lose. But sometimes we get beat up if we are not on the right track. The Lord allows this.

Rom 8:28 And we know that all things work together for good to them that love God, to them who are the called according to his purpose.

And it may have been the refining fire of the Lord also burning out the wickedness from in you.

Mal 3:2,3 But who may abide the day of his coming? and who shall stand when he appeareth? for he is like a refiner's fire, and like fullers' soap:

And he shall sit as a refiner and purifier of silver: and he shall purify the sons of Levi, and purge them as gold and silver, that they may offer unto the LORD an offering in righteousness.

Get on your knees and ask God to forgiveness and ask Him to protect. We will pray for this also. Ask Him what else He wants you to do also and He will tell you.

And the best book to read is the Holy Bible. King James Version. You don't need books, only one. Also if you can download on mp3 and play in your house the Bible, (new testament) it will keep the spirits away and start to bring peace.

Just be patient though. It will take a little time. Bit by bit.

Peter McMaster

----- Original Message -----
From: Eric geoffrey Okello
To: Peter McMaster
Sent: Monday, October 10, 2011 4:57 PM
Subject: Hope all is well daddy!

(Eric is going to a lake in Tanzania to pray)

Praise the Living God daddy and mummy, i am fine and doing well only that money you sent took long to mature, it has matured today and i have just clear off Hotel bills this morning of about $98, a lot of thing happening here daddy, i have a plan to fly to TZ, due no buses over the weekend and its take about 12 hours travelling by bus so had wanted to use Air way but money took long to mature, and now remaining with about $100, Air Ticket is $145 to TZ, i think this will block me to travel to TZ as proposed due transport cost but God knows better me ready to travel!

(He had already prayed for a lake and destroyed their underwater city in the second heaven and it upset some schools these people ran and their children never came home. The schools were taking them underwater. He was off to attack them again)

James went to my home yesterday and he was asking for me according to my wife, two of his friends are in trouble due school demons and some parents want to know were about their children. James is now hiding and he fear he could be arrested any time from now. about 24 parents are claiming they haven got information about their children and where about. this might cause them trouble in short time according to his statements.
thanks daddy and be blessed

CHAPTER TWENTY THREE: THE UNDERWATER MEN

School closed over demons

Lwala Girls' Secondary School in Kaberamaido district was closed over the weekend due to claims of persistent demonic attacks. The district education officer, Moses Ochung, said over 18 students were reportedly possessed by demons, causing fear among students and teachers. He said efforts to chase away the demons using prayers had failed. The decision to close the school was made by the school's board of governors.

News paper clipping

James Umzing and these wicked men ran these schools. They were training grounds for the witchcraft they were involved in, but the Holy Spirit moved in. And as you see, they were powerless to stop it.

> ----- *Original Message* -----
> From: Pastor james Umzing
> To: Peter McMaster
> Sent: Monday, October 10, 2011 7:18 PM
> Subject: good morning pastor Pete
>
> *Dear Pastor Peter McMaster, pray for us and i have repented but no help, three headmasters from different schools we have been operating were rested yesterday due lost of some students and i am sure they are alive but must be under water, some students are agents and we have opened for all of the account number and we do deposit money in their account. after study they becoming full time agents when their parents are not a wear but now there is a problem, some could be in Tanzania and Uganda, my friends came to me yesterday i never wanted to talk to him and said out of the 24 students all the 15 students was rejected from Lake Tanganyika in Kenya and they are free to go to their home. but the one in Tanzania can not come out, we use to ask the queen.*

i have stopped all these but not i am in trouble, i am running i cant even sleep, i have changed my phone number but still my friends use my wife phone number to meet. i am worried i will be arrested and i am innocent. i weant to go and report my friends to local police about what we have been doing and these student could be in those places me i dont know

----- Original Message -----
From: Eric geoffrey Okello
To: Peter McMaster
Sent: Wednesday, October 19, 2011 2:21 AM
Subject: If all gose well, Kakande will face trouble

Some of the people arrested has reported their boss Kakande about his work, even though he too close to the government, his friends has reveal many secrets about him before the law in cluding pastor James. this message was quited by one of them and said all is true, the man said he take students under water and this message below might add more trouble to him daddy

From Red Pepper Newspaper, Kampala, Uganda.

The Kakande Ministries : Prophet Samuel Kakande Marries Fifth Wife

Scandal As Pastor Kakande Weds Fifth Time

And You Can't Believe, All This In 5 Years
Pastor Samuel Kakande of the Mulago based Synagogue Church of All Nations has been exposed as a pastor with excessive libido after he recently walked the aisle the fifth time in just 10 years.

The pastor who calls himself a prophet shocked his followers last Sunday when he paraded a cute light skinned Phillipino as his 5th wife and showed pictures of his secret wedding to her in Manila, the capital of the Philippines.

Kakande took many by surprise when he married secretly a saucy Philippino in Manila town, only to introduce her to his followers during the last Sunday service. The lavish wedding took place in one of the prominent churches in the Philippines. The bride has been identified as Popanes Citia, a famous businesswoman in that far eastern country.

The shock is that Kakande has wed for a fifth time contrary to any church's teaching where an individual can only wed again after the death -and not just divorce- of his or her partner. Last Sunday Kakande paraded his latest catch to his followers after delivering his sermon during the service that ended at about 8pm. The believers jubilated and burst into hymns soon after the controversial pastor had introduced his new catch.

CHAPTER TWENTY THREE: THE UNDERWATER MEN

(There was much more to this article but I wanted you to see where these men are at.)

> ----- Original Message -----
> From: Eric geoffrey Okello
> To: Peter McMaster
> Sent: Friday, October 21, 2011 12:17 AM
> Subject: Pastor James died daddy
>
> *Praise Jesus daddy, i am sad to say this Pastor James died this afternoon daddy he was set free on police bond and went to his home two days ago. According to his wife he went for a meeting in the night (i think he went for their own meeting with his friends and he never reveal to his wife) he came back late in the day very fine according to his wife but he went to rest due they went for the meeting in the night. The wife made food and went to call his husband to come for food at 2pm and found him lying on the bed dead. She can not tell where his husband went and now he is dead. To me i am sure James was killed by poison daddy because he has made a statements revealing their secrets to some people and the .... is connected to some of his friends. I-am sure he died for telling the truth daddy.*

(So James Umzing was killed for his betrayal to the underwater men, or high ranking satanists if you like. But that wasn't the last time they tried to kill our little friend Eric. (They had another offer for Eric but they wrote to me by mistake.)

> ----- Original Message -----
> From: Zingo Moses
> To: Peter McMaster
> Sent: Friday, 3 August 2012 5:16 PM
> Subject: Dear Eric
>
> *Dear servant Eric Okello, I am glad you wrote to me this morning! We only want to support your work in the Lord! The money is ready waiting only your details. God spoke to us to build churches in Northern Uganda and we want to be in partner with you. If you sent me your account details money will be ready next week around 8th August 2012. We shall take you for baptism in Israel for a week as Jesus was also Baptist we shall take you and witness the power of God and where Jesus was Baptist, we shall move round to meet some of our friends and see how they are doing in ministries. We know how much you love God, my friend said you the right person so I have trusted you already. Forward this message to Eric in case you are not Eric. Waiting to hear from you soon!*
> *Dr. Moses Zing*

----- *Original Message* -----
From: Zingo Moses
To: Peter McMaster
Sent: Thursday, 30 August 2012 3:41 PM
Cc: Eric Okello
Subject: Dear Pastor Eric

Praise God Pastor Eric; i am very sorry i am kindly asking you to forgive me, i know i have done many wrong things but i was forced to do so! i am kindly requesting you if you read this message forgive me. i had a car accident few days when you wrote to me last month and you cried because of me i am requesting you to forgive me. my legs!! i have a big problem but God appeared to me and said i should ask you to forgive me. i am now out of hospital but still with much pain i didn't want to tell you this, when you went to Kenya we went to the room you were sleeping but we saw the hotel guard and we went back we wanted to poison you! people used my own money to pay the someone in the hotel to serve you with food and i used my money US$20,000. Pastor Eric so many people are against you, they said you are hard and difficult to be understood, but i now know you a servant of God.

i am requesting you to forgive me and delete this message. i will write to you when i am fine and tell you everything.

(When my wife and I went to Uganda, Eric said, do not eat anything that is offered to you. I just nodded my head. We already knew why.)

That's not quite the end of this episode yet. There was more to come. One thing I have learnt is that Judgement falls very quickly in Africa. And if God wants to clean something up He does.

----- *Original Message* -----
From: Richard Emyedu
To: Peter McMaster
Sent: Saturday, October 29, 2011 12:49 AM
Subject: I cant wait to write this pete

Good morning Pete, pastor closes to Kakande and having churches or over 15000 members in Uganda and we know him as a false prophet died in road accident in Uganda many people feared him with three white pastors. Eric was happy about this message and he told me you gave him some money to go and pray in water where they used to go. He warn Eric that he is young, with a lot of thing, Eric use to fear them but three of them died at once and some white men.

Hope will be on tomorrow's papers trying to check the link I sent you some time back tomorrow

CHAPTER TWENTY THREE: THE UNDERWATER MEN

----- Original Message -----
From: Eric geoffrey Okello
To: Peter McMaster
Sent: Saturday, October 29, 2011 5:33 AM
Subject: four James friends died in accided today

Praise Jesus Daddy; hope all is well; after Pastor James three of his close friends died in the road accident and two USA pastors at the same time. I do not know what has happened but I believe all things happen for the good and we pray for God to receive them into eternal life this is the man who said I am young if you remember about verse I sent to you John 1:1 in 2010….. I think what I went for few weeks ago it's happening now life. God spoke to me and I know God is the one fighting my battle. This are the people who said you can not serve God when you poor and poor people are not the right people of God but when your time comes we all leave earthly things under the sun. He had two harmer car and BMW and houses but today its nothing. Let fight for our life daddy. Its on the head line for today's news paper, I have the names of the American pastors they died together with on mission check on www.newvision.co.ug
hope to update you about this and what has happened later

----- Original Message -----
From: Eric geoffrey Okello
To: Peter McMaster
Sent: Saturday, October 29, 2011 5:39 AM
Subject: Check details on attach file

from www.newvision.co.ug

By Donald Kirya and Herbert Ssempogo

TWO American evangelists are among four people, who perished in a Thursday night accident along the Jinja-Iganga highway.

Dr. Reos Godzck, fellow citizen Leos Both and their hosts namely Bishop John Michael Mugerwa and Ronnie Ssebunya died after a trailer crashed their vehicle at Kakira at 7pm.

According to Jinja police spokesperson, Samsom Lubega, Paul, the driver of a Toyota Super Custom in which the deceased were, attempted to overtake two fuel tankers.

"As he overtook, he realized there was oncoming traffic so he decided to squeeze into a narrow gap between the two trailers," Lubega stated.

Owing to humps on the road, the trailer in front reduced speed and Paul followed suit, Lubega said, adding that in the next few minutes, the trailer behind rammed into the Super Custom.

Godizic, Both, Mugerwa and Ssebunya died on the spot while Paul was rushed to hospital in Jinja. The police by Friday morning could not establish his state.

A fire brigade team from Jinja had to cut the wreckage to extract the bodies. The remains were taken to the city mortuary in Kampala.

From Phoenix, Arizona in US, the two Americans were here on the invitation of Mugerwa of Fast Assemblies Church located in Nkere zone, Katwe Makindye Division, Kampala.

Earlier in the day, they had attended a crusade for married couples in Namutumba district.

Saidi Nyogolo, the driver of the killer trailer disappeared but the police apprehended his colleague, Hamasi Kaizera. Kaizera disclosed that their vehicles contained jet fuel, which they were driving to Entebbe.

South Eastern traffic chief, Washington Labeja, who assessed the accident scene, attributed the crash to recklessness.

The vehicles were towed to Nalufenya police post traffic police continued investigating the tragedy continued. Accidents are among the leading causes of death in Uganda. Thousands of people perish in accidents annually.

Car crash that Eric's enemies were killed in.

CHAPTER TWENTY THREE: THE UNDERWATER MEN

I hope you are seeing the extent of what is happening in the spirit realm, with wicked men associating with devils and demons for their worldly power. But not just in the world, but also to operate in the church. So be very careful of where you go and who you want to lay hands on you. The church is the devil's playground at the moment.

Read your Bibles and ask God for Discernment. You need it. And I'll add this. Almost everyone who I have ever heard tell me they had discernment never did. And "DON'T DRINK THE WATER!!!"

CHAPTER TWENTY FOUR
ANOTHER ONE BITES THE DUST

The next chapter in this saga and I hope it is not too much to handle. It blew me away how God just landed all this in my lap. Exposing it certainly moved me to the next level because I'll tell you something, the devil wasn't happy with me. But God was getting me ready for even a bigger fight than this. This is from my website also. And the reality and understanding of the Kingdom of darkness was coming to me. And I sure would need it.

Here is the story of another who has died coming against Eric and working for the Underwater Men. This was a man called Richard Emyedu who was helping support Eric then turned against him after joining T.B Joshua's group, because he believed that having as much money as he liked he could make a difference.

Richard Emyedu

CHAPTER TWENTY FOUR: ANOTHER ONE BITES THE DUST

But the money was cursed and he fell into the trap of following another Jesus and then persecuting a true believer. I am amazed and the swiftness of judgement in Africa. When God says, touch not my anointed, He means it. (Like when two Catholic priests died on the way to the police station to stop the Otwal Crusade in North Uganda that we held.)

> Heb 10:31 *It is* a fearful thing to fall into the hands of the living God.
>
> 1Ch 16:20-22 And *when* they went from nation to nation, and from *one* kingdom to another people;
>
> He suffered no man to do them wrong: yea, he reproved kings for their sakes,
>
> *Saying,* Touch not mine anointed, and do my prophets no harm.

Richard's life fell to pieces and he could not be talked out of following the money and the false god. Satan hates failure and I believe that the witchcraft that gave Richard the heart attack in the end was sent by the satanists toward Richard and God had removed His protection.

Here is a scripture that most of the church doesn't want to know. This story is also in 2 Chronicles 18. God has had it repeated for its importance. I fully believe that there can come a time when God has had enough. And judgement will come. How severe is according to his will. But I warn you now, don't play games with God.

> 1Ki 22:20-23 And the LORD said, Who shall persuade Ahab, that he may go up and fall at Ramothgilead? And one said on this manner, and another said on that manner.
>
> And there came forth a spirit, and stood before the LORD, and said, I will persuade him.
>
> And the LORD said unto him, Wherewith? And he said, I will go forth, and I will be a lying spirit in the mouth of all his prophets. And he said, Thou shalt persuade him, and prevail also: go forth, and do so.
>
> Now therefore, behold, the LORD hath put a lying spirit in the mouth of all these thy prophets, and the LORD hath spoken evil concerning thee.

Richard was only a young man of about 35 and had a wife and two young children. She left him after he started praying with candles at midnight and doing all these rituals and things that he was shown by the satanists. I am amazed at how strong deception is when it takes hold. And strong deception is not only in Africa. It is amongst most churches here in Australia in some form or another, even RIGHT NOW!!!

> 2Th 2:9-12 *Even him,* whose coming is after the working of Satan with all power and signs and lying wonders,
>
> And with all deceivableness of unrighteousness in them that perish; because they received not the love of the truth, that they might be saved.
>
> And for this cause God shall send them strong delusion, that they should believe a lie:
>
> That they all might be damned who believed not the truth, but had pleasure in unrighteousness.
>
> Mat 24:24 For there shall arise false Christs, and false prophets, and shall shew great signs and wonders; insomuch that, if it were possible, they shall deceive the very elect.

Richard was our friend and named his two children after Poss and myself, when Eric prayed for his barren wife to bear children. He believed that the anointing Eric had came from me, but I believe it came from Eric's fasting and praying and reading his KJV Bible. He went to Eric's wedding also and was a good friend to him.

I had been in contact with Richard for around 5 years back when this took place and saw his giving to the work of God and his downfall. I know many think T.B Joshua is a good man but he is a wicked deceiver. We both tried to talk Richard out of where he was going for around 18 months but these emails are the most recent.

When he tried to give the money he received from T.B Joshua back, he couldn't and he got sick. He was willing one day and like somebody else the next.

Then maybe like Judas, he stepped over the line of no return. God is gracious, but the line is real. Once saved always saved is another demonic doctrine. Christianity is very dangerous when we think we know it all and have it all.

> 1Co 8:2 And if any man think that he knoweth anything, he knoweth nothing yet as he ought to know.

CHAPTER TWENTY FOUR: ANOTHER ONE BITES THE DUST

> 1Pe 5:8 Be sober, be vigilant; because your adversary the devil, as a roaring lion, walketh about, seeking whom he may devour:

> Rev 3:17 Because thou sayest, I am rich, and increased with goods, and have need of nothing; and knowest not that thou art wretched, and miserable, and poor, and blind, and naked:

I was reading a Win Worley book and he said that he was offered riches and fame and whatever he wanted if he would stop doing what he was doing. They even said that he could still do deliverance on some who they gave to be delivered, or all for the show. Any famous names come to mind?

> Mat 4:9 And saith unto him, All these things will I give thee, if thou wilt fall down and worship me.)

> Luk 12:2 For there is nothing covered, that shall not be revealed; neither hid, that shall not be known.

So here is the leader of the gang. His church, SCOAN is on 24 hr TV in Africa and there are many miracles coming from them. They are very rich and build many churches, through which they lead many into error. If you know your Bible you will be shocked at the claim, but many do not and so follow the demonic deception to their own destruction.

T.B Joshuas highly charged demonic poisoned water

Here is some basic scriptures of how we are saved and when and how blessings will come. Not by spraying magic water everywhere. The trouble is that everyone wants shortcuts. T.B Joshua's shortcut will curse you and bring destruction into your life at the least and sending you to Hell is the end goal and Satan's desired result for you.

> Act 4:12 Neither is there salvation in any other: for there is none other name under heaven given among men, whereby we must be saved.
>
> Joh 14:6 Jesus saith unto him, I am the way, the truth, and the life: no man cometh unto the Father, but by me.
>
> Eph 2:8 For by grace are ye saved through faith; and that not of yourselves: *it is* the gift of God:
>
> Act 2:38 Then Peter said unto them, Repent, and be baptized every one of you in the name of Jesus Christ for the remission of sins, and ye shall receive the gift of the Holy Ghost.
>
> Act 2:39 For the promise is unto you, and to your children, and to all that are afar off, *even* as many as the Lord our God shall call.
>
> Joh 3:16 For God so loved the world, that he gave his only begotten Son, that whosoever believeth in him should not perish, but have everlasting life.
>
> Joh 10:9 I am the door: by me if any man enter in, he shall be saved, and shall go in and out, and find pasture.
>
> Joh 10:10 The thief cometh not, but for to steal, and to kill, and to destroy: I am come that they might have life, and that they might have *it* more abundantly.
>
> 1Jn 1:9 If we confess our sins, he is faithful and just to forgive us our sins, and to cleanse us from all unrighteousness.
>
> Mat 6:33 But seek ye first the kingdom of God, and his righteousness; and all these things shall be added unto you.

Now we start with an email from Richard telling us of how he knows that God is protecting him, because of prayer and his obedience. He was supporting Eric and we were all praying for each other.

CHAPTER TWENTY FOUR: ANOTHER ONE BITES THE DUST

Richard had a job building roads and construction and was under divine protection as this next email shows. Richard was travelling in a small van from his work (I have removed all active email addresses, Richard doesn't need his now but it is still monitored)

----- Original Message -----
From: Richard Emyedu
To: Peter McMaster
Sent: Thursday, May 24, 2012 5:37 PM
Subject: Good Morning Pete!

Good Morning Pete, how are you? Eric said you are in another country at your father's home! Pete our God is good, we were ambushed by Al-shabab in Somalia hria road and they fired bullets on us killing three people and injured 4, i was the only one who servived and this is really God. i was in the middle, the driver shot from the arm but he drove us out of the ambush before he collapesd but he is alive he lost blood. thanks for prayers and this is what Eric told me in March Pete that he saw me in dark road and many people were injured i remember i wrote to you.

*thanks, i am fine and now resting home for sometime.
greetings from my family.*

From: Richard Emyedu
To: Peter McMaster
Sent: Tuesday, May 29, 2012 6:34 PM
Subject: Re: Good Morning Pete!

Pete, God is faithful; Ugandan UPDF soldiers killed over 60 rebels in Somalia they are here in Somalia for peace keeping, and they attacked them in their base killing many and injured so many Pete, however they attacked Kenya and with twin bombs injuries many civilian, we have fear they may attack Uganda again but we are praying, These men are bad pete. in 2010 they killed many Ugandan in football. Thanks

i am planing if i get a job in Uganda we shall go back but God is keeping us Pete.

i am happy for all your prayers, its good to serve God and to support the work of God. i do not know what has happened but God protected me and yet my friends got bad injured and they are still in the hospital. i am just thanking God pete

So he loved Eric and knew that he was blessed and we kept in contact lots. But Richard was telling us that he was getting involved with the wicked men who had lots of money and they were building lots of churches in Africa. These were the men who tried to kill Eric. But Richard wouldn't take any notice, he was blinded by dollar signs and fleshy good works. So we tried to warn Richard and he even knew that things weren't right, but open the door to deception and it can be hard to close. Richard received some cursed money from the wicked men then tried to give the money back, he came into trouble, which he blamed on witchcraft from Indian men who he worked with. He took no notice of anything Eric or I told him.

I am only putting the relevant emails here, there were many more exchanges.

> ----- Original Message -----
> From: Richard Emyedu
> To: Peter McMaster
> Sent: Tuesday, December 11, 2012 7:01 PM
> Subject: Pastor, if you can pray for me!
>
> *Pastor Pete, if you can pray for me please pray for me. something is happening to me some Indian are jealous of me at work and they have bewitched me! i wrote to Eric to pray for me also. if i have done wrong forgive me and show me the right way. i tried to go for work two time but I get off the road. yesterday i almost knock my son. my car can not move on road now. Some many things crying in my head, i keep seeing bulls surrounded me all the time. they do not want me to go but to only rotate around. everytime i get in the car i see three bulls in front of me. yesterday i saw bulls in-font of me; i tried to reversed and my son was behind i thought i was knocking bulls but that was my only son.*
>
> *i don't sleep in the night! i hear many things crying, my house keep moving round; bed just rotating whole night. i will leave this job and go to China next year with all my family.*

> ----- Original Message -----
> From: Richard Emyedu
> To: Peter McMaster
> Sent: Friday, December 14, 2012 7:24 PM
> Subject: Good Morning Pete!
>
> *I want to support some churches with this money, i am not sure where to forward this money to since Eric refused! i have contacted TB about it and he said i can use the money to support the work of God. He only*

CHAPTER TWENTY FOUR: ANOTHER ONE BITES THE DUST

> want to meet the pastors i will support with this fund. Eric just has a bad attitude toward this gifts Pete; am working hard to help him out. I will be in Uganda around 22nd but i am still not very fine, we are praying and fasting. My wife is seeing many visions but all her visions not good. We are too praying about it. i will gather some Pastors in my home village and meet with TB, i have never met TB but home to meet him this Christmas break. he seems not a bad man Pete; i have some of his video. The who were against Eric i know them.
> greetings to poss.

I am not sure if Richard paid back the first lot of money. He built 3 churches for these men, usually from donations of $50,000. There are many of these throughout Africa. They think to be rich is to be of God and the bigger the stomach, the house and car, the more blessed you are. Guess where they get that from?!?!?

Richard had just received $50,000 US dollars from Nigeria for Eric but Eric refused it.

> ----- Original Message -----
> From: Richard Emyedu
> To: Peter McMaster
> Sent: Friday, January 25, 2013 4:29 PM
> Subject: Good Morning Pastor Pete
>
> *Good morning Pete, I want thank God for all of you for all your support and time writing to me when I was lost in the bush. I discovered that I was out and I just survived from the mouth of the Lion. Eric wrote to me two days before I got the money and said something was not right with me he talked of a vision he saw about me! But I don't remember his vision but it was something to do with my personal life and my family, after few days Eric became wild on me and told me not to support him in anyway. Few weeks later I felt sick and almost run mad but God delivered me. Every time I asked Eric to pray for me he only tells me I should refund the money that was deposited in my account the $50,000.*
>
> *I became hungry with Eric because he wasn't caring for me that was my thought. Few weeks later you also wrote to me that I should pay back the money I have received! I thought you had planned with Eric not to help me. I used to see bad dreams to make life difficult there were many lizards I could see in the vision. And fighting many bad things, some time driving very dirty black cars, I could not work. When I contacted Eric and refused the money for the fifth time and instructed*

me not to speak to him on phone or to write to him, I went and refunded back the money to the sender. Three days later we went into prayer and fasting after Eric said if I had paid back the money I should pray and fast for three days, I did but I never wanted to hear from Eric since he thought I was bad and refused the money yet I got the money for his ministry; my life changed instantly but still I dint know what I was held up and what happened to me all that was in my mind was that my work mate has done something now improvement since I was at my home in the village Docolo District.

On 11th January 2013, I was invited to go to Nigeria to attend a conference for 2013. In the conference I saw some people that are really bad but Pastors and I used to fear them but they didn't know me but I knew them since they are public figure in Uganda also in the meeting the was about how to win souls!! But what I saw was different, there was a pool with six lizards and everyone was instructed to wash their legs in this pool. It was a six days conference but I took off on the first day. I discovered I was wrong and people were going to use me to harm Pastor Eric. I do not know how I should talk to Eric but I will try.

Pastor Pete, I am sorry, I have wittiness many things with my own eyes

----- Original Message -----
From: Richard Emyedu
To: Peter McMaster
Sent: Saturday, February 09, 2013 6:16 PM
Subject: Good morning Pete

Pete, thanks for writing to me once again, I thought I am alone with my battle but this message has really encouraged me; I didn't want to tell anyone but because of these scriptures you wrote I am going to speak out. I am in a trouble that I do not know how we shall sort it out. Its now three weeks no communication in my house; my wife want to leave me!! I explained everything to her failed to understand me. She said went I went to Nigeria I went under water. She is scared about the money I took few months ago and I returned it back, she just wants to divorce!! She asked me to go Eric's or to call Eric home pray for our family few weeks ago but I cant do this since Eric won't listen but Eric is someone my wife would listen to. I do not know what will happen next. I have got a job in China through some friends but my wife only saying I want to kill her.

Pastor pray for my family and if you can write to my wife Agnes I will forward your message to her. She has no Email address.

CHAPTER TWENTY FOUR: ANOTHER ONE BITES THE DUST

So Richard continues with these men and the secrecy surrounding his life was too much for his Wife Agnes to bear. Richard was torn between his family home and his friends and the money. And it was destroying him.

----- *Original Message* -----
From: Richard Emyedu
To: Peter McMaster
Sent: Tuesday, September 17, 2013 11:30 PM
Subject: Re: Uganda vid and preach

Good morning Pastor Pete and Poss, hope you had a good time in Uganda, this is Agnes, I am asking you to pray for my husband, he is sick and it's now coming to two months! he dose not want me to tell anyone including Pastor Eric and he stopped me from communicating to him. I respect him but I feel we need prayer. Richard has build now 4 Churches in Dokolo and in Kyoga through support from his friends, but since he is not himself, he dose not tell me his plans! sometime he is hard on me. He has his own room and he dose not sleep in my room! He only pray at midnight he buy's candles in boxes and he dose not put light when praying but only candles, when i asked him; he only tells me God instructed him to do so. I am confused and i want to go back to our home. We have everything in the house but no peace Pastor. Pastor pray for us. I didn't have your Email address but today i got access to his Email, he is not around for two days. I don't understand my husband. Do not reply this message I am deleting from sent message also but pray for my family.

----- *Original Message* -----
From: Richard Emyedu
To: Peter McMaster
Sent: Wednesday, September 25, 2013 5:54 PM
Subject: Pastor Pete and Pastor Eric

Good Morning Pastor Pete, I never wanted to write but I must say something to you and to Pastor Eric, If i have done something wrong forgive me!! I have no peace, my wife left me with all my Children! Its now four days I do not know where she is now. Pastor Eric remember how we were close to each other, let's talk. It's now coming to seven months you don't pick my phone calls. since I last met you in 2011, on your Introduction day.

Thanks
your Brother
Emyedu Richard

A reply I sent to Richard.

From: Peter McMaster
To: Richard Emyedu
Sent: Wednesday, September 25, 2013
Subject: Re: Pastor Pete and Pastor Eric

What do you want to say Richard. We all believe that you are in with the wrong men. The money men and underwater men. You are walking in the flesh and thinking it is the Spirit of God. It's not about money, it's about the Spirit of God. Forsake those people, (if you have covenanted with them then this will have to be repented of and renounced, and will be a major battle) and I am sure the the Lord will work it out. He loves you Richard, you don't have to do anything for Him to be accepted. He will exalt you in due time, there is no shortcuts. When we run ahead there is nothing but deception and delusion that may await us.
Pete

Richard keeps asking for help, while still involving himself deeper and deeper into the occult activities of this group. But the money kept coming so his soul ties to the ungodly were strong.

From: Richard Emyedu
To: Peter McMaster
Sent: Tuesday, October 22, 2013 6:54 PM
Subject: Re: Pastor Pete and Pastor Eric

Pastor Pete and Pastor Eric, I know I have sinned and now I have lost all my family; its took me almost two years to realized what Pastor Eric told me. In September 2012, I planned to come and meet you in Kampala but I never made it. I tried to send some money to Pastor Eric but some one was using his Email address, I think I was the caused of it because I gave Eric's email address to someone in Nigeria; he wanted to contact Pastor Eric! but just after few days I heard about what has happened to his Email address but I could not believed he is a bad friend. When I lost my family i cried, but I have discovered something was wrong with me. In my prayer room I was instructed to leave my windows open when praying and a woman is not allowed in the prayer room. My wife wanted so much to see my room but I had my key with me, at mid night I was instructed to set six eggs together and put candle in the middle, and I was instructed to pray at mid night to 2:00am. My window to leave open for the blessing to come into my house. I gave some of my friend my account number but after every month when I check my account i could find more money in my account so i continue in prayer. one day Pastor Eric told me exactly what I was doing but he said he saw a vision! I was scared but I thought God wanted him to know what I was doing since I have been supporting him years back, I wanted to send him money but he refused and stopped communication with me.

Last week, I went to Nigeria and I was instructed to go and be friends some Pastors around me including Pastor Eric! I asked he told some pastors are against us!! I came back home, when I was praying, in the middle of the night using candle light I discovered there was a snake just close to me and that was like a friend to me. I shouted for help. today I am sure I am not following the right way. Pastor if you can help me so that i speak to Pastor Eric, I want him to help me get back my wife. I have build three Churches complete but now I want to tell the Church also. Pastor Eric blocked my Email, I cant send him any message even his phone. I called him yesterday on a friends phone but he was too hard on me.
Thanks you Pastor save my Family.
This the Email address for my wife big sister, you can tell her to come back home (email deleted)

Richard was told to get close to the pastors that this group wanted to infiltrate, including his friend Eric, and lure them into the web with their financial enticements. All the time being warned; and with prayer and fasting going his way, there was a battle.

From: Richard Emyedu
To: Peter McMaster
Sent: Wednesday, December 04, 2013 8:52 PM
Subject: Re: Good Morning Pete

Pastor Pete, today I agreed with all the word Pastor Eric told me and what you said! I never wanted to read any message about my personal life and i thought I was right since supporting the work of God. yesterday I was in Nigeria and i will never go back again. I went there and spoke about my wife who left. And these men wanted to send spirit to bring back my wife! We started praying and I was told to go and bath, here i found three eggs in the basin, they are small eggs. Thanks you Pastor, I want Pastor Eric to come and help me but he dose not talk to me. Tell him i need him to pray for me. I didn't use this water but I will never go back again. All the money that was transfer ed to my account I will refund tomorrow. I met one man whom I know he is not a good man in their and a Ugandan, Pastor Eric does not want to hear only his name so i won't tell him but i met Kakande in the meeting for the first time, planning for 2014 conference

I sent some links to Win Worley booklets to my email list and this is Richards reply. (Win Worley preaches repentance and forgiveness and much deliverance.) These people are told not to repent. Repentance is offensive to them. They just spray with the magic water.

They were now offering Eric $250,000 US. A massive amount. Yes, Two Hundred and Fifty Thousand USA Dollars!!!

> Mar 8:35-37 For whosoever will save his life shall lose it; but whosoever shall lose his life for my sake and the gospel's, the same shall save it.
>
> For what shall it profit a man, if he shall gain the whole world, and lose his own soul?
>
> Or what shall a man give in exchange for his soul?

----- Original Message -----
From: Richard Emyedu
To: Peter McMaster
Sent: Sunday, January 05, 2014 5:56 PM
Subject: Re: Win Worley booklets.

Good Morning Pastor Pete, how are you and the work you are doing, i sheared this message of Win Worley with a friend in the USA, he said win Worley messages are not good and demonic. He told me not to read his messages. I think this man died some years back according to him. Anyway how is Poss and the ministry, I am recovered. Pastor pete, I am concern about Pastor Eric and i don't feel comfortable to see him suffering, i have two Children because of him and your prayer. Recently we collected good amount of money would really help Pastor Eric own a house and support his work of God. We collected with friends people around us US $250,000. I told him to come to my home but he has refused, should I return this money back to people who have raised this fund, I have pastor Eric in my heart and I feel he should have a better life.

If possible talk to him and I can send him the money or I may give him ATM card for easy accessing to the fund. I will be going away to China next week.

I sent Richard the stuff on T.B Joshua and James Umzing, who worked for T.B Joshua, and tried to poison Eric. Richard knew James Umzing and what happened, but still could not see.

CHAPTER TWENTY FOUR: ANOTHER ONE BITES THE DUST

From: Peter McMaster
To: Richard Emyedu
Sent: Sunday, January 05, 2014
Subject: Fw: underwater men

Please read this Richard and think for yourself. Do not run to men for an explanation because thay have lots of money. That can even distort a lot of understanding. You have spoken yourself of knowing these are wrong but you are snared like an animal in a trap. And you are getting used to the cage.

From: Richard Emyedu
To: Peter McMaster
Sent: Monday, January 06, 2014 12:29 PM
Subject: Re: Fw: underwater men

Joshua is not a bad person as people think when you go to his Church you will find all people praising and worshiping God! What many are jealous of is the way God is using him.
When you watch his programs on TV you will realized that he is actually not a bad man. I used to think that way too but I have got to know the truth after some time.
Tell Eric only to refund my money since I am bad I want to leave him alone! I have lost my family!! I found him when he can't even afford food for himself but now he is talking bad on me. I will put him on pressure until he pays my money now and I am going to send him this message.

Richard then wrote to Eric and this is Eric's response to me.

----- Original Message -----
From: Eric Geoffrey Okello
To: Peter McMaster
Sent: Sunday, January 05, 2014 8:32 PM
Subject: Richard called me!

Hope all is well, Richard called me and he was not happy he told me that I said he want to kill me so he told me to refund all his support or contribution of about $2100 in total from 2010 - 2012, he is so hungry of me, but I am wondering someone who wanted to offer me $250,000 and now want his money of $2100. I wish i had money i would give him today. Daddy leave Richard alone demons are controlling him, not himself. Jesus said to His friend, you devil get behind me. If I can only pay Richard what he is demanding I will have peace and I will delete him from my contact list of friends. He said I am spoiling his name that he has joined wrong group etc

I sent this email to Eric with the response I sent Richard..

From: Peter McMaster
To: Eric Geoffrey Okello
Sent: Sunday, January 5, 2014 10:39 PM
Subject: Re: Richard called me!

I just wrote this reply to Richard this morning Eric after he wrote back after he read about the Win worley books. This is why he is angry. I am tired of him not hearing us too. He is full of demons. You cant and dont have to refund what he freely gave. That is ridiculous.

People hate Win worley because of the demons are in them hate him. He was the best deliverance man in the world and known by all the demonic principalities and powers. If somebody is saying that he is demonic then i would run from that person.
Eric will never take your money Richard. The men you are in association plan to kill him. He is exposing their wickedness and you need to wake up also.
They will lead you to damnation if you continue to follow.

From: Eric Geoffrey Okello
To: Peter McMaster
Sent: Monday, January 06, 2014 12:05 AM
Subject: Re: Richard called me!

Oh, I was wondering why he became so angry and annoyed since I don't communicate to him now. God spoke to me about Richard last year and I told him everything but he dose not understand! I have no more words for him, I have done my part; let God do his part now. If he want his money, I will pay God will surely set me free from him.

----- Original Message -----
From: Eric Geoffrey Okello
To: Peter McMaster
Sent: Monday, January 06, 2014 7:37 PM
Subject: Another Battle has started Daddy!

Daddy, I strongly believed that these men are using Richard to convert young Ministers and Pastors to expand their Vision to win souls in their demonic Kingdom. But using money and properties! If you want to that Richard has changed talk to him about the Holy Spirit and Called Jesus Christ to him. He only called Jesus. I think he feared Christ now!

Here is an email about Kafeero, the man who let me preach in his church.

CHAPTER TWENTY FOUR: ANOTHER ONE BITES THE DUST

From: Eric Geoffrey Okello
To: Peter McMaster
Sent: Wednesday, January 08, 2014 9:05 PM
Subject: Re: Fw: underwater men

Richard, many demons entered him and demons controlling him. The only good thing is that God revealed to me at the early stage! and these men are wondering why I am not close to Richard Because they though he was my everything. i can sleep outside but I will have life. This is how they killed Kafero if you remember, he received the blessing and opened doors for the devil, just at night, the man never fall sick but demons killed him like that. I am poor but my Spiritual antennas are up, he can not take me to prison for what? if I will leave the house at God's appointed time. I heard many words but God is with us. I am praying for Richard, that something may happen bad to him so that he may run back to God; like a prodigal Son or Lost Son. Something will happen to him just for him to come back to his sense.

I don't have to stand up for Eric, it seems that praying like he spoke about (this was the first time in six years I heard Eric say something like this) was Richards only hope. I was praying like this also.

> Luk 20:17,18 And he beheld them, and said, What is this then that is written, The stone which the builders rejected, the same is become the head of the corner?
>
> Whosoever shall fall upon that stone shall be broken; but on whomsoever it shall fall, it will grind him to powder.

But Richard became very proud and angry. The fruit of the deception was beginning to manifest in its fullness. These men brought many houses that Eric was renting and threw him onto the street and his family.

From: Richard Emyedu
To: Peter McMaster
Sent: Wednesday, January 08, 2014 6:54 PM
Subject: Re: Fw: underwater men

Not far away, Eric will pay my money and he will be evicted in the house because his house has been bought and I gave him money to buy a house he has refused instead talking evil about me. I am not happy, I don't pray to devil but God. I have a strong feeling Eric knows why my wife left

The anger of Richard reached its peak but Eric was always calm, knowing His God.

Psa 50:15 And call upon me in the day of trouble: I will deliver thee, and thou shalt glorify me.

----- Original Message -----
From: Eric Geoffrey Okello
To: Peter McMaster
Sent: Friday, January 10, 2014 4:26 AM
Subject: Today I visited Police again!

God is God and He is faithful, today I remember some scriptures and I have discovered, every word in the Bible will surely come to past. Richard wanted me arrested the same thing Pastor James did to me in 2009. When he got his friends and they advised him to do so. This time was different; I was called to report to Police, I didn't know why! But on reaching I found the one I used to say my friend there and he really forged statement and words against me. He said I have told his wife to leave him! And now he is suffering and I am spoiling his name. Above all he claimed he borrowed me US$ 2100 and because of that I advice his wife to leaved. On hearing the statement I asked him simple question! I asked him if the evidence for his has claimed!

And he says yes (He has printed some of the Emails) they never allowed me to talk but I told him, I am ready to go to Prison and told him; I will still serve God in Prison. After about two hours, one Police man told me I am innocent. Richard tried to forge a statement but failed and they set me free me and only advised to clear his money. Richard told the officer that I have no money to pay him so I should go and work for him to clear the money for one full year he said. I promised to pay his money, and I know God will surely make it.

The Bible says, thus saith the Lord; Cursed be the man that trusteth in man, and maketh flesh his arm, and whose heart departeth from the Lord. Jeremiah 17:5

Owe no man any thing, but to love one another: for he that loveth another hath fulfilled the law. Romans 13.5

Woe to them that go down to Egypt for help; and stay on horses, and trust in chariots, because they are many; and in horsemen, because they are very strong; but they look not unto the Holy One of Israel, neither seek the Lord! Isaiah 31:1

If God is on your side, people will spend money to kill your dreams, but even in the prison, you will still go with your dreams. No one can kill your dreams

CHAPTER TWENTY FOUR: ANOTHER ONE BITES THE DUST

This was the last I heard for about a fortnight, then this email came from Eric. Richard had died.

> ----- Original Message -----
> From: Eric Geoffrey Okello
> To: Peter McMaster
> Sent: Tuesday, February 04, 2014 5:23 PM
> Subject: Hope all is well with you and the family!
>
> Richard Burial is today, I am going to attend his burial too. the Doctor said heart failure problem, pray for his wife to be strong.

But that wasn't enough for the devil.

> ----- Original Message -----
> From: Eric Geoffrey Okello
> To: Peter McMaster
> Sent: Thursday, February 20, 2014 9:08 AM
> Subject: Prayer for Richard Son!
>
> Praise the Lord God, four days ago one of Richard Son, ran mad, Okello Francis Pete! Some demons were really disturbing him just running and doing much. Agnes called me and yesterday we prayed for the boy he is now fine. Pray for God's protection upon him; it's seem his Father covenanted him. But he is free and we are covering him in prayer.
>
> God bless you.
>
> We are moving on by God's grace, moving from glory to glory

And the Enemy of men, never sleeps.

> 1Pe 5:8 Be sober, be vigilant; because your adversary the devil, as a roaring lion, walketh about, seeking whom he may devour:

> ----- Original Message -----
> From: Okio Joshua Brian
> To: Peter McMaster
> Sent: Friday, March 28, 2014 7:27 PM
> Subject: Praise God Pastor Pete
>
> Greetings in the name of our Lord Jesus. I am a servant of GOD, i want to appreciate you for all you are doing toward serving God, we had a two hours meeting last week about one of our Brother whom he is resting now in HEAVEN Bro. Richard, Richard had a Vision to support pastor Eric and they were close friends, he had placed request

of US$50,000 toward supporting Pastor Eric but we got the money later after when God called him back. We contacted Pastor Eric few days back about the progress and how Richard requested us to support his work. He turned us down by refusing the offer, since this collection was made for his ministry, can we wire this found to your count then you forward to him? Richard had left your contact with us and said you are directly supporting him but you with the work he is doing.

Thanks get back to me.
Your
Joshua Brian Okio

So here is a scripture to end this sad season. I have said all that needs to be said.

> Php 2:12 Wherefore, my beloved, as ye have always obeyed, not as in my presence only, but now much more in my absence, work out your own salvation with fear and trembling.

And just one more email to show that the devil never gives up.

From: Osoco Emanuel
To: Eric Okello
Cc: Peter McMaster
Sent: Friday, 26 September 2014 6:55 PM
Subject: Pastor, praise God

Praise God pastor Eric and Fisherman; I great you in the name of our Lord Jesus, how is the work? Pastor we want to have a good partnership with you in reaching souls! We can support you financially; our vision is to reach out souls. We are willing to offer you free Air Ticket. One of the great man of God in Uganda prophet Kakande recommended you to us. We tried to get you on phone and vain. Can you come to Kampala and we arrange! We need to serve our master together. We shall support you to build churches and supporting you financially with monthly salary.

If you get this message, reply to us, not sure if you getting our messages.

God bless you man of God.
Yours
Emanuel

CHAPTER TWENTY FIVE
RELIVING THE FUN

We were back in Pyengana again. The second trip was over. And we were happy to be home, in the comfort of our own house. We were wondering what the Lord had for us next, or what the next season was He wanted us to walk in.

There was no glory for what we did in Africa. Nobody knew what had happened over there apart from the people on my email list. And they could only read words of a page. And there was no crowd to welcome us home. Which back then was a little disappointing to me, that they couldn't share the excitement of what we saw and experienced.

> Luk 17:10 So likewise ye, when ye shall have done all those things which are commanded you, say, We are unprofitable servants: we have done that which was our duty to do.

But now as I'm writing these words I know why. God had to get us out of the mindset of the world, and even the church. Where it seemed their desire was big groups of followers, and workers, and systems, and religious tradition; all working to a common goal. But if that goal is useless and worldly, then what is the point. All the world is marching to Hell gladly; and with some speed on that. The majority is rarely right it seems even in Christianity, and God just needs willing workers to do his will. And hopefully we did it. It felt like to us that we were exactly where we were meant to be, with no doubts. And we had done the Will of God the best we knew how.

> Psa 127:1 Except the LORD build the house, they labour in vain that build it: except the LORD keep the city, the watchman waketh *but* in vain.

And it wasn't just about doing things for God. We can do all sorts of striving and running ahead and prancing around like we are something bigger than we are, and I had done all that don't worry. But it was to receive also. And we received so much.

God did honour us and taught us so much. He gave us more wisdom and understanding and knowledge and grace and favour. If you pray for those things for the building of the Kingdom of God, then He will supply. And He will send you to work. Even when you least expect it.

> Joh 12:26 If any man serve me, let him follow me; and where I am, there shall also my servant be: if any man serve me, him will *my* Father honour.

If you desire to know God, then He will let you find Him. The path of least resistance in the Kingdom of God is the path of the lukewarm and lazy. The sleepy and the slothful never receive the things of God, because they are not looking. We must be on the search constantly with our eyes open, because He is all around us. And when you begin to realize this, things start to move in a hurry.

> Jer 29:13 And ye shall seek me, and find me, when ye shall search for me with all your heart.

He loves to hide things from us, but to those who are willing to search, He does reveal them. The more we put into it the more we get out of it. Jesus gave us His all, and what will we give in return.

> Pro 25:2 *It is* the glory of God to conceal a thing: but the honour of kings *is* to search out a matter.

God is so willing to bless and to equip those who are wanting. And we were so very much more equipped now from our trip to Africa. But I needed more time in the wilderness to let my soul merge into the Spirit of God, which was a burning fire within me now. It was full of Light and Life and on the next level already waiting, but I was lagging behind.

We had been praying at five am every morning for the hour. When Africans pray, a lot of times they all pray together at the same time. There is nobody leading or people waiting for a turn. There was nobody being greedy for the occasion and praying the long prayers of the Pharisees, looking for the praise of men. It was a time for every single person to put their petition towards God.

Man can ask for us what we need, and although there were targets set to pray for, all asked what they thought was needed. And when agreement was reached in the Spirit, the answers would come. And it was amazing how when the target was hit, then all knew it. The intensity would slow down, even in a few seconds, and then they moved on to the next target.

> Mat 18:19 Again I say unto you, That if two of you shall agree on earth as touching any thing that they shall ask, it shall be done for them of my Father which is in heaven.

So instead of one asking and all agreeing, there are five, ten, twenty, etc, asking at once. And where their prayers agree, and cross over each other on their way to the Throne, God has a lot to work with.

You could hear the ones just learning to pray copying off the elders, and the elders and leaders praying like they were on a desert island, away from everyone, totally oblivious to anything. Stuck in the moment and hitting all targets hard. This is what we both needed, to learn to pray like an African; to make the fire burn in and around us and get the enemy on the run. To be the head, not the tail, to be above and not beneath, smash down strongholds and believe that our words are like swords, and hammers, and can obliterate serpents and scorpions and all that the enemy has.

But also to bring the Resurrection Life, and Abundant Life, into our own little worlds for a start, but then let our faith grow like a tree and start to fight for others also. All by faith, whether in the invisible realms, or right under our noses, where there had been plenty of action this time, way back in North Uganda.

Eric had the meetings in his house where there would be a few come. And they all were struggling. Reima and her sister attended them. They were the Daughters of a Muslim man. He had 27 children. And it seemed that all of them hated him. Reima had just chosen to become a believer a week ago. But she wouldn't renounce Islam. So that didn't matter we thought, give her time. Islam was only a traditional thing mostly in Uganda, with the children just believing to please the parents. And she came in to the meeting one day and sat down.

Poss spoke on being a gentle and caring woman and this convicted Reima who then told us what had just happened the night before. This was amazing. She had got the desire to stab her father to death, so she picked up the knife to do it, but her feet froze and she couldn't move. Down went the knife and her feet became normal again. A few minutes later the desire returned, and so did the frozen feet, straight after the knife was picked up. And it was repeated once more, when she had the desire to stab the nephew for some reason, but she was frozen in the feet again. So the father and the nephew were none the wiser.

I thought "Fair Dinkum, is this harmless looking girl, a lunatic or what"? She was only about 18 or 19 years old. The entire related story was given through a translator, so it was hard to get to know some people, because you were mostly just getting the basic message, and it was hard to get the personalities and character of somebody straight away. I thought she's either crazy or a demon. And I had done deliverance before, a few times, but I was far from expert. And the last crusade, I think God did all that. We just showed up.

This time there was a murdering spirit in this young girl, who was skinny but tall for a Ugandan, being about 5 ft. 10 inches or so. So we laid hands on her and began to pray. Within a minute or two we were chasing her around the couch, me and Eric's wife and some of her friends and stopping her from escaping out the door, which was hastily locked. And it was on for young and old.

I was thinking "Eric mate, where are you when we need you"? He was the expert, not me. I'm only the beginner. I had a head full of teachings but very little experience on demons that would run around and curse and kick and whatever else they could do. And with all the other girls all screaming at this thing in their language saying who knows what, it was madness.

I got the thing down and everyone grabbed a limb or whatever they could grab and we began to cast it out. But some were kicked off and shrugged off and when we thought it had calmed down it would make a bolt for the door. We were just doing our best to hold it for a long time. The whole circus lasted about an hour and a half. But as we were wearing down also, something had to be done. I told Eric's wife Jackie to ask its name. And it gave a name. Reima's sister was there and told us it was the name of a relation of Reima's Father.

And all the girls were puzzled and looking at each other, while trying not to be smashed in the body or head by any wayward kicks or punches that we were all trying our best to not let happen. I also had my Bible and noticed that when we placed the KJV Bible on Reima, the demons would really scream, LOUD. If we were in suburbia in Oz, the cops would be on the doorstep. But in Uganda, it was different.

I told Jackie to ask what it was doing and it said this, too much amazement of all in the room. "I was sent by …….. (Reima's Aunty) through a witchdoctor, to enter into Reima and have her kill her father". So I thought "Wow, what a tactic, get the Niece to be possessed and do the dirty work of the Auntie, who gets off free, while Reima will be doing the time for her".

CHAPTER TWENTY FIVE: RELIVING THE FUN

So we knew it was a curse and broke it. Then called it out by the name it gave us, after lots of abuse and all sorts of things were hurled at it and screamed at it in the name of Jesus. The other women were all having a go at this thing. And then it left. And Reima was OK then. She had no idea what had happened, and was very tired. She did come to the meeting in a couple more days and she was covered in bruises. She had been amazed at the story her friends relayed to her.

But she would not give up Islam. Which I have learnt since that those spirits are so hateful to the word of God. The Bible will actually burn them and also heavy Witchcraft spirits when placed on the person.

I knew that it was no good wrestling demons in people like those people were fighting back. I had to learn how to hold them in the spirit, better than I knew at that time. I had heard of binding and loosing, but never really understood it. But I would learn eventually.

Next was Doreen. She came to the meeting and looked a wreck. Although not a bad looking girl, her countenance was very dark. She needed the darkness gone and she knew it to. Eric was there this time, which pleased me. After last time, I wasn't looking for more excitement than I could handle.

He asked her what the problem was and Doreen and her friend who was adding bits and pieces to the story told him that she was living with a man and couldn't get pregnant. So he blamed her and kicked her out of their hut. So she was angry and went to a bad man who was with Kony for a bit and got pregnant. Then told the man it was him that was a loser or whatever. No doubt a lot of crap went on between them.

Anyway he didn't want her back so she waited until he was in the mud brick hut and she locked the door and lit the grass roof on fire and walked away, not knowing if he got out or not. Or that's what she told us that at least.

So we prayed. And the demon was a little bit longer to get wound up but after a few minutes they were off and racing. We held her down and cast a few out. And sometimes she was raging and sometimes a bit more subdued. But Eric found that she wouldn't forgive, so he had to lead her in a prayer for that.

Also religious spirits were coming up and crossing themselves like Catholics do, as if to draw more power to themselves. And I believe that's exactly what they were doing, because Doreen remembered nothing of this all.

Slithering like a snake and screaming every now and then, it was the sort of show that you would expect in deliverance. In Africa this was the case anyway. Everyone here had been involved in witchcraft and the doors were open in many for their entrance. So the manifestations were varied and violent at times.

But Doreen when she came back to the surface after the demons left wouldn't renounce Catholicism. They are told it's an advantage in life when it is a snare and chains up many in religion. And even when she was being told about how these spirits were manifesting, it didn't matter. She got angry and wouldn't budge. The same as people do here in the west.

Even through those fights that were anything but under control, or so it looked, I learned so much. I had come to know a little of what I had and also what I hadn't, which was a lot better place to be than where I was before. A place where I was beginning to learn the authority I had been given, the very minute I was born again.

And there were others we prayed for, some violent, some not so violent, just thrashing around on the floor screaming like they were being stabbed with red hot pokers or something. Or that's a comparison that I just come up with, because that's how it was.

There were a couple of young boys that were there at one of the deliverances. One was Eric's son and the other his friend who was an orphan, staying with Eric's family. They both dived on a woman who was violently manifesting, and these boys were only small. Innocent was his name and Innocent ended up flying backwards towards the big old couch in the middle of the lounge room where all this was happening, about two good meters from the action, and was a bit wary to return into the affray. These boys as well as the younger ones at times would get up in the early morning, every morning except Sundays to pray for the hour. I suppose they wanted in on the fun bits too.

And all the while a five year old and a six year old were walking around and watching the show, not worrying too much, while Jackie would be breast feeding the baby on the couch and some others cooking in the kitchen.

What the west would consider being like a terrifying horror movie any day of the week, Eric's house hold just took it as Christianity. And Jesus was setting the captives free. Even Poss was starting to get used to it, although it wasn't in her nature to get involved in any world championship wrestling matches with demons from the pits of Hell. But I loved it!

Harmless ladies? No way!!!

CHAPTER TWENTY SIX
TASSIE LIFE GOES ON

It was half way through 2013 and trying to fit back into what would never be called a normal life again. I had seen some real battles in Africa and learned how to pray and was keen to cast out some demons wherever I could find them. There was no voice of doubt anymore when I laid hands on the sick. My faith was high and I was almost at the place where I expected things to happen. Not that it did every time, but I wasn't easily discouraged anymore.

Life slowed down in the sleepy town of Pyengana. We slipped into the country pace, on the outside at least. But I was still praying for an hour a day, reading my Bible and listening to all I could on Spiritual Warfare. I wanted that next level badly. And so did the Lord Jesus Christ. With him sowing into my mind a 40 day fast, and I was not against it.

Even though I'd already done one, I desired to have a bit better attempt with persistent Bible readings and more prayer. So I started after about a month of having the desire. And it was easier this time than the other. I knew what it was about, and while I wasn't praying to get, I was expectant.

I did want to get the darkness out and crucify the flesh, and from what I saw with Eric, who had paid a high price, I knew there was a lot more to come. I wanted whatever Jesus had died for me to have, with many promises quickened to me through the word. Promises that were so big that I thought I was so full of myself to even think that they were for me, but with the right qualities, which were nothing of excellence in me, I knew it could happen.

I'd seen in the Word the ones God had chosen, and I knew He had chosen me for something. That was in my heart, and nothing could take it from me. I was at the point where I was beginning to believe. So the 40 day fast was into the eighth day. And a man I had played football with offered me a painting job. I had done painting in the past and he knew this. But when I said I can't do it he said "Why" and I said, "I've got something else on the go". And that was the 40 day fast. I can remember this clearly now because I thought "The devils in early here after only eight days." And that encouraged me. I was going to make it no matter what.

On the 15th day and I was offered a job that wasn't too bad. It was from a local and he wanted to know why I didn't want it. I didn't know what to say and didn't want to tell a lie so I said, "I'm fasting and I haven't eaten for 15 days" and he replied, "It's a wonder you can even stand up" and I just said "Nahh, it's not that bad". So the Deceiver tried twice in a week and failed.

Every day you know exactly how long you have been going and for how many hours. It is easy to count time down. I was even enjoying weeding my garden to pass the time on my hands and knees. And I was praying more and trying to read and listen to my favourite audio show, Omegaman radio. It was where all the best deliverance ministers on the planet were interviewed and preaching and they were casting demons out over the phone. I loved this and would learn every tactic and strategy to dig them out and put them away.

At about 20 days into the fast I started hearing the word Hobart. And it seemed for the next week that it was getting louder. It became so obvious that I said "Righto God, I'll go to Hobart. I finished the fast and felt really good. I lost over 25 kgs and got down to a weight I was when I went on the scales at Collingwood at 15 years of age. I was 88 kgs again and I felt like a young bloke. So I started exercising and running and weight training again.

I knew some people who were running a halfway house down near Hobart and they said I could go down and help. But it ended when they realised I had too many prior convictions to be able to go into the jail to interview those who were looking for a place to stay. So after 3 months I went back to Pyengana. This felt right anyway.

But I did get a taste of things with some good fellowship and a few people to experiment with in deliverance, and I was seeing results. We need to exercise our faith by doing the works, and I had teamed up at times with a man who was keen to learn all he could. It was fun praying with him, most of the time.

Once he prayed for a young woman who was very troubled that he met here in a church and thought she needed some prayer. And the demons went off and he couldn't control them. Poss and I were just driving down to Hobart and he rang me and said, "Where are you, there's a demon going off here and I need some backup" all the while, the demon screaming in the background.

So in about half an hour we pulled up over the road and about 50 meters up the street where the parking was ok, got out of the car and could hear the screaming. I thought, "Wow, it's a wonder the cops aren't here".

We walked in and here's Alan, I'll call him, with the younger woman and a friend of his trying to hold her on the couch. She was cursing and screaming and trying to bite and bashing her head on the floor and kneeing herself in the head and the man who was helping hold her had never seen anything like this in his life. And I'm not sure if Alan had either.

Alan said when I walked in, "You're in trouble now demon the backups arrived". I thought "Yeah, I hope you're right Alan". So it was on, trying to cast out the demon. It would come up for ten or twenty minutes then go down, and all would be well. They weren't coming out though.

Every time the demon would go down the girl, (we'll call her Ellie), would go straight to the cask of wine and take a big swig and then talk for a bit. But she didn't want to be a Christian. She didn't want to repent or do what was required to weaken the hold they had on her. And when we would start to pray again the demon would be off and out of control. It seemed that nothing we did worked.

By now Alan had rang an old Pastor who came to look but he couldn't help either. And then the cops showed up, which was only a matter of time. With the demon screaming so loud, we were wondering what took them so long.

But when they walked in the door there were about six people there then. And Ellie was having one of her quiet times. The demon was subdued, but still lurking down low, and not happy. The cops charged in, obviously because somebody must have thought someone was being murdered and all were in peace.

Ellie was standing there with a glass of fruity lexia or some poison like that. And they questioned her and went. And the old Elder statesman was there to explain that "All was OK, the young girl has some problems and we are just helping". This happened twice more in the next hour or two.

CHAPTER TWENTY SIX: TASSIE LIFE GOES ON

Just before they would walk in, the demon would go down, and whatever the outside world thought was happening in that small one bedroom unit, seemed to be a false alarm. Then the cops sat up the road for a bit and finally left.

We must have worn the demon out enough for a longer rest in the middle of it all. But when it did surface, it was so violent. The Old Pastors son showed up who was a hard man. He had been inside jail, and a fighter and no fear of anything. But when the demon in Ellie went off and he was trying to hold her, he was hiding behind a cushion on the couch trying to protect himself and knowing that what he was wrestling with was not the girl he knew.

The demon was speaking to us all, cursing and trying all the tricks to lead us off the path, pleading to the women there to help, but all the while with a sly grin of a liar that was not very smart was upon its face. And it was playing every game in the book.

Finally it was quiet and we left to go the 40 minutes to where we were staying. The Pastors son was a friend of this girl and offered to sit around and watch her for a bit. He rang after a couple of hours and said "Can you come quickly; this thing is on the loose again". He was a backslidden Christian but after watching this, he did want to know more about what was happening and how these things operate.

One thing about deliverance, when you see it and a different entity controlling the person, all of a sudden the world becomes a different place. And if the demons are telling you things that no-one else knows then that can be very spooky. Along with all the threats of death and destruction they spew out. But the devil is a liar.

So Poss and I went back in and Ellie was being held in a fashion on the couch. And she started screaming again at about one thirty in the morning. So the old mate who was holding her was on a good behaviour bond and was worried if the cops come in and see this then they would lock him up for sure. But he didn't want to leave her like this.

So I grabbed a pillow and put it over her mouth to muffle the screams. In Uganda it didn't matter how loud the screams were. If you said to anyone it's a demon, they understood. But here was different, so very different. The demon used a tactic that I thought was very clever to get rid of me.

It went down in the fight and when Ellie came up she thought I was trying to smother her. For this I couldn't blame her. And then she was going to call the cops. So the old mate with the cushion that was stopping the demon from head butting him had to explain this to her. The devil is a nasty fighter. So we left late in the night and we were worried about Ellie for a while.

Poss and I went back to Pyengana and I came back to Hobart a few days later after a three day fast. We had a lot of ripe raspberries so Poss packed some and I was going to give them to Ellie on the way through town. I called in and her boyfriend was there. He had heard what had happened. And I said it was the demons.

He didn't believe in demons so I said, "Check this out mate, this is us in Africa, casting demons out". I'd got a few short videos of what was happening at Eric's place, and he could see the comparison. And then I did something stupid. Ellie walked over and said, "Give me a look" as she was wondering what the screaming was on my phone. And stupid Pete showed her. "Oh Nooo…….." I thought as the demon manifested immediately. "Oh God, Noooo….not again" I thought, if not said out loud.

The boyfriend and I picked her writhing body up off the floor and put her on the couch and had some restraint upon her. She was a petit little thing, but the last session two large men were struggling to hold her and three could manage a little easier, but with an effort, that's for sure. Praise God, I had listened to a teaching by a man called Jozef Jazinski only a few days earlier. He was a deliverance minister who was a big one of my favourites. He had just given a talk on Binding and Loosing.

> Mat 16:19 And I will give unto thee the keys of the kingdom of heaven: and whatsoever thou shalt bind on earth shall be bound in heaven: and whatsoever thou shalt loose on earth shall be loosed in heaven.

"What you bind on earth will be bound in Heaven" he said. I wasn't trying to jump ahead into loosing anything yet, that was still a bit complicated for me. I still had to sort this binding thing out.

With me in my life, I had been gullible at times and getting led astray and believing stuff I should not have believed and being deceived and deluded in the past. But it did seem that with the same belief, or faith that I had to swallow a camel, I could take the Word of God and believe it, a lot of times without question. This was a gift or talent or whatever you want to call it that I had. I would receive by faith. And it was easy. And with all the Word I had read, if three times the New

Testament and once the Old Testament every year, I would have been up to around 40 times New Testament and 13 or so the Old.

But that formula, while I still kept it, was beginning to be all over the place and now I would just read where led. And sometimes just opening the book would set me off or I could hear scripture references or words from scripture to direct me. The book is alive, as is the Author.

So Jozef had said that when we bind something, an Angel can come and wrap it in chains. Chains were mentioned in the Bible as chaining up demons so I thought, "Fair enough". No question needed. Here it is in the Word, and if Peter knew about this and Jude, the Lords half-brother, then why not.

> 2Pe 2:4 For if God spared not the angels that sinned, but cast them down to hell, and delivered them into chains of darkness, to be reserved unto judgement;

> Jud 1:6 And the angels which kept not their first estate, but left their own habitation, he hath reserved in everlasting chains under darkness unto the judgement of the great day.

I could see that these chains were pretty good thing to believe in.

> Rev 20:1-2 And I saw an angel come down from heaven, having the key of the bottomless pit and a great chain in his hand.

> And he laid hold on the dragon, that old serpent, which is the devil, and Satan, and bound him a thousand years,

Jozef also mentioned that the chains will last as long as your faith will allow. It could be for minutes, to weeks or more. So I was armed with some knowledge that I was busting to test out.

Then Omegaman the radio host asked Jozef a question. "What if we bind and they don't get bound?" That had happened to me too. Jozef had the answer. He said "If the devil is testing you out and trying to steal your faith and making something that is not that big in front of you look so huge that you just get discouraged and give up, he will do this. He will line up spirits on the surface and when you bind one or cast one out the next one will surface and pretend that it is the same demon, and tell you the same, so as to make you think that you are failing, and give up and run away with your tail between your legs."

Anyway that's the sort of thing I heard. Because I had been there a few times now. He continued, "So when you bind the demon, say, I bind you also, and you and you too, until they stop." And I was thinking "This bloke is such a mighty man, how long would it have taken him to work this one out". He made it sound like it was almost like common sense, and I took it as such. Then in a few days I got to test it out. Isn't that an amazing coincidence? Nope! That's God.

So I said to the demon, "I rebuke you and I bind you, and you and you and you and you." I was picturing five of them lining up. Immediately the demon went down, or away or was bound and gagged or whatever happened to them, and I was thinking "Wow it worked" but still not expecting miracles.

Then I started to say "Ellie, come up, come up Ellie, come up", and she came up. All this happened in about a minute and a half. Not the tens and twenty minute bursts of insanity that we had gone through a week or so ago. She came up and was looking around and wondering what was going on, but seemed fine.

So within another minute, I said to the boyfriend, pointing at the raspberries, "give her some of them when she comes around properly" as he was still amazed at what he had seen happen with the demons getting bound and then the calling of his girlfriend back up from being unconscious to awake.

But what was going on in my head was, "Quick, get out of here now while those things are bound before you stir em up again." So Pete, the big bad demon slayer, although gaining a quick victory, still bolted with the tail between the legs. And got while the gettin was good!!!

Also I did know that there is abundant more spiritual strength with a three day fast. So that combined also with the tactic of Jozef of the binding, it was a great display of control over the enemy, even if just for myself. I was pleased to see it, that's for sure.

We never heard about Ellie again and hope she's OK. Without repentance there is no freedom.

CHAPTER TWENTY SEVEN
ANOTHER FIGHT TO PICK

We were back at Pyengana for 12 months in 2014, waiting for a direction from God to move to Hobart. But there was another fight that He had planned for me and this time I wasn't too fearful of it. I knew that it would be exciting at times and at others draining and other times the roller coaster would show up and I'd be seated right up the front. But I had been battle hardened by now more than anyone I knew personally, in Australia at least, and was confident that God could deliver me, no matter what was coming against me. And every battle had an end and a purpose.

> 2Co 4:16-17 For which cause we faint not; but though our outward man perish, yet the inward *man* is renewed day by day.
>
> For our light affliction, which is but for a moment, worketh for us a far more exceeding *and* eternal weight of glory;

I had an understanding of what peace fasting could give and the strength and power it brought also and the warfare I could pray was enough to get most things on the run quickly. I had got the nod to uncover the darkness that I had seen in Africa, not to mention here in the western world where this deception was spreading also. And I was keen to get moving with it.

I rounded up all the emails that you read in some previous chapters and put them on my website. I also made some videos of what I had filmed in Uganda and from other sources as well. And of course it never went down too well with some of the millions of followers of T.B Joshua.

I had a fairly good idea of what would happen and I was right. The curses started coming. No doubt straight from the source and straight from the followers, who thought it OK to curse me in their comments on YouTube and by email straight out. But I wasn't in fear this time around, it was a simple task of just breaking the curses in the name of Jesus, or a lot of them anyway. Most never had much behind them, but that wasn't the case for all of them.

There were lots of people wanting Eric's phone number, email and address and it got to the point where I couldn't trust anyone. I had to pray and ask God to show me who was who. And He did, and still is. I need this so much now still. The devil is a serious foe.

There were all sorts of new devils in my dreams and lots of fighting with Africans and Whites trying to spear me and stick pointy things into me and throw things and feed me stuff like nasty meat and all sorts. And also animals and demons trying to rip, tear and devour me however they were assigned to do and with whatever they were equipped to do it with. But God never let me fall once. I knew how to pray them away and they rarely came back twice in a row. It was rare actually to see the same spirit or person twice. Never three times. I don't think they were that stupid.

Sometimes they would get through and I would wear one or two and I would have to get out of bed and pray for a few minutes or so until I felt the peace return. Or nullify the hit on me until something came out in coughing that had landed in me and needed to be expelled like that. Once it took me an hour in the morning to get something off me. As I had to go to work, I was praying under my breath in the milking shed for half of that hour before it left. It was some sort of fear thing and it was a little difficult to shake.

If you don't feel right in anything, treat it as a demon, or a curse, which are assigned demons. Again the results will surprise you. I saw scorpions as big as dogs standing in front of me, spraying stuff out their tails at me and huge meter long spider legs trying to come through my window at night. I never told Poss a lot of these things but she is in a place now where it won't bother her, especially after what we saw happen with the massive war we have just came through lately. But I'll get to that.

Plus there were still lots of uncovering of the things that the Lord was wanting me to deal with in myself. I knew I had to clean my act up to as quickly as possible, or I would be minced meat for a demons dinner. All the time I was pushing to be more obedient and turning away from fleshy chains that still surrounded me at times and that was a fierce battle also. But I knew the power of repentance and trusted in the Blood of Jesus Christ.

> 1Jn 1:9 If we confess our sins, he is faithful and just to forgive us *our* sins, and to cleanse us from all unrighteousness.

It was on for young and old some nights, and to be praying at least an hour a day was a necessity that I had worked into my walk with the Lord Jesus Christ that was not too hard to do now, but so essential now to my survival. Not that I could keep that religiously. Sometimes it couldn't be done if we were travelling, but whenever I got an opportunity, I treated them like Gold.

I said before, new levels, new devils, and these ones weren't happy. But I was happy that they weren't happy. I felt like I was playing a part of the plan of God, and was sort of becoming used to the solitude of the work. Poss was always there to encourage and to put me in my place if my head swelled, and again I am very grateful to God for her.

The demons came again to hold me in my bed but they didn't scare me at all now. The night terrors were not that terrifying any more. I did wonder though how they were getting in because I knew my defences were up and there was fire around always with the prayer and the KJV audio Bible playing most nights all night. But I figured this is one way that God used to keep me on my toes.

Because I did in the past not like to overdo things, and would just get to a certain level then put myself in cruise mode. And I was continually asking God to not let me be comfortable there ever. So He didn't I believe, and still hasn't.

I was of the thought that only the most powerful of the Witchdoctors and satanists could astral project from Africa to Tasmania and still cause trouble so that helped me believe that I was not going to get overwhelmed. And I wasn't. Because from the crap getting hurled at me on the internet, there was a multitude that hated me.

Pity I couldn't say that about being overwhelmed when I uncovered the hornets' nest that is in Tasmania itself. They were right on the doorstep constantly for months. In the spirit at least but I'll get into that later. And no doubt a part of the trouble I had been copping for years.

There were still many fasts done to break sticky oppression and it worked well, and some longer ones in between. A twenty one dayer would keep the devil from the door for a much longer time than just a three dayer.

And this little battle with the underwater men went on for six months or more but was slowing down a bit. I had been breaking all witchcraft curses and sending them back to the senders, to reveal to them that they should not be cursing believers. And because I never knew who these people were, I didn't do this in a very vindictive way. I knew it wasn't personal so I was never against the people, most of the time.

But sometimes I would pray that the curses would be sent back to the demonic instigators that were using the deceived people to send them. And I knew it would filter through the whole group.

I had this dream once that showed me this. I had been going through a few weeks of oppression. Not too bad but just a constant heaviness that was not normal and I couldn't shift it. I can't think now of what prompted me to pray like this on this certain day? I probably copped some spears and arrows in a dream and was just going to return them.

I started praying, "I break all witchcraft curses coming against me in the name of Jesus Christ and I return them seven fold back to the sender". It was according to these scriptures and it wasn't personal but it was serious. I knew they hated me because they hated the Lord Jesus Christ, and I was a servant of His.

> Gal 6:7 Be not deceived; God is not mocked: for whatsoever a man soweth, that shall he also reap.

> Psa 79:12 And render unto our neighbours sevenfold into their bosom their reproach, wherewith they have reproached thee, O Lord.

I was in the lounge room throwing back invisible spears in real life, acting it out prophetically, and with a strong desire to break the powers down that were now harassing me, and the Name of Jesus Christ was behind the power returning the spears of course. And I already knew that prophetic actions in the natural can move into the spiritual. Like the leaping for joy and brushing dust off the feet.

And before I was saved I was playing with invisible swords and could see their purple slashes cutting across the darkness of my closed eyes when doing the stupid rituals or whatever they were, without any idea or knowledge or foundation under my feet.

So when I saw this scripture below, which I had read many times, and there were others in the Word too like this, then I had no question of the effect of this action I had undertaken this day. I had no doubt. My God is a God of War. And we operate in faith.

CHAPTER TWENTY SEVEN: ANOTHER FIGHT TO PICK

> 2Ki 13:15-19 And Elisha said unto him, Take bow and arrows. And he took unto him bow and arrows.
>
> And he said to the king of Israel, Put thine hand upon the bow. And he put his hand *upon it:* and Elisha put his hands upon the king's hands.
>
> And he said, Open the window eastward. And he opened *it.* Then Elisha said, Shoot. And he shot. And he said, The arrow of the LORD'S deliverance, and the arrow of deliverance from Syria: for thou shalt smite the Syrians in Aphek, till thou have consumed *them.*
>
> And he said, Take the arrows. And he took *them.* And he said unto the king of Israel, Smite upon the ground. And he smote thrice, and stayed.
>
> And the man of God was wroth with him, and said, Thou shouldest have smitten five or six times; then hadst thou smitten Syria till thou hadst consumed *it:* whereas now thou shalt smite Syria *but* thrice.

So I did this in my daily warfare prayers against a foe whom I knew not but had an idea of where they were coming from and that was Africa. Apart from the Rosicrucian witches that would show up now and again and others I had upset it was sometimes hectic but a lot of quiet times as well.

I prayed that the devils workers own spears would return and go through their own necks. According to this word I had read. Reading the Bible is very dangerous to the devil and his demons. No wonder he stops most Christians from doing it. And he works very hard to steal the faith from those who do.

> 2Sa 22:38-41 I have pursued mine enemies, and destroyed them; and turned not again until I had consumed them.
>
> And I have consumed them, and wounded them, that they could not arise: yea, they are fallen under my feet.
>
> For thou hast girded me with strength to battle: them that rose up against me hast thou subdued under me.
>
> Thou hast also given me the necks of mine enemies, that I might destroy them that hate me.

I also read through Psalm 35 aloud and for half an hour or so, then that night I went to bed and had this dream.

I was standing behind a large tree just a little wider than myself, and I was too scared to move because I looked around it and these dark men, not dark in skin but it was like they were shadow men. They were black figures, who were shaped like people and moved like people. And they were throwing spears every few seconds at the tree and hitting it very hard that I could hear the "THUD, THUD, THUD. And they were hitting their target from about 20 meters away almost every time.

I was hiding behind the tree too scared to move and I was thinking, "If I try to get away from here, they'll nail me for sure". So I couldn't move. Then all of a sudden the "THUD, THUD" stopped. And the men started to walk not straight towards me but on an angle where they stayed the same distance away. There was a tall skinny man and a short fat man. I saw some of the spears lying at the base of the tree I was sheltered behind and ran and grabbed a handful. About seven of them I could see.

I threw them as hard as I could in one handful and one spear went straight through the neck of the tall skinny devil or demon or the Avatar of the witch behind it or whatever they were. And he just fell straight onto his face. And I thought, "Beautiful shot, that'll teach em". Then a loud voice spoke and it said, "You've just killed a Prince." And I woke up and thought "Wow, a Prince hey. I must've given those spears a fair throw with some spiritual weight behind them. That should stuff up the plans of the enemy for a bit then."

I knew it could have been a principality that was taken down and I was pleased. They are the highest of the hierarchy of demonic spirits with many under their control. Then the oppression I was under was gone and all was good for a bit. I did wonder if I actually killed it or it was the plans and purposes that were killed. I was hoping for both.

> Eph 6:12 For we wrestle not against flesh and blood, but against principalities, against powers, against the rulers of the darkness of this world, against spiritual wickedness in high *places.*

So with victories like this I was gaining confidence in the warfare prayers I was praying and I was beginning to understand how God could use His people to break the strongholds not only in ourselves and for others also but in all sorts of places and in and over all sorts of areas, if we were led to pray by Him and He was in those prayers. I'd already seen how the young nobody in the world called Eric had made a mess of the underwater kingdom single handed. I do know that many in Africa are praying against these imposters also, so am pleased that the Lord Jesus was happy to reveal these hidden things to me and that God was encouraging me and making me set my sites a bit higher than the standard aim of western Christianity.

And from knowing the Word, I knew that all the trials and tribulations I was going through was for my benefit and for the benefit eventually of so many that were tormented and struggling. Or that was my heart's desire. To bring as many into the Kingdom of God as I could and help them to also believe. Knowing the Word did help me cope with a lot, but some things were painful and frustrating.

Especially watching people who the Holy Ghost was leading into the wilderness away from structures and traditions of men, for their learning and to gain strength, just as I had received going through it, but they never had the strength to stay. And so become fearful and discouraged and lazy and crawl right back onto the pew that chains them back down in the systems and crushes all life out of them.

Right back to where the devil wants them. The breakthrough was in their grasp and they melted. But many do not even come this far and are unaware of any Abundant Life outside the box.

> 2Ki 19:3 And they said unto him, Thus saith Hezekiah, This day *is* a day of trouble, and of rebuke, and blasphemy: for the children are come to the birth, and *there is* not strength to bring forth.

And the opportunity is missed. And mostly from what I have seen, never returns. What a downer! Even now as I write it makes me heavy.

CHAPTER TWENTY EIGHT
42 DEGREES SOUTH

Poss and I had decided to go to Hobart. It was the beginning of January 2015. The pull in my spirit was far too strong now to stay in the quiet country town, so we decided to rent a unit and move down. And see what happened. Not being one to procrastinate in the things of God, and not knowing how many days were in front of me, I didn't want to waste any time. And it was time for a new season.

I was praying to God about what were we going to do and got this Word for Hobart. Notice the scripture reference. Hobart is 42 degrees south of the Equator and it was the beginning of 2015 that we were venturing down.

> Isa 42:15-16 I will make waste mountains and hills, and dry up all their herbs; and I will make the rivers islands, and I will dry up the pools.
>
> And I will bring the blind by a way *that* they knew not; I will lead them in paths *that* they have not known: I will make darkness light before them, and crooked things straight. These things will I do unto them, and not forsake them

I was thinking that this meant God will straighten out the religious systems in Hobart and bring change. I wasn't sure how but was looking forward to it. I was wondering if it involved me or not. But I was thinking most likely it did somehow, if He had given me the Word.

> Amo 3:7 Surely the Lord GOD will do nothing, but he revealeth his secret unto his servants the prophets.

Now I'm not saying that I'm a Prophet. God does speak in parables to me a lot and sometimes straight forward, but I believe this is normal in a relationship for His servants to receive. I think if I was a Prophet then things He tells me would not be so cryptic at times. I do know a less

CHAPTER TWENTY EIGHT: 42 DEGREES SOUTH

than a handful of people with a real prophetic gift, and I do not have that.

On the drive down to Hobart on the first day we were moving, the man called William Lau from USA who gave me the training of the Elijah Challenge, who trains believers how to command healing to the sick; that I had found invaluable in Uganda when we went, rang me and asked if he could bring his teaching and if we could host. He had a week off in September in between conferences and would be in Australia doing nothing for that week. And because I had shared with him what happened in Otwal crusade a few years back, I suppose he thought I may know people who would want the training that I found to be so good.

But I never knew anyone much in Hobart and I told him this. But I said that I would look and try and round some people up to do it. It was very early January and the training was going to be in September. So I though surely this is too good to miss so I said yes with the Isa 42 word in my mind. And being half way down on the very day we were moving excited me because of the timing.

So we get to Hobart in a one bedroom flat in Lindisfarne. This was it for at least nine months. But we did stay for 12 all up. It was the first night in Hobart I was asking God "What do you want me here for, or what's the plan?" and I had this dream.

I was looking at four or five, I know there was four at least, (so I say four main ones and one not as prominent) swimming pools. Each had a massive crocodile in them. Then the dream went to a lot larger pool like a big 25 metre long Olympic one and a massive crocodile was filling that pool. Then a woman came prancing down beside it dressed in a ballerinas tutu as I was standing there. She jumped onto the gigantic crocodiles head dancing about and went down its back hopping and skipping as if it was nothing and not a care in the world. I couldn't believe it how she was so brave, stupid never came to my mind.

Until she got down it's back a fair way and just kept dancing about, fell off it's back near the back legs of the giant beast and into the water and sunk. I was standing there thinking with a bit of a panic for her "How can I save her, how can I get into the water with that thing and fish her out"?

Then I looked and I was holding a pitchfork. I woke up and knew the interpretation immediately and that God wanted me to remove the beasts with the pitchfork. So I did a lot of warfare and asked God to roll them over so I could get at the soft spots underneath to fish them out and then asked Him to show me what is in the bottom of the pools and the picture came of the pool being dry and a meter deep or so of dead men's bones. The church in this city is filled with Pride/Leviathan and that there are four main culprits and one not quite as bad as the other. But the Strongman over them all is the same.

> Job 41:34 He beholdeth all high *things*: he *is* a king over all the children of pride.

The ballerina was a picture of those who enter and treat things as a big game and party and they are devoured and sunk in the stinking stagnant waters of Leviathans lair. And they don't even know it.

> Jer 5:26-31 For among my people are found wicked *men:* they lay wait, as he that setteth snares; they set a trap, they catch men.
>
> As a cage is full of birds, so *are* their houses full of deceit: therefore they are become great, and waxen rich.
>
> They are waxen fat, they shine: yea, they overpass the deeds of the wicked: they judge not the cause, the cause of the fatherless, yet they prosper; and the right of the needy do they not judge.
>
> Shall I not visit for these *things?* saith the LORD: shall not my soul be avenged on such a nation as this?
>
> A wonderful and horrible thing is committed in the land;
>
> The prophets prophesy falsely, and the priests bear rule by their means; and my people love *to have it* so: and what will ye do in the end thereof?

So within the first two days I had something to pray about, and go through the prophetic motions of pitch forking the giant beasts out of these places called church. I did have a look about some of the places that were meant to be all the go, but found them mainly dead and lifeless, with things built on hype and regurgitated theology that was binding people in chains and brainwashing and mind controlling the masses. These had no different structure and religious process than the smaller groups up in the North East I had attended.

Once I went to a testimony breakfast and a something followed me home after a conversation with a man who was high up. It was a spirit of offense. And it was so sticky. It took me half an hour to get rid of it through warfare. And I found out soon after that the man who I got it off, who used to be a Pastor in this big church, had offended many. But the poor bloke didn't even know he was wearing it, and who knows, maybe didn't care?

I also went to another large church once and the feeling of fornication there was so dirty I wanted to leave even before I sat down. But I sat through it just to see how much worse it could get. Stupid me!!! When men who are put in charge don't do the job or are of a wrong spirit, it filters down throughout everyone who has given him or her right to control them or council them or whatever you want to call it.

I have seen the clones being built and moulded to a desired shape and everyone acts entirely how they are programmed so as to not rock the boat. And every group has their own characteristics, some Godly, some demonic. And the scales tip the wrong way a lot of the time.

> Mic 3:11 The heads thereof judge for reward, and the priests thereof teach for hire, and the prophets thereof divine for money: yet will they lean upon the LORD, and say, *Is* not the LORD among us? none evil can come upon us.

The second night, I decided to pray against Mona, Museum of Old and New Art. All I knew at the time was that they were a perverse group who would put filthy things on display and the place was devoid of all moral standards. And by around two or three in the morning I knew I had hit a big target, and it wasn't very happy with me.

The dream was this. I was standing in a doorway overlooking a neat green lawn about 50 meters to a lake or calm sea. And there was a small boat pull up with two or three men and with them was a big green demon. This demon was so angry and jumped from the small boat and charged at me at full pace. And I'll tell you something, when something is around eight foot tall, they can move along pretty well.

So within seconds it was almost upon me and I looked and I was holding a large kitchen knife. Now the demon was very ugly and had horns and it was a female too. It was the same dirty green colour as the Hulk in the movies. Some may say I have been watching too many movies, and I probably have done that too. But when I warfare now in prayer, like I told you before, I get confirmation of the damage I have done or God gives me the moving images of the targets in full colour a lot of the time.

I did ask an ex High Priestess of the Tasmanian Satanic coven in 2018, that we helped to escape and helped deliver her, which fight is still ongoing, and we are about to get into that bit, what its name was and she said, "Its name is Hagith. It only shows when there was real trouble and things had to be dealt with."

So I was standing there without any fear and watching it bound toward me and the place where the knife had to go for the main damage was right up between its legs. But I couldn't do it. I'm not sure why. As the demon looked a little like a human having one head and two arms and legs, but it was green, eight foot tall, and through the vicious snarl I could see it's pointy teeth showing with which probably was about to take my head off. And very ugly too but I still had too much compassion for this thing to do the job I was meant to. Then right at the last second I woke up.

I did do the prophetic actions of what was needed when I awoke. Maybe God was sparing me the trauma of the sight of close up warfare. I still don't know. That never worried me before. I was disappointed a little knowing that a good blow in the second heaven could have destroyed that thing then and there. I was also wondering why I had compassion for this demon. It could have been because it was a female maybe? Or could it have reminded me of an old girlfriend I once had……..err……, calm down….., that's only a joke people, to lighten up the story. It worked for me anyway!

So Mona was a target then, but I was to find out a few months later how much. There was so much spiritual oppression in Hobart. It was unbelievable really, compared to Pyengana. Which Poss was still travelling back the four hours every week to work her three days in the St Helens Hospital Kitchen.

I had to travel back every fortnight for the three days to escape and get a rest from the weight of whatever it was trying to crush me down in this city. I was doing a three day fast every second weekend while in Hobart just to keep my head above water. It was so intense. I could pray and there would be release but it was like lighting a candle in the darkness and then the candle would burn out and the darkness would descend again. Then the three day fast would restore the candle to give a fortnight light.

I did pick lots of other spiritual fights with my anointing oil and prayer walks. The big Tasman Bridge where many were jumping to their deaths I had seen as a stronghold and so walked across it several times.

CHAPTER TWENTY EIGHT: 42 DEGREES SOUTH

There were some main positions around the city where I was led to go like parliament house and the big roundabout on a major intersection. Also I was going past in a bus and saw a massive snake wrapped around the roof of the Bahai temple. So it needed a bit of anointing oil around it too.

There was also the Dark Mofo festival by the satanists at Mona. They all cram the waterfront and put on their perverse displays they call art, but a lot are to mock the church and are Aleister Crowley rituals. I could see this, having a little understanding of things from the past.

They actually got a very high ranking witch called Marina Abramovic (I never knew how high just yet though) down to Tassie to do some rituals and shedding of blood in Hobart. She had videos of her cutting inverted pentagrams into her stomach with razorblades and all sorts of wicked and perverse things she would do. And this lady was, in the name of art, a main attraction.

There were also a big nude swim on a public beach and the climax was an Ogoh Ogoh. A huge Idol of a demon that everyone would cast their cares upon and write down their worries and stuff and poke it in this beast, then the satanists would parade it down the street and burn it in a ritual. Just to mock this that was done by our Saviour Jesus Christ.

> 1Pe 5:7 Casting all your care upon him; for he careth for you.

Poss at the Ogoh Ogoh

Everything was a blasphemous mockery of His work and meant to be offensive some way to the Christian God. But some on the local council and the politicians may be in on the game, and with financial support there is probably no doubt about it.

So I made a website exposing all this and left it up for 12 months. That may not have helped me with the pressure but I was at war, so whatever came, I would have to deal with.

Airport advertisement for Mona Museum

Flying in and out of the Hobart airport, one could see this advertisement bold and anything, right when you walked in off the plane. It would have been around four meters wide by one and a half high.

I know these are nowhere near as heavy as what is going on in other countries, but this was my home state now and I could see the satanic agenda to knock down righteousness and draw people into a huge snare of enjoying witchcraft. Again I say; Satan is a dirty fighter. And most people in the church had no idea.

So the war went for 12 months. I did venture into the belly of the beast of Mona Museum once with Poss and did a prayer walk through it. It was pretty bad and very dark and twisted. But one consolation was that Tasmanians were allowed in free. So that helped me decide to go and visit and hopefully stir some things up.

The main Hobart museum in the city was not much better. We did get a home group together that people seemed to enjoy. I was showing them things they were not used to but they seemed to enjoy the teachings and the prayer times. Sometimes it was only a small number and sometimes two or three handfuls.

CHAPTER TWENTY EIGHT: 42 DEGREES SOUTH

Sometimes those that came were a handful to handle. With some abusing me before they took off. I knew it was the demons within them though, so wasn't too worried. Most of these people had come out of the church and had their eyes opened a little. Some more than others though, which made things a bit easier.

The time was coming up to September and William and his wife Lucille were coming for the Elijah challenge training. I knew the devil didn't want this in the church. And there was an extra crushing weight of oppression on me and all sorts of junk getting thrown around in my head. I was being told to do a 21 day fast but was trying to avoid it, still continuing the three dayers almost every fortnight. But the pressure overwhelmed me and I started. And when I got through it I was ready for this fight.

I know every time I gained strength, the thing trying to hold me down was defeated. I may have been a long way from the top of the Mountain, but I was moving forwards. But it was an invisible battle again. And I wasn't going to whinge to anyone. I did get a little proud of how I could push back the enemy all by myself, and hadn't had any help for years. So I was reluctant to ask for any. But once I was under a massive load and I got the people of the home group to pray. I was thinking just before humbling myself to ask for prayer, that most of these people don't know enough about spiritual warfare to be able to get much on the run.

But I did ask and although most of the prayers were simple, I know God worked through them. Maybe because of their compassion for me, we were close with most of them, and also I would say that my humbling of myself to say that I was struggling was the main thing that the Lord wanted me to do. And it taught me a valuable lesson. None of us can do it alone. Maybe for a bit, but don't ever think that the prayers of others are not worth much. And it was a lesson I needed, because what was coming, I was asking every man and his dog to join in to pray against this enemy. I was at times desperate for help. Some joined in and I am grateful.

We found a place to hold the Elijah Challenge meeting, which was a Korean pastor's church in the Hobart CBD. He enjoyed it too. But there was little interest anywhere. And even mockery and slanders. But I was expecting that. We made flyers and handed them out here and there but the best way to get rid of them was at a picture theatre when there was a Christian movie on. I thought this was good because groups from every church all over the state were coming and we could hand out one flyer to twos and threes and more.

Two evenings we got away with that and then we were banished from the picture theatre the next day and banished from the car park the day after. But we had handed out over 200 flyers which would have reached over one thousand people.

Also I emailed all the churches but got no response. And out of all those flyers, only one person wanted info. This was the state of the church in Hobart. But God is watching.

So William came and there were around a dozen who did the training. And they got to practice praying for the sick with each other and on the final night they could pray for those who came for the healing night. And there were some who had never prayed for anyone that prayed for people and they were healed. And all were very much encouraged. And we were all very happy. But it was a very few in number that attended.

I was asking God why the people didn't come when it would have lifted the church from death to life and He showed me. The very next weekend there was a woman who is associated with what I would call false Prophets. She was speaking at the Grand Chancellor Motel. And she charged $50 a head and there was no meal or anything.

This reminded me of when Eric had told me Benny Hinn hired out a soccer stadium in Uganda and charged $50 a head to preach. That was around a month's wages there. I will say no more about this, because it won't be good.

And here's the judgement that may be awaiting some of those who willingly stood in the way and that spoke evil of Gods work. I'd already seen Him Judge very swiftly in Africa, and even though it was a lot slower here in Australia, I had seen it come here, and I had seen people die, some I never mentioned here.

> Hos 4:6 My people are destroyed for lack of knowledge: because thou hast rejected knowledge, I will also reject thee, that thou shalt be no priest to me: seeing thou hast forgotten the law of thy God, I will also forget thy children.

One more thing I will add was a dream for a house church in the Hobart area I had received. It was going well with many numbers, but no-one here showed up at the Elijah Challenge meetings either. I was not upset, only disappointed. Not for the people in charge but those who are hungry and looking for more of God but not receiving it. Just getting more of the same milky substance mixed with fairy floss as the

CHAPTER TWENTY EIGHT: 42 DEGREES SOUTH

system is dishing out. I knew where to find the meat, but the meat was too much for most to handle.

> Heb 5:12-14 For when for the time ye ought to be teachers, ye have need that one teach you again which *be* the first principles of the oracles of God; and are become such as have need of milk, and not of strong meat.
>
> For every one that useth milk *is* unskilful in the word of righteousness: for he is a babe.
>
> But strong meat belongeth to them that are of full age, *even* those who by reason of use have their senses exercised to discern both good and evil.

And I was given a dream for one of the men who were in charge of this group. I had met him a couple of times and he was bolder than most. Telling things how they were so I had a hope that this dream may encourage and help him. But the dream, I only received it and all I had to do was deliver it. This was late 2015 and I had the dream while still in our flat. And I prayed about sending it. But we moving back to Pyengana so it took a week or so to get to.

> G'day .... (Name removed)
>
> *I wrote this letter below on the morning of the 14th Dec. But I have prayed about sending it and still feel I have to. Today is Tue 22nd. And although you are not directly in the dream, it is for the body and strong leading to share with you.*
>
> *It was good to see you again at the .... (place removed) residence where the gathering was on Sunday night. I know that everything happens for a reason, so to be seated next to you was ordained and I believe that I need to share this with you.*
>
> *I entered the house at around 15 past 7. Around 5 minutes off the finish of a weeklong fast. I was fasting to crucify flesh and also believed that that same week I would receive Knowledge of His will for direction. And as we had driven From St Helens to Launceston there was no order in this timing.*
>
> *I did hear that you had been fasting for some answers to go forward with but sitting next to you I could feel your need and your searching for an answer for the Hobart Church. I could also feel that you were not getting any answers, or nothing that was fulfilling your wish for direction for the body in this town. I felt a heaviness or frustration or something like this as you look for the next step. Or a wilderness we could say.*

This was no word of knowledge or anything, just an inside observation.

As I looked at the people I could see that they were from different places and have different ideas and I believe even one small group chasing a different spirit. And I did not envy your task. But they are gathering together and hungry. Looking for answers also.

I do believe that you have an important role in Hobart as I have heard you preach twice and am impressed with your boldness to go where most ministers fear to go. Something that the Church desperately needs.

Anyway I had a dream last night and I believe I have to share it with you. Especially after the talks by the Indian people saying it's time to walk in your God given authority and power.

I know the Word says that,

Jer 23:28 The prophet that hath a dream, let him tell a dream; and he that hath my word, let him speak my word faithfully. What is the chaff to the wheat? saith the LORD.

Jer 23:29 Is not my word like as a fire? saith the LORD; and like a hammer that breaketh the rock in pieces?

And that dreams rely on the correct interpretation and a small margin of error can upset the whole thing. So a dream is reliant on the interpretation totally, unless obvious and non symbolic. (Like getting shot in the guts!!!)

Firstly, I grew up on a sheep farm that my Father owns and his Father before. He now runs 2500 sheep and am well aware of the references that Jesus spoke of when he spoke of sheep and goats. Have dwelt on the spiritual reflection many times.

The dream.

I was shearing sheep in my Aunties woolshed and I had shorn 70. The wool was full of grass seeds and things and one particularly nasty grass seed we called a corkscrew. They are a little over an inch long.

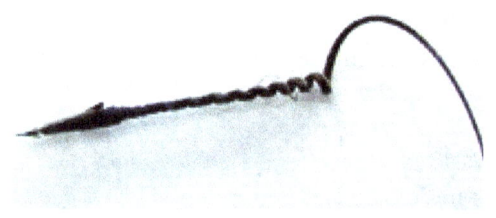

CHAPTER TWENTY EIGHT: 42 DEGREES SOUTH

These would screw in then the points would go into the skin on a sheep's back. And there were many.

On the next stand was a woman that grew up in the small town I lived in and she had had many men. Mainly young ones that came from other areas, especially in her young years. She had shorn only two sheep and asked if I could show her how to shear more. I said go and ask Graham (this was her husband in later life who died in a car crash soon after the wedding, he was a shearer, much better than I) And after I said it I was thinking that he is so proud and self centered that he wouldn't bother or take the time anyway. And I did not want to be involved with this woman in anyway.

The dream ended around four thirty and I woke up. Not long after I arose and prayed for the interpretation and as it was unfolding I had your name in my spirit and I knew I was to give it to you.

The interpretation.

Aunties woolshed. Represents Hobart. It was a small distance from home. I was sent to it to work as I was sent here to work.

Shearing sheep. Every year a sheep needs to be shorn, or they get very scraggy and full of thistles and things, if on rough ground, or away from a shepherd. Also a shorn sheep is much whiter than an unshorn. Or spiritually cleaner. These sheep were full of thistles and corkscrew. This represents the oppression and torments the body is in because of demonic oppression, torments witchcraft, fear, discouragements and so on.

The harlot. This represents the current state of the church. She has many lovers and sticks around until the next one comes who looks sweeter than the other. As the doctrine of demons and the ear tickling deceivers that has led the bride into apathy, slumber, sloth, wrong attitudes and motives and so on.

The husband. Now dead. Represents a christ who is still on the cross. A christ that is not interested in his bride. No resurrection power, and no relationship. A false christ, and them, full of doubt and unbelief in the one they serve, at work here, by not asking. Even though in the natural he was a lot better shearer than me.

This is what I believe that a majority of the church are following. Because of things like no repentance and no crucifying of the flesh then the relationship with God is very low. Although wanting to believe, they have stopped asking. (obviously demonic oppression, blockages and hindrances, discouragement and again unbelief, deception and delusion can be at work here also.)

Numbers. According to E.W Bullinger Two represents. We have seen that One excludes all difference, and denotes that which is sovereign. But Two affirms that there is a difference—there is another; It is the first number by which we can divide another, and therefore in all its uses we may trace this fundamental idea of division or difference. The two may be, though different in character, yet one as to testimony and friendship. The Second that comes in may be for help and deliverance. But, alas! where man is concerned, this number testifies of his fall, for it more often denotes that difference which implies opposition, enmity, and oppression.*

So with the brides lack of understanding at the least, or even rejection of the truth, (see Hosea 4:6,) she is not at all effective in setting the captives free and working the good works that are waiting for her as was in the ministry of Christ.

Luk 4:18 The Spirit of the Lord is upon me, because he hath anointed me to preach the gospel to the poor; he hath sent me to heal the brokenhearted, to preach deliverance to the captives, and recovering of sight to the blind, to set at liberty them that are bruised,

Luk 4:19 To preach the acceptable year of the Lord.

Seventy represents Again Bullinger. 70 is combination of two of the perfect numbers, seven and ten. Hence 7 x 10 signifies perfect spiritual order carried out with all spiritual power and significance. Both spirit and order are greatly emphasised. To shear seventy sheep in the natural in a day is about the average for a brand new beginner. And in the Kingdom of God I am only a sixteen year old.

But called into the wilderness at 4 yo by an audible voice, I have been through a bit of testing and all the trials with little help from man, but mainly from above. And far away is the belief that I have attained perfection, or the saying that I know it all, but I believe that my focus on learning spiritual power and authority of the believer is a must for all Christians, so they can stand in the day of trouble that is close at hand. And with the thinning of the veil between us and the second Heaven happening at a faster rate than ever before (Rev 12:12, Dan 7:25) and the web of witchcraft controlling minds and dulling the sensitivity of all men (see web and net background on US dollar bill) many unprepared will fall. 2 thess 2.

CHAPTER TWENTY EIGHT: 42 DEGREES SOUTH

Then after understanding it's use in our own life, it can be used to do the works that are waiting in others. Even the greater works! This seems to be the only area that has not been explored in the whole body of Christ to it's full potential, be it because of fear and doubt, confusion and doctrinal error.

After praying for God to confirm in the Scriptures, He led me to two chapters in Amos, Ch 4 & 5. Read them and I'm sure you'll get the idea. The body is weak, sick and dying and it needs to learn to stand and fight. Going around the mountain is no longer an option, but we must begin to ascend. Heb 12:18-29.

And I have enclosed what I believe to be part of an answer to this what I have put forth for you. Because I know that in the dream itself is no real direction.

So that's the dream. Whatever your opinion and actions, soldier on!!!

Praise the Lord.

Peter McMaster

I enclosed a Win Worley Mass Deliverance DVD and an Elijah challenge DVD. And so I tried to inject a desire for Deliverance and Healing that was desperately needed in the body of Christ, which was bruised and battered and far from resurrecting in Life and Power.

I never heard anything back but wasn't anxious about things. I only delivered the word, just like I had to some small churches in the past. But I have heard since that a wrong spirit infected that meeting and it closed down also. And when I say this it is not with any joy, I can tell you.

And the enemy was a lot more at play in these churches down here in Hobart than what I knew at the time. There was way more to all this than what met the eye. And over the next couple of years it was to be exposed. And then it became the fight of my lifetime. Or to this current time right now.

CHAPTER TWENTY NINE
THINGS WARM UP

The 12 months in Hobart was over and I was fairly glad. It was like a holiday in one way for Poss, as she had never lived anywhere bigger than St Helens, which is only around three thousand people, if that. But I was looking forward to just having the peace and quiet of the country, and escape that oppression that was down there in Hobart. I was very tired of all the fasting. And I came back and relaxed as much as I could. I was wondering how we could ever go back down there and live under that sort of spiritual pressure. I wasn't looking forward to any return in the near future that was for sure.

Some of the people in the group were missing us and as they had been beginning to grow a little it was sad to leave them. I was praying for them to hear from God in dreams and they had started to have prophetic dreams and that excited them a lot. And I had got them to fast a little. Which things were slow at the start but when they saw miracles at the Elijah Challenge they started to believe.

With one girl who was cooler than lukewarm doing only a one day fast, the first in her 15 years that she said she was a believer, and even had some chocolate in the middle of it but went through to the end told us that she heard a voice speak to her and it said "Today I am well pleased". I told her that was God. Why don't you fast again? And she tried again, and even after hearing God speak, couldn't make even 24 hours. And she eventually slipped backwards. There was no strength.

Another had lots of problems but couldn't do a one day fast. I was praying for him from our Pyengana farmhouse home, four hours from Hobart now and a voice spoke within me, the still small voice of the Holy Ghost and said very clearly, "Those who will not stand will fall."

When we separate from the pace of the world and focus on Gods things, we will begin to hear this voice. And sometimes it is easy to hear. Instead of wanting Jesus to come with a trumpet sound and knock on our door in his crown of thorns and say, "This is what I want you to do", and make a big thing about it, God works the other way.

> Ki 19:11-12 And he said, Go forth, and stand upon the mount before the LORD. And, behold, the LORD passed by, and a great and strong wind rent the mountains, and brake in pieces the rocks before the LORD; *but* the LORD *was* not in the wind: and after the wind an earthquake; *but* the LORD *was* not in the earthquake:

> And after the earthquake a fire; *but* the LORD *was* not in the fire: and after the fire a still small voice.

I knew that this person was going to find things difficult in the near future, and he did. They can't understand that if they would put effort into God He meets them half way. His rewards are great and well worth every effort we put into Him. But they had no faith and I was amazed to see them revert back to old habits that I had been trying to help them break and return to the Santa Claus teachings they had been feeding on over their Christian lives that gave them a massive false sense of security.

> Heb 3:12 Take heed, brethren, lest there be in any of you an evil heart of unbelief, in departing from the living God.

I had found some people hard to deal with, and some spiritually lazy, and was wondering, "How am I ever going to be a Pastor God, if I can't, and do not want to, deal with people anymore"? I was still a little heavy from all the fighting and a bit discouraged. But now I see what I did. I did things according to how I thought they should be done. I was still striving and running ahead and that had to be worked out of me. And God began to say, "Don't you go to them, let them come to you". And though it sounds easy, it is very hard to turn from a direction that you have told yourself is the way it should be. And when we think we have everything worked out, we probably are way out.

> 1Co 8:2 And if any man think that he knoweth anything, he knoweth nothing yet as he ought to know.

> Isa 55:9 For *as* the heavens are higher than the earth, so are my ways higher than your ways, and my thoughts than your thoughts.

God knew my heart though. After all He was the one who said "Open new doors and new doors shall be opened".

He had not told me to stop this yet. But with the Word of letting people come to me, that made things so easy for me. I trusted God to bring people that needed help, and I would help them. I had prayed, "God, give me the real hard cases that no-one else can help, and I will do my best to help them. If I am Anointed and a Pastor, then you will help me to do this." Wasn't long and I was regretting this prayer. LOL

Another thing I needed to repent of was picking fights in the spirit without asking God if He wanted me to go to war with those strongmen and territorial spirits and Principalities and whatever else I had been waving my sword at. So I just said "from now on God, I'll just wait for your Word of knowledge and your go ahead". I definitely didn't want to have to fast every fortnight, just to stay afloat.

So God honoured those prayers, like I said He knew I just wanted to help people come to know Him. After what He did for me, I cannot but say, that the best thing in the whole universe is Jesus Christ and his Freedom and Life and His Truth and Peace and Joy and Hope and Love. I just wanted everyone to know this. I had started to pray deliverance and healings over the phone with some good results, and more people were ringing me. There were some people coming also that we would pray deliverance on as well and that was good.

But things were still too slow for me. I had to get into the mode of being patient. It wasn't a roller coaster of emotions and fears and doubt that I was on, that was mostly conquered long ago, but it was about how much sitting around waiting for God to act instead of myself. I knew the Word and I wanted to fulfill it.

> Jas 2:17-20 Even so faith, if it hath not works, is dead, being alone.
>
> Yea, a man may say, Thou hast faith, and I have works: shew me thy faith without thy works, and I will shew thee my faith by my works.
>
> Thou believest that there is one God; thou doest well: the devils also believe, and tremble.
>
> But wilt thou know, O vain man, that faith without works is dead?

But I also knew what the Lord had told me, so I decided to be patient.

There were a few weird things going on though. I was always putting my faith to work. After seeing what Eric had done with the bees, I thought why not here. We had some mice and rat problems and they

CHAPTER TWENTY NINE: THINGS WARM UP

were chewing through things they shouldn't have so I cursed the vermin from coming on the property. Some Tasmanian Quolls moved in under the house. That solved that problem.

Also a tiger snake was crawling across the back cement one day and a cat we had saved from the pound that wasn't very friendly was hitting it on the back and it turned around and left. Poss saw it all happen. She is terrified of snakes. And Poss had seen another tiger snake slither under my workshop. I was away working and came home and prayed that God would drive it from our land or kill it or whatever I came up with. I didn't like snakes much either. I treated it like a demon. I loosed confusion and blindness on it and give it the works. Then I went and set rabbit traps and rat traps around a saucer of milk to catch it if I could.

Poss was out the back and the snake came out from under our house disorientated and it was like it was blind. She screamed and I was there in a few seconds and watched it bumping into the wall of the house and the back steps into the house. It was the strangest thing. And as the shovel was right where it slithered to instead of about 150 degrees of open space it could have went into, I thought, Praise the Lord.

I would watch the animals for strange movements. I grew up on a farm and knew how animals behaved. Some were really strange. And after Africa, I was watching even more for signs of God in everything, and also the enemy.

I was at my Fathers place and in the bedroom about two AM in the morning I woke up and there was a bat flying around. I thought how weird is that? I wasn't spooked though. I knew all the doors were locked and there is a lot of mice running around the farm so Dad had blocked every hole up in the house so tight that an ant would be struggling to get in. So I got up and prayed and then chased the bat around for almost 20 minutes before I could catch it and put it out the window. If bats are blind then its radar was pretty good. Dodging everything I threw at it. I soon forgot about any possible curse while running and jumping around that bedroom, chasing what I thought may have been some demon or witch, trying not to wake my Father up in the room next door. And I was praying in the name of Jesus Christ, just in case. Does that last sentence make me sound like an over reacting paranoid lunatic or what? LOL.

I'm imagining right now if my Old Man had caught me chasing it and I told him "I'm just gonna dispose of this demon or witch Dad, don't worry". But that was my life and still is. Although not being able to speak to many about this, it is good just to get it out. How you take it is up to you.

Another time when we were fighting the Tassie witches, (I'll get into that next,) there was a really big black cat hanging around, and it was out the back real close to the door. And nobody close owned a big black cat. This was not scared of me and the way it looked at me reminded me of the big ugly dog in Uganda. I thought it was really strange. And it just walked off when I saw it from about five meters away like it owned the joint. So I went and prayed about this one and treated it like an invader and the very next day it had been splattered on the road out the front of the house. I thanked God just in case it was Him who cleared this thing away. This happened at the height of the battle with the satanists that I'm getting to very soon.

I had been praying warfare for a few minutes and I heard some strange noises coming from our laundry. And during those months there were lots of strangeness going on so I didn't know what to expect. I went out and walked through the wide open door and an owl was flying around into the walls. It was very odd behaviour, and the noise only started when I started praying. I caught it though and let it go.

Spooky owl

Anyway back to the story. One girl from Qld rang me and she was suicidal and they on the verge of going into the psych ward. She had been a witch. We'll call her Dianne. An ex drug addict, been in jail and she had been around biker gangs and seen some nasty things and done some nasty things. She also said she was taken to a ritual and saw a sacrifice and was fed human meat as a five year old. But it was a Sunday school that she was attending at the time. She believed that her

CHAPTER TWENTY NINE: THINGS WARM UP

sister was fed the same. And the sister was a witch also and she owned an occult book shop on the Gold Coast. But Dianne needed help. So we prayed over the phone. And things were moving and she was getting a little freedom. She had a 17 year old son also.

Dianne was easy to talk to and honest about her past and she was really struggling and thought that people were out to get her. And maybe they were? We said to come down to Tasmania to stay for a little, and she came with her son. We did intensive deliverance on her and got out many spirits. They were screaming very loud as they were coming out, and talking all sorts of crap. We were praying most days for an hour or two at least. When people are infested with witchcraft, there are so many demons they are impossible to count.

God was giving me many dreams and words of knowledge about her and she was getting many visions about things also, and hearing the spirits name themselves in her head, and sometimes out loud. It always helps when the person getting deliverance lets the deliverer know if something is going on. So keep asking the person if anything is happening or if they are hearing anything. Look for clues.

There was something that made things difficult with this deliverance and this was the timing of this. Two days before Dianne got to our house, I made a video exposing the satanic coven in Hobart that was running the Dark Mofo festival over the days leading to the winter solstice. And I had uploaded it and sent it to my email group and a lot of churches and it got about 160 or so hits in a couple of days. Then the satanists saw it. And I knew it was them because of the comments that came on the video. I had to shut them off. I wish the Christians networks were this well connected.

Massive jump in views of dark Mofo video.

And poor old Dianne landed in the middle of this. She did have trouble sleeping and was not very co-operative at times and her son threatened to kill me once and hid in the bedroom playing video games all night and sleeping all day when the Dark Mofo satanic festival was in full swing in Hobart.

And because Dianne's third eye was still partially open she said she was seeing astral travelers lined up around our boundary fence a lot, and other things hanging about.

And some of the things she was seeing I had been seeing in dreams also. So I knew some of it was real.

And the day that Herman Nitsch performed the satanic slaughter of the bull ritual in front of a couple of thousand people, mainly satanists from all over the world, and it was a massive ritual, I could feel it's effect, even in Pyengana. It was an open mockery of Jesus Christ's shed blood. These people were starting to offend me and annoy me. This is the reason I made the video.

Also the Uniting Church in Tasmania was complicit in this by letting a band called Night Terrors play satanic music in six or seven churches between Hobart and Launceston. They were creating a song line or dragon trail. A path created in the spirit realm to connect South Tassie and North Tassie together. Under the demonic influences that were being pushed in the South.

Tassie is covered in blood rituals   *Weirdness under Hobart CBD*

CHAPTER TWENTY NINE: THINGS WARM UP

Dianne stayed for the two weeks. We baptised her in the river and the demon froze her body standing in the river. I used the baptism to bring the spirits to the surface and cast them out. We were in the freezing river and the demons were saying "Its Holy water, its Holy water" and we couldn't get her down forwards in the water. We tried for a few minutes and had to do something else. So I spun her around and dunked her quick backwards and when she came up she let out massive screams of the demons fleeing. It was very fortunate that we were a long way from any other humans; otherwise they may have thought we were murdering her. I used this tactic again after that with some others. It worked well. And anyone else doing a baptism should use it too. It's a good opportunity to get the spirits on the run. See The Last Reformation by Torben Sondergaard.

One thing Dianne wouldn't do was let me return curses. Every time I would pray that all witchcraft go back to where it came from she would stop me. Now she knew little of the Word of God but at times was hungry for understanding. And at other times would be telling us how things worked. It would have made me pull out my hair if I had any. I had to juggle between her deliverance and not offending her. And it was a struggle.

She did have an idea of where some trouble was coming from but didn't want them to get hurt. And she was at times so oppressed. I tried to explain, if somebody is throwing rocks over your fence all the time, some of them will hit you. And if you don't throw them back sometime then they will just continue on and on and nothing will change. And it's not just you that they are throwing these rocks at.

> 2Th 1:6 Seeing *it is* a righteous thing with God to recompense tribulation to them that trouble you;

But she wouldn't listen and there was a game going of tippy toeing around a woman that was deep into witchcraft and liked to control the show. So in the end after two weeks I had enough and we sent her home. We did stay in contact with her for a little while and she was a lot better than before she came. And after a few weeks back she said she did return the curses and overnight two thirds of her problems left. I will add I have never been convicted of returning curses to the senders. I put one dollar in a poker machine once walking through a pokey room to our car when we stayed in a hotel room one night years ago and the conviction almost crushed me. But there was a time coming that I started doing this with vindictive motives. Because the battle became very personal and then things changed a bit. Doors were opening for demonic access into my life and into the person we were trying to help.

But Dianne was friends with another witch who was struggling really badly. And she was in Tasmania. Dianne told her to ring me for some help. And if I thought I knew stuff about the enemy, this woman had lived in amongst the worst people for decades and her job was mostly to destroy the church, I realized I knew very little.

And with me praying to God to take me up another level, He certainly answered it. This fight was going to last every day and night for months to the extent that I slept in my clothes for about four months straight, when I could sleep.

Can we have one Voodoo Doll with the works thanks. This hit hard!

Nasty surprise

CHAPTER THIRTY
WICKED WITCH OF THE WEST

Dianne had told Jill to ring me and she mentioned that Jill had told her she was a High Priestess in a satanic coven in Tasmania. I was of the opinion that the people who delve into witchcraft and new age all had some official idea in their head that they were someone of high rank. Be it a self-appointed delusion or inspired by others and whether in this life or as some of the troubled ones I had run into, a really high profile from past lives.

Not that I believe in past lives, the Bible tells us that we only get one go at life, but these people have been deceived by vain glory and delusion to make them feel better about themselves.

> Heb 9:27 And as it is appointed unto men once to die, but after this the judgement:

But when Jill rang me one afternoon in late 2016, she didn't seem to have any self–promotion in her. Or any rebellion or judgements or anything that I could see that would make her look like what she told me she had been in the past. Jill was friendly but she was struggling, with life and death, and was very open to anything I could do for her.

Jill had been in hospital for ten weeks now and during that time said she was on life support. She was telling me some things she had been involved in and I knew that if they were real witches and she had been a real satanist then there would be a lot of curses flying her way. Jill wanted to confess things to me and from what I was hearing I had to say, "Don't tell me, tell God, I don't need to know".

Dianne had told me a little about what Jill was involved in and even Dianne was a bit shocked, which amazed me a bit, because Dianne was no Mother Teresa, I can tell you that. So I led Jill in a repentance prayer and told her to repent and say sorry to God in her mind about the things she knew she had done that were wrong. And she did this. It took a couple of minutes and all was fine.

She had been attending a small church which the satanists would not target, because there was little life and less than eleven people attending. Any numbers less than that they wouldn't bother with.

But this did give her a little strength and I am positive that even this desire to put in an effort to find God, had put a stronger hedge around her than without, even though she said she couldn't take communion and had to pour the drink down her boot and stash the biscuit or whatever they were passing around there. And she couldn't read the Bible or pray or do anything much in the way of Christianity. And this she had been doing for a couple of years. There must have been such a battle raging in Jill for that time; I was impressed that she could do this.

I have to say this that the people running this church could not tell that they had a real High Priestess of a massive satanic cult in their midst for that time, and that is a shame to them. But they would not have been able to help anyway, believing the things they believed, and working to the theology they had been fed in the cemetery, errr, whoops….seminary.

We started on the forgiveness prayers, and this was a little more difficult. I led her to repent for holding un-forgiveness towards anybody. Now I know Satan is very vindictive and his followers are usually the same, and have an elite mindset where revenge is necessary and judgement must come. But even little old Christian bowling ladies can get this resentment and bitterness and it will affect them so bad.

I already gave the scripture of the tormentors in an earlier chapter. The ones that Jesus said the Father will send to us if we don't forgive. And most believers have no idea that this is in their Bibles and that is very sad. It's a big open door for curses to enter and to cling to us and then the bitterness in the spirit will cause our bodies to break down in some way. The hedge was broken in Jill and her past was catching up with her.

> Ecc 10:8 He that diggeth a pit shall fall into it; and whoso breaketh an hedge, a serpent shall bite him.

This had in my mind no doubt; a lot to do with her old friends, and her old boss Lucifer, telling those friends to kill her through the witchcraft, black magic and voodoo curses that they were experts at. And this is the same for anyone coming out of Satanism. It is only by the Power of the Lord Jesus Christ that can lead them out of the darkness and protect them so the enemy cannot kill them. There is no escape otherwise.

CHAPTER THIRTY: WICKED WITCH OF THE WEST

> 1Co 1:18-19 For the preaching of the cross is to them that perish foolishness; but unto us which are saved it is the power of God.
>
> For it is written, I will destroy the wisdom of the wise, and will bring to nothing the understanding of the prudent.

When we begin to put in the effort to look, no matter how off track we think we may be, Jesus Christ will appear in some way or another and start to lead us into the light.

> Joh 8:12 Then spake Jesus again unto them, saying, I am the light of the world: he that followeth me shall not walk in darkness, but shall have the light of life.

Jill had told me in other phone calls down the track a bit that the people she knew that tried to get out, all committed suicide. And she was involved with this Coven almost 30 years so she had seen a few die. Whether it was shooting suicides or hanging or running a car into things at high speed, she never knew anybody that had escaped. So it was surprising that she had made it this far. I was quickly realising that this woman was no little teeny bopper lighting candles and the incense and reading a few tarot cards.

I led her in a prayer of forgiveness. "Repeat after me Jill, I forgive those who have hurt and disappointed me and I let them go and ask you God to bless them." She said some of the prayer, "I forgive those who hurt and disappointed me and ask you God to forgive…..ughhh, I can't say it. I knew this was going to be a struggle.

"You have to say it Jill. If you can't forgive then you can't be forgiven. The Word of God makes that clear. Let's try again, say this, In the name of Jesus I forgive all my enemies and ask you God to bless them." She had trouble saying Jesus and could not ask God to bless them.

I know how hard this can be, I went through this. But she was trying ever so hard so I asked the Lord to help her through. And she got it out and struggled naming some names and there was one name that she couldn't forgive and said so. "I can't forgive Jarrod" she said. "He has done some horrible things to me." And from what I heard in later phone calls and deliverance prayer times, I couldn't blame her.

Jarrod was the High Priest. He was the enforcer. He came from the USA and is now here in Tassie to promote this filth and corruption. I was going to have a few fights with Jarrod in the near future in the spirit and I got to see him around four or five times in dreams and visions, and knew exactly who and what he was.

Jill said that Jarrod, as punishments for being late or doing something wrong in the group, would put petrol and oil in her eyes, pins in her feet, and nails through her armpits and tied her to a power pole naked once and whipped her with thorny blackberry bushes. Not to mention the wet wooden skewers shoved under the fingernails. I had known bikers and criminals in the past, and even they have some morals, but doing this to women was a very low act. But this was the world she chose to be in. After drinking that blood at the first meeting, and going through the initiation ritual that was it. Her soul was sold to Satan.

I had to pull her up a few times as she wanted to tell me more, but I needed to keep my sanity and did not want to form any judgements about her. It was Jesus who brought her to me to help. If I had any bad taste in my mouth about anything she had been doing then how could I help? Jesus had forgiven me and I knew He would forgive Jill.

But I never knew anything about Jarrod yet. I just knew that she hated this man for some reason. So I persisted and said, "You have to forgive him Jill. It is essential so you can be healed". I knew without doubt that this hatred for this bloke and some others had to be dealt with before any healing would take place. Jill's heart was bad; her liver was in bad shape, her pancreas and her spleen and her intestines also. The curses hurled at her were doing their job. That was obvious also.

Because I had learnt that if my heart gets jumpy and starts to play up, I break all curses and it will come right usually under a minute or any other strange pain or suffering I learnt to deal with like this also. And mostly they will go quickly. So with every one of those problems in her, this stumbling block had to be dealt with or she was going to die. And at this lowest point in her life, she was willing to try.

"I forgive Ja....... Ughh, can't do it" she said. You have to do it Jill, "Lord, give her strength" I said as I wrestled with the resistance in her in the invisible realm. "Lord I forgiiiiiiive Jaaarod, ahhhh" with a sigh of relief as if she had conquered the unclimbable mountain.

"I bind the strongman in Jill as your Word says Father and every wicked spirit within her right now in the name of Lord Jesus Christ."

> Mar 3:27 No man can enter into a strong man's house, and spoil his goods, except he will first bind the strong man; and then he will spoil his house.

I was in war mode now and could feel the presence of God and the Holy Ghost fire all over me. I knew there was victory coming, but not to what extent and didn't care. This enemy was going to get a flogging.

I knew that this was something ordered by the Lord and a good work He had prepared for me at this exact time.

> Eph 2:10 For we are his workmanship, created in Christ Jesus unto good works, which God hath before ordained that we should walk in them.

"I break all witchcraft curses, black magic and voodoo that are coming against Jill, all hexes and vexes and vexation of spirit I rebuke you and break your power. The Lord Jesus Christ rebuke you." I started attacking the enemy hard. "Every curse be broken now in Jesus name and I loose the Holy Ghost Fire to burn up all chaff, and everything that offends in the Kingdom of God. I break all chains and every yoke of bondage and slavery I smash now in the name of Jesus".

"All walls and bars and hedges and fences and gates and dams be smashed to pieces. I loose destruction on every destroyer and spoiling on the spoilers. Every vindictive power, the Lord Jesus Christ rebuke you. You must leave now. Get back to where you came from or to the feet of Jesus Christ to be made His footstool and never return".

My faith was high to fight for Jill and I was using the sword of the spirit which is the Word of God.

> Eph 6:16-17 Above all, taking the shield of faith, wherewith ye shall be able to quench all the fiery darts of the wicked.
>
> And take the helmet of salvation, and the sword of the Spirit, which is the word of God:

I believed this scripture and used it to break off the word curses off Jill, which would have been numerous, and I told the demons the same.

> Isa 54:17 No weapon that is formed against thee shall prosper; and every tongue *that* shall rise against thee in judgement thou shalt condemn. This *is* the heritage of the servants of the LORD, and their righteousness *is* of me, saith the LORD.

I rebuked not just the spirits but also the sickness and disease and the mental anguish and torments and every other thing that was held back by the un-forgiveness and commanded Jill's body to be restored. I knew that the Grace of God was on Jill because of the moaning and groaning and the deep coughing that she was doing and I knew that I was hitting them hard with the same compassion for the tormented and tortured that I had with my Mother.

I still hated the devil and I wanted him out of this person's life. Otherwise I knew that she was dead. This time though I was not a novice. And I was putting all I had learnt and practiced and believed into this. I was surprised that with the amount of coughing that the nurses didn't go to see what was wrong with Jill, but like the cops at Ellie's place, I know the Angels were working here too. As I had prayed that God would send a sufficient number to help here too.

I was asking Jill throughout what she was hearing, because she had been in contact with these entities and communicating with them, and now they were ripping her to bits. It was no strange thing for her to hear their voices. "They are saying you're a traitor and calling you all sorts of names, and they hate your guts". I said, "Good, I hate their guts too." And I knew I was hitting them.

These spirits that were coming out though were not the ones that she took years to get in the bloodletting rituals and sacrifices on the high places around Tasmania. These were the demons assigned to the curses that were causing the sickness and the disease. Not that I knew about Jill's past yet, but it didn't matter. One demon out is one less in. And they were moving. So for 20 to 30 minutes I kept praying with for her until she stopped the coughing and groaning and she said she felt very light and very well. She believed she was healed and so did I.

I said you will probably be able to get out of hospital tomorrow. But she wasn't so full of faith. The doctors let her go after a week. But they made her take a wheelbarrow full of pills home with her. The thing is, they couldn't fix her, but the Lord Jesus Christ worked through me to help her. But the doctors will take the credit. And even when they see miracles like this, they still do not believe.

And I believe that Satan can see blessings that are meant for us, and he can stop them or delay them. And he can also make us impatient and run to man earlier than waiting for God who has prepared the answers for us. So there are a lot of times we as Believers, are too impatient and choose the worldly choice and then Satan sows the ungodly answer into our minds to make us not grateful to God.

Like what happened way back with my Mother and her saying it was the chemo that helped her. The devil will often give another alternative. But with Jill, this was never going to happen. She knew Satan was out to kill her now and had totally rebelled as much as she knew how.

CHAPTER THIRTY ONE
THE WAR BEGINS

I spoke to Jill a few times after the prayer and then she said she was doing OK and we stopped communicating. I thought, "Praise you God. That was good about Jill. Thank you for healing her, and thank you for using me in this work too". I was very encouraged, as I always am when we see a healing and deliverance. We can use this encouragement in future battles when we need it, because sometimes encouragements are few and far between. I learnt this by this Word. David had to do this also.

> 1Sa 30:6 And David was greatly distressed; for the people spake of stoning him, because the soul of all the people was grieved, every man for his sons and for his daughters: but David encouraged himself in the LORD his God.

I think it was about three months or so before we spoke again. I was praying a little for Jill but I thought she must have been OK. But, things were about to get totally out of control. Like a full on horror movie, and I was in the middle of it as a big target, which I could've gone without. But somebody had to enter this fight, which in the end wasn't just for Jill, but for so many more.

Around twelve years before this I received a prophecy from a man called David. He was the Tasmanian head of FGBMFI. And even Bill, the Australian President of the whole organisation said that David's gift was real and if he ever prophesied to me then I should listen real well. David had prophesied to Bill that he would be President and Bill found that hard to believe. Bill was only about five feet tall and very chubby and although owned a business, was not polished like you would think his position required. But God doesn't deal that way.

Bill became President and could communicate with the average person on the street no problem. God can use this, and He did. Anyway the

Lord spoke through David, "Son, I am calling you to war, I will prepare you and equip you and you will smash down satanic covens and bring many witches out of darkness." And he went on but I was stuck on this first bit so I never got the rest. I wish it were recorded but it wasn't. While he said the first bit I was thinking, "Awww, is this true, sounds a bit scary, they'll be hard to deal with", and my mind was full already, even with this first sentence.

A complete meaty meal in a few seconds which filled me so I couldn't take any more in. I used to think about this and when Dianne came I thought it may be happening but it is sure going on now, but the coven is yet to be smashed, although it has weakened greatly.

So very soon after Jill's healing I received another prophecy from someone who I know hears from God. He spoke and said, "I will put you into the mouth of the lion, you will break out its teeth and choke it and feed off the honey." And straight away I thought, "Yum, I like honey; that sounds good." So I think that softened the first bit a lot then and there.

But within a couple of months, all thoughts of what the honey could be and how sweet it was going to taste and how blessed I will be and how nice life would go from then on, and everything would be rosy and I would live happily ever after, left in a hurry, even overnight, LOL. Sometimes we let so much crap run wild in our heads. So the honey went out the window, and I ended in the lion's mouth and he was chewing as hard as he could!

I got the desire to forward this prayer to Jill after a couple of months of no contact. I had got it off the internet years ago, and prayed through it when the Rosicrucians were giving me a hard time and believed it helped a bit. I had not heard from Jill though and didn't know how she was going. So I sent it by text.

> *This is a very powerful prayer against Witchcraft and with fasting even more powerful.*
>
> *This prayer can shut down Witches and Satanists forever. Being that this prayer basically shuts down the senders of the hexes and vexes by returning their evil to them sevenfold. I turned this prayer into a blessing that they would need to turn to Jesus for their own curse to be removed. This would be saving them from HELL and being saved from HELL is a blessing.*
>
> *Father, In the name of Jesus Christ of Nazareth, I plead the precious uncorruptable blood of Jesus over myself and my family and everything*

CHAPTER THIRTY ONE: THE WAR BEGINS

that belongs to us. I ask for giant warrior Angels to be loosed from Heaven to surround and protect us. As your war club and weapons of war I break down, undam, and blow up all walls of protection around all witches, warlocks, wizards, Satanists, and the like, and I break the power of all curses, hexes, vexes, spells, charms, fetishes, psychic prayers, psychic thought, all witchcraft, sorcery, magic, voodoo, all mind control, jinxes, potions, bewitchments, death, destruction, sickness, pain, torment, physic power, psychic warfare, prayer chains, and everything else being sent my way or my family members way, and I return it and the demons to the senders right now!, SEVENFOLD, and I BIND it to them by the blood of Jesus!

Father, I pray that these lost souls will find the light of your Son Jesus. Their own snares and traps have been set against themselves. In the name of Jesus Christ of Nazareth I now loose them from all mind control of Satan! Father I also ask that you Bind the Holy Spirit to their hearts as a guide to your Son Jesus. So they may be set free from the bondages of Satan.

In Jesus name I pray Amen

And she replied before the day was out saying something like this.

"Thank you so much Pete, I am amazed at your timing. I was about to go and do a three day fast today and start a ritual up the hill and shed a heap of blood and give it back to those Fu@#$^&* Bas#$*&@. They have been hassling me for weeks. But I said the prayer and things feel a bit better now." I thought, "That's good. They may lay off a bit now".

But…… That very night I had this dream. There was a car and a big snake was looking for an entry point in the lights and under the bonnet. A man with long blond scraggy hair and a long face came and he had some snakes in a bag. I said in my dream, "Careful mate, those things can bite". And he replied "I know; I've been bitten so many times already". Then I thought, "Well why do you play with them?"

Next second he had a big stick, grabbed the snake off the car with it and held me down face first and was shoving the snake on the stick into the back of my neck trying to get it to bite me. I was thinking, "If I lay totally still it won't bite me, and as soon as I get up from here I am going to punch him straight in the head."

But I woke up and broke the curses and prayed some warfare and thought what was all that about. But I did loose civil war and division into the camp that he was with, not knowing if he was a demon or witch.

I thought, "Not sure why he picked me for his target but I'll send him against his own".

> Mar 3:24-25 And if a kingdom be divided against itself, that kingdom cannot stand.
>
> And if a house be divided against itself, that house cannot stand.

And the next night I saw him in a group attacking a little short bald man with glasses, who didn't look very happy. And I knew that God was showing me that the prayer had worked. And I continue to pray that God would send strife into this unrighteous group as He did here with these wicked men according to His will.

> Jdg 9:23 Then God sent an evil spirit between Abimelech and the men of Shechem; and the men of Shechem dealt treacherously with Abimelech:

So my wife and I realized that there needed to be some hands on deliverance and decided that we should travel the three and a half hours to where Jill was and do this for her.

> Jas 5:14-15 Is any sick among you? let him call for the elders of the church; and let them pray over him, anointing him with oil in the name of the Lord:
>
> And the prayer of faith shall save the sick, and the Lord shall raise him up; and if he have committed sins, they shall be forgiven him.

And as we were travelling across the top of Tasmania Jill rang us and said, "Those pricks are driving around my house and tormenting me, be careful". We arrived on edge and I wasn't sure if a physical confrontation would come or not but when we got there all was quiet.

But she did meet us at the door with a pair of scissors hidden in her hand ready. She was very much on edge also. I knew the long haired man had something to do with her and I said "Who is the long haired tall blond man with a long face". And she gasped and said, "That's Jarrod, how do you know that? He was just driving around the house here".

I said "He attacked me with a bag of snakes, the same night you prayed that prayer." Jill was amazed that I could see these things. She had the divination gift that was esteemed in the satanic coven, but did not really think Christians could see anything. I was amazed at their

CHAPTER THIRTY ONE: THE WAR BEGINS

network and how they seemed to be a step ahead, and I learnt that they were always watching. Anyway we prayed for Jill and heaps of demons came out by deep coughing and wheezing, so deep that we were hoping that they weren't going to suffocate her. And when she could say Jesus and hold the Bible we left.

She was happy and at peace and we were happy too, but all of us exhausted. The first meeting took about four hours. But that wasn't the last time we prayed for Jill. And it wasn't the last time Jarrod came to visit, Jill or Me.

The next time I seen Jarrod was a few days after when I had just put anointing oil around the house. I saw him in a dream or a vision. I knew now that he wasn't a demon. I was in bed but don't know if I was asleep or not. He was walking around the house where I never put any oil which I hastily did the next day. And when I put it there I didn't go lightly with it.

A voice spoke to me just as I went right around the house and finished with the place I'd seen Jarrod. "You're going a bit far now, aren't you?" it said. I knew it wasn't my thought and I knew it wasn't God interrupting my faith in action. So I laughed and rebuked the demon. And said, "You're an idiot demon" thinking how stupid it was, trying to get me to stop what I was doing.

But the battle was on. I heard God speak and had many dreams and words of knowledge in visions and pictures in the next few months. I heard the enemy speak one day soon after this first or second hands on session with Jill, whether witches or demons saying, "You're going to die tonight". And the same afternoon God spoke and said, "They have called a multitude after you". So that night I was ready.

I prayed like never before. It wasn't their threat that fired me up as much as it was God giving me the warning. The devil is a liar but when God says that they are coming then I listened. So I started praying and focusing on the warfare and protection and the destruction of this coven that now I knew that they were out to destroy the church. I had a bit of practice just before this, praying things through. God had told me to pray for America a few years before, but I always had thought that America was doomed and that He was going to judge it.

I listened to the doomers and fear mongers too much and had little to pray about except to wake up the believers. But three months before the USA election I had asked the Lord who the Strongman was over the New World Order. And He said straight away' "Amalek". Amalek was an old King who gave the people of God a lot of trouble. And the Amalekites would scout around the edges and pick off the sick and dying and young and weak. And I could see the connection easily.

So I started praying for at least half an hour every day. I made sure I never missed. I was following the election and could see the fight between good and evil playing out and I knew that if Hillary Clinton got in, that would be it, all over. So I was praying that Amalek would be destroyed, like this prophecy says he will be.

> Exo 17:16 For he said, Because the LORD hath sworn *that* the LORD *will have* war with Amalek from generation to generation.

> Num 24:20 And when he looked on Amalek, he took up his parable, and said, Amalek *was* the first of the nations; but his latter end *shall* be that he perish for ever.

The spirit of the Amalek was still at war with the people of God. And I believed that the Lord had just given me the go ahead to attack this Strongman and Principality. I was faithful and prayed it through and also through the debates with Trump and Clinton and kept it up for two and a half months straight. Not one day off. And about two weeks before the election, I got a massive release after only 15 minutes or so of prayer. And I knew straight away that I had done my bit and that Donald Trump would win.

Now I know that there were thousands of people praying for Trump and fasting and praise God he won the election. I told my father and others that he was going to win but they thought I was mad. They were blinded by the mass media garbage and I can't blame them. They were hammering Donald Trump as bad and still are; all part of the Amalek spirit. Before the election I had found out that Clinton's right hand man John Podesta had connections with Marina Abramovic and that she had connections with people in Tasmania who ran Dark Mofo, and at the time the Pizza Gate scandal and the other scandals were happening.

And I was beginning to see that the people from Mona Museum had friends in high places. And that Tasmania was the tail of the Amalekites with all of them real Luciferians, or devil worshippers. That would sell their Grandmothers for gain. And Jill had been high up in this. Jill told me that she was paid to go into the churches and

CHAPTER THIRTY ONE: THE WAR BEGINS

curse them and that she would drink blood and fast three days then go in loaded up with demons and assign them to the weakest people there with the intention of them not getting any help and walking out worse than they were when they entered.

She said she could see the auras of those in sin and there were different shades and colours for certain sin. She knew who was fornicating and in adultery, to addictions and mental torments, and she would assign demons accordingly. And they would bring in luke warmness and apathy and confusion on the Leaders and Pastors. And in 20 years of doing this all over Tasmania, she was only caught out twice.

She also said that there were 20 to 30 others that were doing it every weekend also, a combined effort to destroy the church. And they are still working at it. Hard! Jill said that she could see that the majority in the big churches were in sin in some way or another. She also said that she could see the Angels standing next to a lot of people but they would not do anything. And because those people had open doors and they were in agreement with their sins, they were open game.

> Isa 66:4 I also will choose their delusions, and will bring their fears upon them; because when I called, none did answer; when I spake, they did not hear: but they did evil before mine eyes, and chose *that* in which I delighted not.

Now I do believe that God will give grace for a season and conviction of sin will occur. But continuing in these sins and searing the conscience will grieve the Holy Spirit and then ears will become deaf and the slippery slope has been reached. It will be all backward from then on, once the conscience has been seared from any sin, and the conviction of the Holy Ghost stops. Have you been wondering where the power and authority is in the church? It has been stolen from under our noses.

Now Jill's third eye was opened long ago. She said she was raped at eight to eleven years old by her grandfather and asked God for help. When this never happened she called out to Satan and the grandfather was dead in a couple of months. So she worshipped Lucifer and built a shrine in her room which her mother liked very much and was happy with her divination gift, which her mother had also.

Jill was also raped by 16 men once at a young age and she hated everyone, which is a good asset for a real satanist witch. And she hated Christians even worse because she hated God. Jill's divination gift was working as a young girl and she had seen where a murdered girl's body was and told the police. She was right, and when the satanic group found out, they invited her to the meetings which were mainly new age, but eyes were on her.

She was asked soon after, because her gift was very accurate, if she wanted to join the group. She was made a promise by a man that nothing would ever hurt her. So she drank the communal blood and that was it. Deeper and darker she went. And it got as dark as you can imagine, and I won't go into details except that some of the spirits that we drove out, took years of rituals and bloodletting and sacrifices to get in. She became high Priestess because of her desire to succeed and because she wanted the devil to love her.

But with the death of her mother years later she started asking questions. And now all her old friends wanted her dead. She had broken the oath and that was it. No return. Just Death!

Jill at the shooting range. Getting ready for a spiritual war

CHAPTER THIRTY TWO
GONE NUCLEAR

The threats kept coming. I heard this loudly not long after the other threat, "We are going to kill you tonight." They failed the first time but this one was still taken seriously. They did try the first time and it was heavy. You could feel the darkness in the atmosphere but I had prayed for a couple of hours this time and stayed awake most of the night on the ready. There was an air of thickness and darkness and heaviness as they were trying to steal the peace. But I had the sword out and I knew that I was a going to be a handful for however many were coming at me. More than a handful for them I hoped.

> Jos 23:10 One man of you shall chase a thousand: for the LORD your God, he *it is* that fighteth for you, as he hath promised you.

Over the next few months there were strange sounds and animals acting weirdly. A half dead snake was on the road out the front, still squirming right in the middle of our driveway that had been run over one day as we returned home from a trip to the shop. We could see Gods protection there, as I was trampling serpents and scorpions every morning, and not just them.

> Psa 91:13 Thou shalt tread upon the lion and adder: the young lion and the dragon shalt thou trample under feet.

I was using these scriptures a lot. Seeing how it was ordained from the beginning that we could bruise Satan's head with our heels. I was certainly doing the prophetic actions for these two scriptures and believing it. And it felt good. Try it!

> Gen 3:15 And I will put enmity between thee and the woman, and between thy seed and her seed; it shall bruise thy head, and thou shalt bruise his heel.

> Rom 16:20 And the God of peace shall bruise Satan under your feet shortly. The grace of our Lord Jesus Christ *be* with you. Amen.

Whether it was the anointing oil line, the wall of fire or the hedge of protection I prayed up every day, I don't know. I knew God was working and fighting for us and was fairly confident that the enemy would have to struggle to get through the defences.

> Zec 2:5 For I, saith the LORD, will be unto her a wall of fire round about, and will be the glory in the midst of her.
>
> Job 1:9-10 Then Satan answered the LORD, and said, Doth Job fear God for nought?
>
> Hast not thou made an hedge about him, and about his house, and about all that he hath on every side? thou hast blessed the work of his hands, and his substance is increased in the land.

I had numerous attacks in my dreams that I had learned to cancel out long before this fight, and had seen many things trying to get over the oil line I had put out, and also demons sitting in trees watching us in my visions and dreams, and strange birds watching me in the daytime that would leave when I rebuked them. It was exciting at times but scary at others.

I had learnt to watch everything for signs of God and signs of the devil from our trip to Africa. Not that I was paranoid. It was the opposite. Here is the scripture following the second find of the 26:18 numbers of fire that I had the night I was born again. And when I read them it had entered me, even almost 20 years ago, and it was a promise that He made and I believed it was mine.

> Deu 26:19 And to make thee high above all nations which he hath made, in praise, and in name, and in honour; and that thou mayest be an holy people unto the LORD thy God, as he hath spoken.

God was at work constantly. I trusted Him and knew He would not give me more than I could handle. And I knew I was well trained for the fight. I had ramped up my praying to two to three hours a day and never slept out of my clothes for around four months. I could feel them coming at times or God would wake me up and warn me, and at other times Poss and I would get really bad acid reflux that would warn us they were about. Plus we were praying for Jill over the phone and had to fight for her also. And she was copping it worse than us.

So I was standing in the gap. I wasn't going to see the devil win, No way! I wasn't worried for us nowhere as much as I was for Jill.

CHAPTER THIRTY TWO: GONE NUCLEAR

She had no idea how to resist or stand and was stuck in the middle of this fight for her life. God had looked for a man and given me the task, and I didn't want to let him down.

> Eze 22:30 And I sought for a man among them, that should make up the hedge, and stand in the gap before me for the land, that I should not destroy it: but I found none.

Jill was copping visits from them in vehicles, driving around honking their horns, burnouts and putting curses in her letterbox and into her backyard. Not to mention the invisible visitations which were many, to me, and no doubt they had a spiritual highway straight to Jill's place. But we were fighting for ourselves and for Jill, praying so much and fasting, and with God keeping us a step ahead.

I began to see that Jill was a catalyst in the middle of all this to bring this entire Tasmanian coven down. And I had set my mind to cut the tail off Amalek in Tasmania. I loved this place and was getting angry at what they had been doing unnoticed for decades. And I believed and still believe that God had ordained this time, and that He is going to destroy this group. All over the world!

The first few curses they threw were hitting very hard. It was hitting Jill and the assigned demons were entering because of anger issues and her desire for revenge, and it was hitting me hard too, maybe because of the fear of the unknown. I didn't know what these people were capable of and they were on my Tasmanian doorstep. Not coming from the mainland or overseas.

The reason they want to take Tasmania is because you can drive across the top and also from top to bottom in five hours or so. They could be anywhere in the place in half a day. But I also thought a visit in the natural from them would be unwise, but I didn't know how stupid they were. First curse hit us very hard. Jill could read this and she said it basically read "You and your new friends are dead".

But the day we got it we drove to Hobart for some strange reason, and in the night visions, God took me around to the Witches places to mock them. Something I wouldn't have done, even if I could. I was walking in their houses and onto their properties and saying things that I can't remember now but they were not happy with me. And there were a lot ended up chasing me. But He stood me behind a glass screen and nothing could touch me. And they were filthy angry, especially the crazy women, so vicious.

Death threat

They come at me hurling all sorts of things at me, words and objects. I woke up and prayed for about 20 minutes and went back to sleep. No dramas then. Jill said about the attention she was getting in the natural, that she had never seen them operate like this before; out in the open. She said they never had to.

All movements were done by word of mouth, nothing written down and no phone calls. She had seen many people perish by curses and rituals done against them through sickness, disease and accidents, and they had been so successful that coming out of the darkness to harass in the daytime and in person was never done. So she knew they were getting desperate. And that encouraged me to keep ramping up the intensity of the fight.

In everything that I saw as a weakness in their attacks I used for myself as an encouragement. There were many fights at night in the second heaven while in my dream state with weapons and hands and fists and feet at times. I was also rebuking small groups of them in the name of Jesus and they were cringing in foetal positions on the ground and other times loosing upon them the terror of the Lord and same thing, there was cringing and real terror. Not a good look in a group for high and mighty devil worshippers. If you don't understand, pray about these scriptures.

> 1Co 15:32 If after the manner of men I have fought with beasts at Ephesus, what advantageth it me, if the dead rise not? let us eat and drink; for to morrow we die.
>
> Jer 32:21 And hast brought forth thy people Israel out of the land of Egypt with signs, and with wonders, and with a strong hand, and with a stretched out arm, and with great terror;

CHAPTER THIRTY TWO: GONE NUCLEAR

> Gen 35:5 And they journeyed: and the terror of God was upon the cities that *were* round about them, and they did not pursue after the sons of Jacob.

None of this was my idea when I sleep. I just go to sleep and I get to see what is happening, but my body is taken over and I have no say although I do feel emotion while being there. But as for having a will to do this or that, it's not there. So for those who say I must be astral projecting, it is nothing like it. If you hear of those who visit the Courts of Heaven, Beware! That is a demonic thing picked up by the churches.

There were also the usual dreams of guidance, instruction, warnings, council and words of knowledge for others. So I wasn't living in one big nightmare, only some of the time. LOL. But we were winning!

> Joe 2:28 And it shall come to pass afterward, *that* I will pour out my spirit upon all flesh; and your sons and your daughters shall prophesy, your old men shall dream dreams, your young men shall see visions:

I had been on the devils list for a while now, even in Tassie. My wife stayed in the Grand Chancellor Motel in Hobart one night around 12 months before all this after booking well in advance. She found a dirty brown feather stuck in a newly made bed. It seemed these people had eyes everywhere and were in high places.

This blood curse was done early on in the fight by two younger witches that Jill knew. There was the top ones coming against her for a start, then lower ranked and then lower again, every time Jill would give me their names, I could pray and target that individual.

Jill's car

Other times like I said, I would describe them to her as they came at me in the astral plane and she knew who they were. None of this was strange to either of us. She knew the game from her perspective and I understood it from mine. And I was winning a lot of battles and when I would fight the ones she knew and win, they would not return.

I was not sending death curses but with warfare against their strongmen and even this against the humans, which I have found effective. You know, it's one way or the other into the kingdom of God, and I know I was brought in by the latter here.

> Luk 20:17-18 And he beheld them, and said, What is this then that is written, The stone which the builders rejected, the same is become the head of the corner?
>
> Whosoever shall fall upon that stone shall be broken; but on whomsoever it shall fall, it will grind him to powder.

And every time they would land one with a night terror or a curse in Jill's letterbox, we would have to cast the spirit out of Jill attached to the curse. The open doors were obviously the large demons within, which were getting weaker all the time, and also her desire for revenge, but she would ring us and we could cast them out after 15 minutes or so of warfare over the phone. Some of them were not happy and let me know with a few or more expletives.

It seemed if they came in recently, they had no legal rights. I am no expert and I was just going as I was led. Jesus Christ is the deliverer. I was just the worker, and I felt like a blind one half of the time. But the other half, I was seriously on the job.

We did go back to Jill's a few times to lay hands on her and do some heavy duty work. We drove the three and a half hours and once we had arrived and there was blood dripped on the doorstep. And the man running the small church came and I was burning the curse in the side garden after cleaning up the blood. It was written on some paper that was stuffed in the door

I told him what had been happening for a couple of months now and he was surprised. I said she is loaded with spirits. He said, "No, once you are saved you can't have demons". I said "Come inside and you will change your mind within ten minutes. And we started to pray and the demon came up and was saying" Help me, help me Adam, tell them to stop." It put on quite a sooky act.

And Pastor Adam believed that the spirit talking through Jill was Jill.

And I could see that so I kept telling him it was the demon speaking and he didn't believe me. So I had to think what to do, and quickly. He was looking like he was going to stop us and stuff everything up so I said, "Who is Lord demon, who is Lord"? The demon started to cackle and said "Lucifer is lord" to the shock of Adam.

Obviously a demon will never say Jesus Christ is Lord. This is a good way to test the spirits and see who is on the surface.

> 1Co 12:3 Wherefore I give you to understand, that no man speaking by the Spirit of God calleth Jesus accursed: and *that* no man can say that Jesus is the Lord, but by the Holy Ghost.

Then it was on for young and old. The fireworks had begun. It had stopped hiding and was now on the surface fully manifesting, spitting and kicking and cursing and speaking in weird languages and calling for reinforcements. We had been to Jill's before to cast out the demons and got many out. Some of them named themselves and put up quite a fight and hundreds came out just by deep coughing.

But now they were almost gone, with the bigger ones forcing them up to save their own skin. The spirits were telling us things that only we knew and also telling Adam, the old pastor what he had done in the past to which he was quite surprised. He was amazed now and I got him into the fight, which he took to like a man.

It was good to see an instant change in his theology. I knew he would have to change his mind. Experience is of more value than any theology. And now he had some. So that session finished a few hours later and we were all exhausted. And Poss and I drove back happy. But that was far from the end of it.

We received a curse in the mail that hit me so hard. I was very impressed with the dark power behind it. Although it was just a heap of weird writing like German or something but it was so heavy. As soon as I opened it, "BANG" it hit me like a ton of bricks. I walked into my shed to get a lighter to burn it and couldn't find one so I stuffed the letter in my top pocket and was going to walk inside with it and the Lord spoke loudly and said "Don't take it inside". So I left it outside, went and got a lighter and broke the curses and prayed as it burnt. Half of the heaviness left and there was a lot, and half I couldn't budge. I prayed for two hours and it was stuck on me.

A friend called Abel in Sydney who is a street preacher rang me the next morning and said "Hey Bro, what's going on down there? The

Lord took me down last night in the spirit and your house was full of darkness and I walked around for an hour rebuking demons and covering everything with the blood of Jesus. I'd never done that before. And I went to go outside when all the dark had left and the Lord told me, "I didn't tell you to go outside." Abel continued in his Kiwi accent, "It was all so strange, but so heavy man."

I told him what had been happening and then he understood and entered the battle with prayer back up. Thank you Jesus. He definitely brought in some help when it was needed.

> Lev 26:6-9 And I will give peace in the land, and ye shall lie down, and none shall make *you* afraid: and I will rid evil beasts out of the land, neither shall the sword go through your land.
>
> And ye shall chase your enemies, and they shall fall before you by the sword.
>
> And five of you shall chase an hundred, and an hundred of you shall put ten thousand to flight: and your enemies shall fall before you by the sword.
>
> For I will have respect unto you, and make you fruitful, and multiply you, and establish my covenant with you.

I had a handful of people praying also by now. I was praying with a man called John who understood some things about this fight as he had trouble with this group himself in the past. He was keen to help and once as we prayed warfare for about 40 minutes against this coven and for the church, my anointing oil turned blood red. I was amazed and God confirmed its use and that He was in this war that was going on. All these things comforted me and I never felt alone at all.

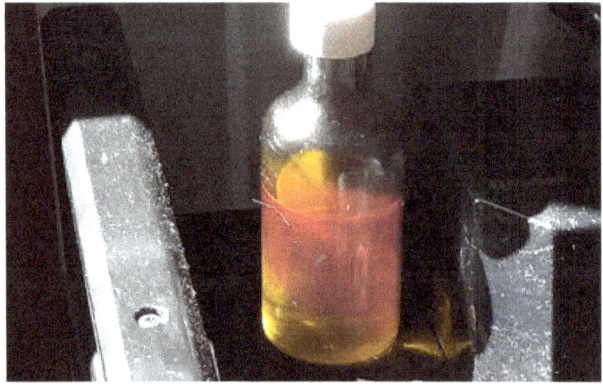

Anointing oil turns red

CHAPTER THIRTY TWO: GONE NUCLEAR

We had made lines around Jill's house that the witches couldn't step over on the road out the front and on her front porch also. When she was hit hard by a curse and couldn't say Jesus, she said that she had to go out the back and smoke her cigarettes. It was too uncomfortable near the oil. And if she put even one toe on one drop, even in her shoes, it would burn her.

She said once when I gave her some oil at a time she wasn't doing too badly and before the line, that a high up satanist knocked on her door and she threw some anointing oil on him. She said he reacted like it was a heap of scorpions.

Oil line

There were two of her old companions showed up one evening as Jill was out the back having a smoke and she heard them calling from out on the road. Her house had about a 5ft fence and she walked over and saw them on the far side of the road. They couldn't get any closer because of the oil.

This is the text I received from Jill the next day.

> *Pete PLEASE stop whatever you are doing!!!!! Went out for smoko, Garry & Karrwen promised the oppression would stop if my mate (being you backed up) They weren't joking*

They had no desire to back off Jill. They were getting hit hard and this made me smile. It was far too late to stop and I was not in the mood to relinquish all the ground we had gained, for peace with the devil. Or I could put it exactly what I thought, "You idiots, as if." Once Jill told me another head honcho pulled up with four others in the car. Three men in black hoodies in the back and they tried to get her in the car. They put the curse in the letterbox that morning and she got the mail and opened it and it landed, then the demon was near the surface. The plan was that it would be strong enough to get her in the car. But the Lord was working. She had enough strength to resist its control.

She said she went out to the shed and filled a tennis ball up with petrol and put a wick in it and walked back out the front and lit it and threw it in the front seat. But it didn't ignite in the car, only when they went into a panic and threw it out onto the road. Which I thought was disappointing.

I prayed about the man I heard was driving and I had already seen him get a touch up. Without knowing he even existed, I'd asked Jill who the tall man was who looked like Dr Chris on the TV. I'd seen him get hammered in a dream after praying this following.

> Amo 9:2-3 Though they dig into hell, thence shall mine hand take them; though they climb up to heaven, thence will I bring them down:

> And though they hide themselves in the top of Carmel, I will search and take them out thence; and though they be hid from my sight in the bottom of the sea, thence will I command the serpent, and he shall bite them:

> And though they go into captivity before their enemies, thence will I command the sword, and it shall slay them: and I will set mine eyes upon them for evil, and not for good.

There are many Imprecatory prayers in the Word. In the Old Testament they were used against natural enemies and in the New Testament era now we use them against the spiritual entities that trouble us, because we now have the authority to do so. But if the witches like to play their games in the second Heaven, or the astral plane, then where those demons inside them are getting the beating, then the ones who are hosting them are going to wear some damage as well.

It got to the point where the demons could not be cast out over the phone anymore. The little ones had fled or been forced out and the big ones had more control when they manifested. Three times they told me to F#$% off with a little more abuse than that and threw the phone and then proceeded to smash up Jills house. That was hard with the phone ringing and no answer and us knowing that a demon had now taken control. Actually it was near terrifying. But we had to trust God. And we would pray hard also.

CHAPTER THIRTY TWO: GONE NUCLEAR

Jill would wake up soon after collapsing on the floor or the couch with no knowledge of what happened, and there would be something smashed or damaged. Bibles ripped and things strewn around in certain rooms. So it was too hard now, we had to travel.

The demons were strong and it seemed as soon as we got a heap out after the visit the satanists were back on the job putting them back in through the curses, whether in the letterbox or through other means in the night time. I had to give them credit, they were determined, but so was I.

I made the oath long ago that I was going to give the devil as much trouble as I could and this was my big chance. And when I saw in a dream that Jarrod was over right next to my Fathers place doing some sort of ritual in the spirit, the fight turned nuclear.

I was not going to let their ugly vindictive ways come against my family. So it was on. He got some special prayer, as well as the others who God had shown me their faces. And I was still learning their names when describing them to Jill. And most of the ones I was shown in my night visions were the ones who were visiting her and had been associated with.

> Pro 21:18 The wicked *shall be* a ransom for the righteous, and the transgressor for the upright.

When I saw them and was told their names who they were, they were falling quickly. I saw Jarrod on the TV, talking up Mona Foma. He was one of the spokesmen. And his real name was something else. Jill told me Jarrod was his Witch name. So I found out his real name and sent his picture to all on my email list.

I know he would have got severely chastised for this and when Dark Mofo came around, that he was one of the main organizers of; he had run away back to America. This suited me. I hope he never comes back. And if he does, well…

The lights were blinking at home, the big one on the lounge room ceiling and the lamp at times during prayer. I was sleeping on the couch or fully clothed under a blanket on the beds in the house for months, and also getting up at 11 or 12 most nights to pray. Between 12 and 4 in the morning was the time mostly that the action would occur. Not every night or even every second night, but there was no telling when they would come. There was a sense of suspense about for the few months and it was a burden I had to bear.

I did pray for Jill once over the phone when she was desperate and I was working, and her nose started to bleed and the room she was in filled up with blowflies. She wasn't surprised though. She said at some of their rituals, blowflies had swarmed around, even at night at four in the morning. She took a selfie and you could see the blowies in it around her when she sent it to me, and the blood pouring from her nose.

Jill was so strong. I was absolutely amazed at her strength. How she would get knocked down then get back up. Many people would be in the psych ward after the first round or two. Jill was a fighter. I knew this already but when we visited her once to pray she could hardly walk because of a sore knee that she hurt in a bit of a barney with a couple of high ups.

She'd already told us that Jarrod and some loud mouth woman came that she knew to threaten her and she hit Jill so Jill beat the crap out of the woman and kicked Jarrod in the testicles. I just told her that I can't blame her, but inwardly I was thinking, "Well done", which is not really the righteous response. But sometimes the righteousness and patience was being tested severely. And even after the scratches and the bites that the demons left, that would just come out of the blue, she would recover in remarkable time.

And Poss and I were there with her when some scratches came, twice. Once we had just started deliverance prayers and another a lot later. The second lot are pictured and she received this threat in her yard two days later. They had threatened her about the oath she had taken but couldn't get to her. The Lord had protected her many times now. If they could have, she would be dead. And she knows it.

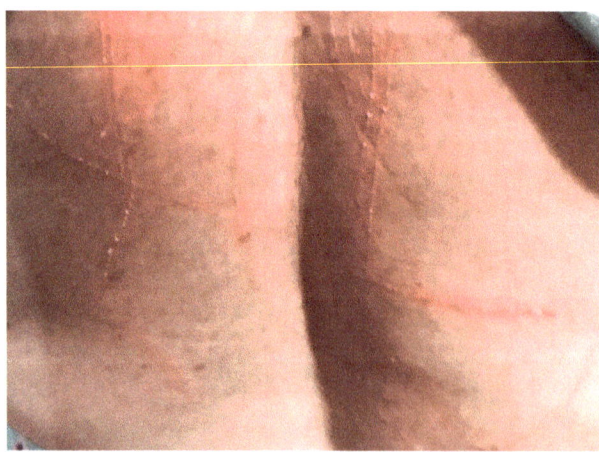

Demon scratches

CHAPTER THIRTY TWO: GONE NUCLEAR

Also she had no brakes on her car when her son got in it to drive once, but she had just driven for three and a half hours like that with no problem. God was and still is working.

We had to laugh at the spelling of some of the curses we were getting; it seemed that the apprentice satanists were on the job. This one was received only two days after the scratches appeared. Amazing how they can see. People worry about the technology, but these witches have that as well as eyes in other places.

Air raid

One time we went we went to Jill's we found a letter in her letterbox and it was a curse. And I burnt it and broke the curses and was teaching her to do the same. That was on a Thursday of a long weekend. Then we received one exactly the same but ours had been posted.

I had covered the letterbox with oil and we had tongs and lighter ready every day we checked our letterbox. And this time I burnt it off our property and broke the curses and it only took half an hour to get on the move, which was still a fair time though, but they were weakening.

And the third one we got after we had stopped the mail being delivered to our house, and it stayed in the post office. So when we had got home after two weeks away it was waiting for us. They had posted it hoping that our friend who was looking after our house may take it inside we thought.

Anyway I got it from the post office and it read, "We are still praying for you and the hard up ones" written in the same black pen with the sticky tape on the envelope back and no return address.

I took it down to under the bridge in St Helens and burnt it, breaking the curses then urinated on it and kicked the ashes into the water. That only took ten minutes to clear off, plus got a bit of a laugh as well.

> Col 2:15 *And* having spoiled principalities and powers, he made a shew of them openly, triumphing over them in it.

I thought, "How stupid are these idiots". We'd been away on the mainland for two weeks and I had let up on the on the warfare a bit against this mob and they greet me with this. "You should have let sleeping dogs lie". I thought. Or even better here,

> Pro 26:17 He that passeth by, *and* meddleth with strife *belonging* not to him, *is like* one that taketh a dog by the ears.

Peace flowers

The enemy was playing all sorts of games. Cursing Jill one day and trying to woo her the next. But I kept telling her to destroy everything. Even the expensive gold and silver jewellery they were leaving. I found one lot in the garden on a deliverance mission that must have fallen in there, when one satanist tried to get over the oil line and must have thrown it and it landed in the bushes next to the porch steps. It was a steel web ring. I broke the curses and burnt the ring in the cardboard box and the ring disappeared before the box was burnt.

Once they got a hit on Jill and the demon was at the surface. Her unsaved husband and son could tell something wasn't right and old Pastor Adam who was called to the house was told bluntly how bad he was and that he was full of BS, but at least he knew what it was that was talking to him now.

CHAPTER THIRTY TWO: GONE NUCLEAR

Curse on car and vial of blood thrown in car open window

They had seen Jill's eyes turn black also a couple of times. The Husband, Son and Pastor Adam had all seen this. So we go up there after Adam said to get us up to help, and Jill had gone to the occult store and bought some rings. One was a pentagram and the other just a shiny stone. I could tell when we arrived that she wasn't going well and could not go near any of the oil around the place or say Jesus or touch a Bible.

But she was still in her body resisting the things on the surface that had been speaking to her during the night like they used to, and she had been speaking back to them. And this is what was texted to me from Jill the day before we got there.

> *Things a lot more pressured after we spoke Pete.. I felt a strong presence so I asked " who should pass theee and bring troubles in the physical form"? " it is I aquiel as you well know, before & now " /*
>
> *Tu saves como yo soy, tu saves quien soy*
>
> *I can speak in many tongues now Pete, many tongues*

We told her that the pentagram ring had to go and she was obedient with little resistance. But when I tried to get the innocent looking ring off her that was bought from the same shop, the demon manifested immediately and clenched her fist and it was a struggle to get it off. It had no legal right but with the jewellery it did.

So as long as she had that on and she was in rebellion to Gods word, it could stay. But as soon as the jewellery came off it had to go. And it was fairly easy to cast out and remove, only being there a couple of days, although it did resist with physical violence and more, for about half an hour.

So ladies, be careful what jewellery you wear. Also perfumes and lipsticks have curses attached to them. Ask yourselves how do they make you feel when you wear them? I did hear a testimony from a man who was involved in a lipstick factory in Africa. They were putting human blood that was crawling with demons in them.

This may have been the last two days we were there at Jill's place before the strongman came out. Six hours one day we were with her, about five praying, and five hours the next day with about four hours praying. We were enjoying the times that Jill was on the surface and it was easy to tell the difference. She was happy and had so much knowledge about the enemy, I was fascinated, and learning so much. I discovered so many tactics and strategies and our faith had just skyrocketed through all this and our trust in the Lord.

> Pro 3:5-6 Trust in the LORD with all thine heart; and lean not unto thine own understanding.
>
> In all thy ways acknowledge him, and he shall direct thy paths.

We were tested on the very last day when we were getting the second last demon out, we believe she died twice. Her eyes rolled back and we could only see whites and she stopped breathing for a couple of minutes, and the thoughts coming in both my head and Poss' that were so loud and damning were saying, "You've killed her. She's dead. You're going to be in so much trouble". We were looking at each other and we knew how serious this could get.

So I started to rebuke death and Poss was calling her back and then she started to breathe again. Praise God. What a relief! I knew of this scripture beneath and I had seen this before after a large demon had come out, even out of me while doing self-deliverance in the past.

> Mar 9:26 And *the spirit* cried, and rent him sore, and came out of him: and he was as one dead; insomuch that many said, He is dead.

But this time there was no demon that had left. They were just trying their hardest to kill Jill and destroy Poss and myself.

So Jill was up and talking and we were relieved and we thought we have to get this demon out. So we started praying again. And it happened again. Eyes rolled back and white and no breathing. But this time I just commanded the spirit to let her go and loose her and it only took a little under a minute this time and Jill came back to the land of

CHAPTER THIRTY TWO: GONE NUCLEAR

the living with no recollection of anything. But it was spooky I tell you that. I was thinking it may be good to raise the dead, but not much fun if you have killed them first. LOL

After about five or six months, the last strongman was out. There were so many of them. They would put up massive fights and be kicking and screaming and punching and spitting and cursing and crying and begging us to leave them be. Some of the names were Legion, Leviathan, Beelzebub, Ashteroth, Baal, Belial, Molech and Abaddon, which are demons from the Bible. And many more that are not mentioned in the Holy Book.

They were all resisting as much as they could, but with the name of Jesus, they could not stand, and one demon that took Jill even years to receive, was kicked out in 20 to 30 minutes. I think that was Beelzebub, the one that gave her more divination powers, as did Ashteroth. Beelzebub is also called "Lord of the flies" and maybe this is where the blowflies came from earlier on.

> 2Ki 1:2-4 And Ahaziah fell down through a lattice in his upper chamber that *was* in Samaria, and was sick: and he sent messengers, and said unto them, Go, enquire of Baalzebub the god of Ekron whether I shall recover of this disease.
>
> But the angel of the LORD said to Elijah the Tishbite, Arise, go up to meet the messengers of the king of Samaria, and say unto them, *Is it* not because *there is* not a God in Israel, *that* ye go to enquire of Baalzebub the god of Ekron?
>
> Now therefore thus saith the LORD, Thou shalt not come down from that bed on which thou art gone up, but shalt surely die. And Elijah departed.

We got Ashteroth out one day and then she got hit with a letterbox curse a few days after. I had lost count on the number of times I told her to let her husband check the mail, but she said he would only worry. I had to show him the pictures in the end and tell him all of what was happening. He didn't want to know but he had to join in. He had seen others try to deliver Jill in the past and they failed and things only got worse for them.

Anyway a week later Ashteroth surfaced again after the curse and I said "Ashteroth, we cast you out last week, how did you get back in?" And with a cackle it looked and pointed in the direction of the letterbox. That is when I told the husband that if he wanted his wife to come right, he had to check the mail every day when he got home from work. And he did. Don't ask me how this relationship ever worked. It was very strange and amazing to Poss and me.

> Jdg 2:12-13 And they forsook the LORD God of their fathers, which brought them out of the land of Egypt, and followed other gods, of the gods of the people that *were* round about them, and bowed themselves unto them, and provoked the LORD to anger.
>
> And they forsook the LORD, and served Baal and Ashtaroth.

Now these spirits choose who they entered and dwelt in. And Jill had become a willing recipient and their home that they didn't want to give up in a hurry. So they were trying everything to hang in there.

The name Abaddon was coming up near the end. Whether it was the demons calling out to their master or Abaddon himself we don't know. But this one took some time on one day and never came out and then on the next day it surfaced again and was a stubborn one to move. But with lots of persistence it came out. We just kept beating it with the Word of God and with our determination and the name and authority of the Lord Jesus Christ obviously, it weakened and left. It was a very sticky one though. These crazy satanists were playing with the real stuff, and losing their souls to these entities, who have so deceived them and led them into their traps. Very sad to see how they have been so blinded.

> Rev 9:11 And they had a king over them, *which is* the angel of the bottomless pit, whose name in the Hebrew tongue *is* Abaddon, but in the Greek tongue hath *his* name Apollyon.

The Deliverance was so exhausting but so rewarding. To be fighting the Principalities that I had read about in the Bible and winning was a great thrill. We were extremely grateful to those who were interceding for us while this was happening. Only a handful, but they believed, and that was enough. When we got Leviathan out the second last day, I showed her this picture. It is in St Helens and it blew her away. It was the image of the spirit that she had taken in to herself to give her pride among the group.

Jill was getting visions while in deep deliverance and hearing the names of the demons and she would relay these to us when she was on the surface, and we could use them like the words of knowledge they

CHAPTER THIRTY TWO: GONE NUCLEAR

Leviathan

were. Demons will give up their names or call for higher ups to help and God can give pictures or words of knowledge to any of the workers also. It's a faith builder all around, and at times very enjoyable.

I said to God late into the last day, "How much longer?" We'd already been battling the day before and almost four hours this day. And He said, "Half an hour". I was so glad to hear that. So in the last half an hour the last to go was a demon called Aquiel. It is the god of Sundays, that works against the church to destroy it. This is the spirit that stops people from going to church and the main one behind the work it had Jill do when she was a satanist.

In the end it was crying and complaining that it couldn't be saved and moaning that it wasn't allowed into Heaven and was trying to bargain with us. It was crying out, (I beat them up so bad with the weapons of the spiritual warfare) . "Please let me stay just two minutes more, please, please". And I said "You gotta be joking demon, you have to go, and right now your two minutes are up" and with that it left in a heap of deep coughing and she was free from all the Satanism spirits that had entered. Praise God.

There is so much more to this story and I may write another book when the Coven here is totally destroyed. Please pray for that. Not the book, but the destruction of the satanic takeover aimed at Tasmania, because they want the whole state. But not while I'm here they're not.

> Eze 3:17 Son of man, I have made thee a watchman unto the house of Israel: therefore hear the word at my mouth, and give them warning from me.

CHAPTER THIRTY THREE
A DIFFERENT BATTLE

With the majority of the satanist spirits out of Jill and her ability to say Jesus and read the Bible now strong, we thought we had crossed the mountain. But it wasn't over yet. Jill was telling us of how her and her possessed friends would do rituals in the high places and shedding blood, and in parks, schools, playgrounds, bridges, accident spots on the highways, water supplies and obviously the churches.

I knew what Satan was and now I can see how he spreads himself on the earth through his workers. All conned and filled with false promises of spending eternity in Hell on their own little thrones. Jill was going not too bad. And because the enemy failed in the job of loading Jill up again with the devils that were tormenting her, they started to curse her health, which they were already doing but they seemed to focus in on it more, with Jill spending more and more times in hospital.

Her liver was failing, and her pancreas, spleen and heart were playing up. It seemed that every time we would gain ground she would be going well, then the devil would have his go and the doctors then would want to see her and run tests. So basically she was tested right after the enemy hit. I had seen the coincidence, but Jill was having trouble believing that God was on her side.

I did constantly remind her that without God she would be dead, and that He knows what He is doing. He is not just working with Jill; He is working with all Jill's family and the doctors and everyone involved with this struggle, for whatever reason He liked. I do believe with her returning to the same hospital for sometimes weeks on end made the doctors confused. They had put her on so much medication, and she had a monitor in her heart. No doubt after the healing the first time when she was bad then all of a sudden could go home, they would

CHAPTER THIRTY THREE: A DIFFERENT BATTLE

have took the credit for all their meds. But if she did die when we prayed for her, and we thought she had, twice, then that would show up on the heart monitor. And they would tell her it's urgent and treat her as a guinea pig with all their poisons.

Once Jill went in to hospital and hadn't had a bowel movement for 16 days. And it took them until about 10 days before they gave her anything for it. And it still didn't work for another six days. She also had a problem called Barrett's mucosa. It was really bad reflux. I knew it was a curse because we figured out that a lot of the times she got it, Poss and I got it also, at exactly the same time.

Jill also got some horrific nightmares of death and destruction aimed at her while she was in hospital. All designed to break her down and lose all hope. And no wonder the bad dreams came. Dark Mofo was on again, and every witch in Australia was most likely attending, although, this year wasn't as bad as the last, and I knew they were getting weaker. And I did believe that, and still do. Right now there is little oppression, apart from the lights flashing a couple of times writing these last few chapters. And we are in Hobart now, so I can't blame any dodgy wiring in the old farmhouse now.

I had been praying a lot that the enemy's council would be foolishness, and I believe it had just come to pass in a big way, for the world to see.

> 2Sa 15:31 And *one* told David, saying, Ahithophel *is* among the conspirators with Absalom. And David said, O LORD, I pray thee, turn the counsel of Ahithophel into foolishness.

Because what they had done in Hobart was so extreme and foolish that it worked totally against them. I do believe that the prayers being prayed against this group were intensifying and that they had lost face with their followers in Tasmania. Not just because of their defeated attempts to destroy Jill and even myself, but no doubt because everyone that did partake in cursing and attacking the righteous and failed would be most likely punished by the enemy severely for those failures.

Jill knew what they did to those who stuffed up their orders. So in a big final push to show how clever they were and how much they thought they owned and ran Tasmania, they did this. They put up 3 blood red inverted crosses that were 20 meters high, down on the Hobart waterfront. And finally some of the church people woke up.

Satanic crosses, Hobart waterfront.

I know the satanists believe the church is full of hypocrisy and those who are sheep and asleep and probably with good reason at times. The hypocrisy in men who pretend to be righteous has been around for as long as man has been here.

> Rom 2:24 For the name of God is blasphemed among the Gentiles through you, as it is written.

Although some didn't want to see or even think that the devil may be real, and said so in the papers, a lot signed a petition about these things. And it got up to over 20,000. The Dark Mofo's put one together and they got around 5,000. Even with all the witches walking around the streets they could not get as much support as they thought they could. And the Mayor Ron Christie was saying things like it's got to go, we don't want this in Tasmania. So some people are waking up. Praise God.

Once Jill got out of hospital she was very low. And when she was low, the enemy would enter her a lot easier than normal. She was on a downer about God and wondering why He didn't just sort the people out who were against her and then everything would be just sweet. I said "He doesn't work that way". But it seemed that nothing I could say was helping and it was another worry that we had to pray about and deal with.

God told me to step back from her a little while so I didn't contact her for a week, which was hard. I did want to stay updated and know what to pray for, but I trusted God, and stepped back. Jill rang after a week and said she was so low that she knew she needed help and turned her phone off for that same week, which would have worried Poss and me to be getting the message bank for a week.

CHAPTER THIRTY THREE: A DIFFERENT BATTLE

But we had been told not to contact. Jill said she got on her knees and started to pray to God, and God showed up in the Spirit and blessed her with peace and gave her a taste of His real presence, which was so good for Jill and for us. Now the God she had been told about, the God who had been healing and delivering her and protecting her, had all of a sudden become so real. He was now Jill's God.

This was such a blessing and a massive shift in the momentum of this fight. Now Jill knew that God cared for her and she had felt the love and it was something that she desperately needed. Thank you Lord Jesus. We continued to break the power of the curses coming against her over the phone and were praying healing to her a lot. We were much time in prayer for her recovery, along with the prayer warriors on the job too. It did seem as if the enemy was getting weaker and weaker, with the visitations slowing down and were fairly powerless mostly.

Jill could say Jesus now and read her Bible without wanting to throw it away and tear it up. Jill's husband was still going through the mail and screening it and this shut one of their avenues down. Jill was very curious and she knew it, so she had to resist that desire to check the mailbox. And she did, which was a big relief for us.

They were still throwing curses over the fence and following her around at times and she was still angry with them and still looking for revenge, which was a door open in itself. I had taught her to pray and break the curses and she was growing strong very quickly. What took me well over a decade to learn, Jill was learning in months. But there was still something that she had to let go of.

I was telling Jill to send the curses back to the sender, and because of the viciousness of the spiritual attacks, Jill was getting very vindictive against the enemy. One curse hit and she started shaking very badly. And it lasted for almost two weeks or so. We saw her and prayed but the shakes continued.

Usually when we prayed, if there was anything in Jill it would come out by her coughing it out. But the shakes stayed. I thought if must have been the side effects of the pills they had her on. So we just treated it as that. But we learned soon enough the Truth, praise God. Here is a dose of what she had to take 3 times a day. God help anyone who is in this snare.

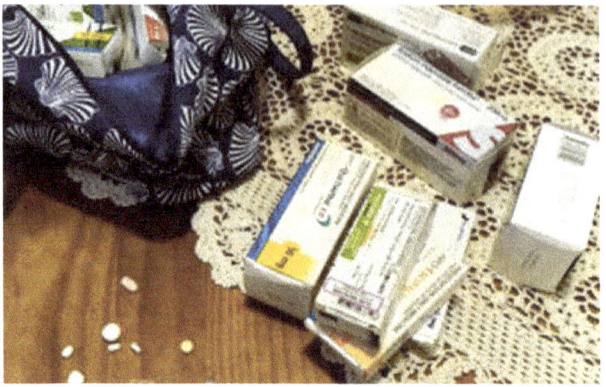

Breakfast

Poss and I were talking about Jill's shakes after we had seen her. And others who she had met said they had seen them too. It was even in her voice, it was weak and a little bit like you try to talk when you are shivering cold. Not quite that bad, but getting there.

We were praying and then this happened which gave the game away that the devil was playing here. Jill was called into the specialist. And I got this text from her. This wasn't long after the scratches on her back and the threatening letter in the last chapters, after Jill had shared some of her story with others.

It was backlash for sure and revenge and retaliation from the enemy who is desperate to keep the hidden things in darkness. But before this happened Jill was saying to me, "I hope I don't get scratched again", and more or less expecting a hit from them in retribution. Apparently that is how the devil keeps all his workers, petrified against resistance to his orders and his will. I was thinking of this scripture, possibly the open door for this but I'm not sure. It did happen anyway.

> Job 3:25 For the thing which I greatly feared is come upon me, and that which I was afraid of is come unto me.

And fear is a spirit. We had cast out a fear of death from Jill early on. But they were still attacking, as they do to all of us.

> 2Ti 1:7 For God hath not given us the spirit of fear; but of power, and of love, and of a sound mind.

There are many types and functions of fear. And they keep us in much bondage. What are yours? Rebuke them and tell them to leave in Jesus name. The freedom is waiting there for you.

CHAPTER THIRTY THREE: A DIFFERENT BATTLE

> Heb 2:15 And deliver them who through fear of death were all their lifetime subject to bondage.

Anyway there's your mini sermon for the week, back to the story.

Jill had just returned from the Doctors. She knew where the trouble was coming from.

> *Just got home. Not good news. Last blood check did not come out so well, can't remember the fancy condition as a result, urine has blood in it & heart not in an unstable beets grrrr. He wants to change meds & upped my strength in a few medications. Dr asked (....Husband) if he was OK with me going back into hospital!!!!! Dr phoning me on Monday to see if meds have helped, those lousy %#@+* are on the attack again!!! I keep praying every day for my health to be cured so I don't understand why God is allowing this? In away, I was expecting another attack of some sort but not this. They are getting through I'm sure to keep my mouth shut with a vengeance.*

She was angry again and disappointed about her sickness and discouraged. This battle was going on for months as well with physical, mental and spiritual attacks on her constantly. I was amazed how she kept pushing on. It was an absolute credit to her. But I could see the anger in this text that I hadn't seen in Jill for a little while and I got suspicious.

So I could see un-forgiveness in her springing up again. Then Jill went to a church in a nearby town, but she went alone. Usually she went with somebody else if it was to visit another place. When she gets in there and sits down the back, she sees two of her old friends come in to curse the place. And she said, "I saw Cynthia and Mark in the church, that they were cursing the whole way through and I didn't know what to do. They were staring daggers at me and I was staring them back."

Jill felt so bad that she didn't do anything. But she did tell some of the attendees afterwards about this, but in some places, that would mean nothing. Jill was angry on Sunday arvo and rang and I prayed for her. I reminded her that she had done this thing for many many years and that they were under instructions to do this by their masters. I said that you would have totally upset their concentration and they probably failed and she knew what happened to those who failed.

So I led her in a prayer of forgiveness and got her to forgive and she asked God to bring them out and save them. And it was genuine I felt so we prayed and got some spirits out. Here are the texts that went on the next day.

How do you feel today Jill? Good we hope.

You have no idea just how much I am greatful THANK YOU to u lovelies

I'm feeling much more peace with all that's going on. I know those who are against me will change their tactics that I'm not familiar with. I guess its a time of testing & will do my best to not leave an open door, especially after you prayed & what came in & around me with oppression. I can't thank you enough as I probably would have been ten times worse today. I'm also really grateful to those who are holding me in prayer. I've unloaded every action & thoughts over to God. He will take on the fight to bring healing & keep the enemy a million times away. Thank you both for your prayer, discernment & encouragement AMEN

That night I read about Jesus asking God to forgive the men who were responsible for crucifying Him and Steven who said much the same about his stoning.

> Luk 23:33-34 And when they were come to the place, which is called Calvary, there they crucified him, and the malefactors, one on the right hand, and the other on the left.
>
> Then said Jesus, Father, forgive them; for they know not what they do. And they parted his raiment, and cast lots.
>
> Act 7:59-60 And they stoned Stephen, calling upon *God*, and saying, Lord Jesus, receive my spirit.
>
> And he kneeled down, and cried with a loud voice, Lord, lay not this sin to their charge. And when he had said this, he fell asleep.

Then Jill got another curse thrown over the fence the next day into her backyard, most likely from the two in the church the day before, but she rang me straight away and I told her to burn it and not open it. I was amazed at how many of them she opened, and then paid a price and wished she didn't. But with this one I was with her on the phone and she burnt it and we broke the curses and asked God to cover us in the blood and I told her about what God had shown me and that we had to forgive them. I prayed and she was coughing things up. And she felt a lot better again. But I was unsettled and started to pray at home about the letter.

CHAPTER THIRTY THREE: A DIFFERENT BATTLE

I forgave them with the above scriptures still in my mind, and then I started coughing up things. And I knew straight away what was happening and why. So I rang Jill and explained what the devils tactic was against us and we both repented for sending the curses back with a desire for revenge and retaliation. And then Jill started to cough really deep. And this is some text messages that went on between us after this. The shakes that she had for around two weeks disappeared as well.

I explained the trick of the enemy. And now we shut the doors of un-forgiveness then we had to keep them closed. I think Satan was sacrificing many so we would fall into a trap of a root of bitterness. But praise God, He was with us and gave me the understanding of what was happening.

> *Praise God Jill. Thanks for letting us know. The main thing is that we need to keep the doorways and foothold the enemy uses to access to a minimum. Then it doesn't matter what tactics they use, we are clean and mostly untouchable. So the main tactics are for us to open the doors. But always be wary.*
>
> *I coughed up a little more after talking to you Jill and yawned a bit. It was about that letter or one of them maybe the paper plane. But something came out. Better them out than in. Hope your shakes are gone forever too.*
>
> *I'm so sorry that you were under an attack Pete. I'm pleased tho that you got those entities from hell. I to have been coughing off & on. (… Husband) noticed & made a comment about it by thinking I had a chest infection.. Threw the authority of Jesus, no more coughing today. I'm praying harder for you & Poss. I had that gut feeling that you was under attack when you said that you was coughing. I feel sure that they would be finding new tactics in their curses. My shakes have totally gone, with much thanks to you both praying for me. Now I will up my praying for you both.*
>
> *The spirits are coming out Jill. Don't hold them in by not coughing. We are OK. I prayed and know what's happening. If we just send the curses to the feet of Jesus and not back to the sender then it will stop our vindictiveness toward them, looking for revenge. I have been coughing up a few too this morning that may have had this legal right. I think we both have truly forgiven them and God is cleaning us out. Praise the Lord*

God gave us both deliverance from a lot of things that were hanging around within us. Praise him. And we learned a valuable lesson.

> Rom 12:17-21 Recompense to no man evil for evil. Provide things honest in the sight of all men.
>
> If it be possible, as much as lieth in you, live peaceably with all men.
>
> Dearly beloved, avenge not yourselves, but *rather* give place unto wrath: for it is written, Vengeance *is* mine; I will repay, saith the Lord.
>
> Therefore if thine enemy hunger, feed him; if he thirst, give him drink: for in so doing thou shalt heap coals of fire on his head.
>
> Be not overcome of evil, but overcome evil with good.

God teaches us so much. Most can't get over a hurdle, let alone a mountain. But if we persevere, the answers are always there. I did have a dream in the next couple of nights of me rebuking two people in the name of Jesus Christ, and they were with others and just cringing in terror on the floor. I told Jill what they looked like, and I already had a good idea of who they were, Cynthia and Mark.

So now we had moved to Hobart. God told us through prophetic words not to yoke up with anyone. So that suited me. When we got here I started noticing all this ugly graffiti with no meaning on power poles and signs, especially on intersections. They were everywhere, hundreds and hundreds, mostly in black. I knew they weren't right.

Hobart Hexes

I asked somebody that knew and they replied, "Hi Pete, its a hex, curse on ill health & death eg cancer heart attack, stroke, car accidents, not a good message for the unknowing victims. So this is another work we have to do, apart from all the others. But now I feel that the teeth are busted out of that lion and the choking is underway.

The pressure is nothing like it was in 2015. Whether that means I have gained strength or the enemy is failing. Or perhaps both, it doesn't matter. I'm in this mode now.

> 2Ti 2:3-4 Thou therefore endure hardness, as a good soldier of Jesus Christ.
>
> No man that warreth entangleth himself with the affairs of *this* life; that he may please him who hath chosen him to be a soldier.

And I won't rest until the enemy is scattered and driven out of the land, because the consequences of failing this are not very good, at all!

> Deu 28:7 Num 33:55-56 But if ye will not drive out the inhabitants of the land from before you; then it shall come to pass, that those which ye let remain of them *shall be* pricks in your eyes, and thorns in your sides, and shall vex you in the land wherein ye dwell.
>
> Moreover it shall come to pass, *that* I shall do unto you, as I thought to do unto them.

But I have this promise also that is true and I had seen many times before, and I know I will see it again.

> Deu 28:7 The LORD shall cause thine enemies that rise up against thee to be smitten before thy face: they shall come out against thee one way, and flee before thee seven ways.

But I do remember this. I had also learned to not be overly happy when an enemy was judged.

> Pro 24:17-18 Rejoice not when thine enemy falleth, and let not thine heart be glad when he stumbleth:
>
> Lest the LORD see *it*, and it displease him, and he turn away his wrath from him.

EPILOGUE

This has been the happenings so far. Some will continue, some will end and more may come. And I'm excited about that. I desire to do the will of Him who saved, delivered and healed me. I know He will lead me into the greater things He has for me.

> Joh 14:12-14 Verily, verily, I say unto you, He that believeth on me, the *works* that I do shall he do also; and greater works than these shall he do; because I go unto my Father.
>
> And whatsoever ye shall ask in my name, that will I do, that the Father may be glorified in the Son.
>
> If ye shall ask any thing in my name, I will do *it*.

I trust my God. And that is the main thing. If anything fails I know it is not His fault, and it may be part of His plan. I am beginning to understand that. And I am still only beginning to know Him. But the more I know of Him, not just His love and grace and mercy, but His chastisements and discipline and expectations of us and how we are to walk, then He becomes not just a God but a Father and a friend as well.

> Jer 9:23-24 Thus saith the LORD, Let not the wise *man* glory in his wisdom, neither let the mighty *man* glory in his might, let not the rich *man* glory in his riches:
>
> But let him that glorieth glory in this, that he understandeth and knoweth me, that I *am* the LORD which exercise lovingkindness, judgement, and righteousness, in the earth: for in these *things* I delight, saith the LORD.

How well do you trust God? How well do you know God? Do you feel forgiven and feel that the Creator has made his home within you in the deepest parts and loves to be with you?

> Jer 31:33-34 But this *shall be* the covenant that I will make with the house of Israel; After those days, saith the LORD, I will put my law in their inward parts, and write it in their hearts; and will be their God, and they shall be my people.
>
> And they shall teach no more every man his neighbour, and every man his brother, saying, Know the LORD: for they shall all know me, from the least of them unto the greatest of them, saith the LORD: for I will forgive their iniquity, and I will remember their sin no more.

Christianity is a relationship where you know He cares about everything you do and that He has a greater purpose for you than just that of following men and following your own desires. He so wants to share Himself through us and that is the greatest blessing that anyone can ever have. To know that the Creator God wants to use us in our own free will to change the hearts of many and bring eternal life into their lives. There is no greater work.

> Joh 17:21-23 That they all may be one; as thou, Father, art in me, and I in thee, that they also may be one in us: that the world may believe that thou hast sent me.
>
> And the glory which thou gavest me I have given them; that they may be one, even as we are one:
>
> I in them, and thou in me, that they may be made perfect in one; and that the world may know that thou hast sent me, and hast loved them, as thou hast loved me.

The Lord God Almighty will lead us into the truth and onto the path He has for us. And there is one special path that He has for you. It is there waiting. Follow Him and you will find it.

> Rom 8:14 For as many as are led by the Spirit of God, they are the sons of God.

He will lead you into Life. The abundant life He promised. And you will begin to bear fruit.

> Joh 15:4-8 Abide in me, and I in you. As the branch cannot bear fruit of itself, except it abide in the vine; no more can ye, except ye abide in me.
>
> I am the vine, ye *are* the branches: He that abideth in me, and I in him, the same bringeth forth much fruit: for without me ye can do nothing.

> If a man abide not in me, he is cast forth as a branch, and is withered; and men gather them, and cast *them* into the fire, and they are burned.
>
> If ye abide in me, and my words abide in you, ye shall ask what ye will, and it shall be done unto you.
>
> Herein is my Father glorified, that ye bear much fruit; so shall ye be my disciples.

Don't put too much trust in man,

> Jer 17:5-6 Thus saith the LORD; Cursed *be* the man that trusteth in man, and maketh flesh his arm, and whose heart departeth from the LORD.
>
> For he shall be like the heath in the desert, and shall not see when good cometh; but shall inhabit the parched places in the wilderness, *in* a salt land and not inhabited.

Trust in God and your life will be filled with His life.

> Jer 17:7-8 Blessed *is* the man that trusteth in the LORD, and whose hope the LORD is.
>
> For he shall be as a tree planted by the waters, and *that* spreadeth out her roots by the river, and shall not see when heat cometh, but her leaf shall be green; and shall not be careful in the year of drought, neither shall cease from yielding fruit.

Learn not to fear man.

> Pro 29:25 The fear of man bringeth a snare: but whoso putteth his trust in the LORD shall be safe.

Be wary of other men's motives concerning your life. They may think they own you.

> 2Pe 2:3 And through covetousness shall they with feigned words make merchandise of you: whose judgement now of a long time lingereth not, and their damnation slumbereth not.

Be honest with the Lord Jesus Christ. We all struggle with things. Work on removing every obstacle and He will work with you. Get yourselves free of the restraints of religion and tradition and find life. It's not in the places most men will tell you.

> Mat 16:24-26 Then said Jesus unto his disciples, If any *man* will come after me, let him deny himself, and take up his cross, and follow me.
>
> For whosoever will save his life shall lose it: and whosoever will lose his life for my sake shall find it.
>
> For what is a man profited, if he shall gain the whole world, and lose his own soul? or what shall a man give in exchange for his soul?

Lose your life to find it. That's hard to get your head around. To me who over indulged in life almost past the place of no return it may have been easier than others to turn this way. And now with no addictions and every lust mostly under control, there is life to be found. And it is His Life.

All is being restored. My body, soul and spirit and the things around me are being renewed also. My mind, my will and my emotions are coming under control. My memory is being restored and I am being blessed with wisdom and understanding and knowledge. There is nothing better on this planet and the world cannot give this. The roller coaster of life is becoming a smooth ride.

> Rom 8:11 But if the Spirit of him that raised up Jesus from the dead dwell in you, he that raised up Christ from the dead shall also quicken your mortal bodies by his Spirit that dwelleth in you.

And when we come into alignment with His Will then He will lead us to others who we can help. Then the gifts will manifest and we start to see the miracles and the healings and deliverances that we only hear or read about.

If you have got this far and do not feel that you are a Christian then right now, ask Jesus to be your God if you never have, and repent of all sins that you know you have done. Forgive everyone that has hurt you or disappointed you and ask God to bless them. Then go through this prayer and believe it. I am asking it for you. And I know that my Lord and Saviour is working right now!!!

Final Prayer

Father God, in the name of Lord Jesus Christ, I ask you to bless with abundance those who have come this far. I ask you to open their eyes to see You more clearly and open their ears to hear You more clearly. Open their minds to perceive and their hearts to receive directly from You. Give them more wisdom and understanding and knowledge of Your Will for their lives.

Grant them strength, might, power, love and soundness of mind, to enter the wilderness and conquer the enemies that await them. Then come out with power. Let them not be stagnant or lazy. I bind slothfulness and the lukewarm attitudes and loose upon them the unquenchable fire of the Holy Ghost, right now, to burn up all the chaff and everything that offends in the Kingdom of God.

Fill them full of life and love and abundant joy and peace as they travel the narrow road that leads to life. Let them walk in the armour and with the sword of the Spirit and shield of faith that will quench every fiery dart of the wicked one. Help them stand and to fight and to overcome, and become the head and not the tail, to be above and not beneath, as they stand on the firm foundation of your Word.

And in the name of Jesus Christ I stand in the gap and repent for the sins of the ancestors down to the tenth generation, all the sins of idolatry, witchcraft, lust, pride, anger and rebellion. All chains be broken now and leave as well as all yokes of bondage and slavery to anything not in the Kingdom of God.

Father I ask You to break every curse over their lives as they repent and forgive and renounce every work of the wicked one and I command all witchcraft and black magic and voodoo curses to be broken right now and leave the people and never return. Hexes and vexation of spirit leave also. Sickness and disease I curse you now and command you to shrivel and die as did the fig tree that Jesus cursed. I curse all demonic fruit right now in Jesus name.

Fear and anxieties leave and all depressions, hopelessness and suicidal thoughts I rebuke you and command you to go now in Jesus name. I smash down all satanic altars over all here and loose desolation into the kingdom of darkness that is about them now and smash with the hammer of God's word, all walls and bars and gates and hedges and fences that surround them and are blocking and hindering any and all growth.

I loose torment on every tormentor and spoiling on the spoilers and destruction on every destroyer now in Jesus name and command you to leave NOW in Jesus name. The Lord Jesus Christ rebuke you.

Lord Jesus save them and bless them. Clean them up and use them and grant them Eternal Life. In The name of Jesus Christ I bind this prayer upon you all NOW. AMEN.

www.ingramcontent.com/pod-product-compliance
Lightning Source LLC
Chambersburg PA
CBHW051936290426
44110CB00015B/1998